No God But God

FAITH MEETS FAITH

An Orbis Series in Interreligious Dialogue

Paul F. Knitter & William R. Burrows, General Editors

Editorial Advisors

John Berthrong

Karl-Josef Kuschel

Diana Eck

Lamin Sanneh

Felix Wilfred

In the contemporary world, the many religions and spiritualities stand in need of greater communication and cooperation. More than ever before, they must speak to, learn from, and work with each other in order both to maintain their vital identities and to contribute to fashioning a better world.

FAITH MEETS FAITH seeks to promote interreligious dialogue by providing an open forum for exchanges among followers of different religious paths. While the series wants to encourage creative and bold responses to questions arising from contemporary appreciations of religious plurality, it also recognizes the multiplicity of basic perspectives concerning the methods and content of interreligious dialogue.

Although rooted in a Christian and Maryknoll theological perspective, the series does not endorse any single school of thought or approach. By making available to both the scholarly community and the general public works that represent a variety of religious and methodological viewpoints, FAITH MEETS FAITH seeks to foster an encounter among followers of the religions of the world on matters of common concern.

FAITH MEETS FAITH SERIES

No God But God

A Path to Muslim-Christian Dialogue on God's Nature

A. Christian van Gorder

ORBIS BOOKS

Maryknoll, New York 10545

Founded in 1970, Orbis Books endeavors to publish works that enlighten the mind, nourish the spirit, and challenge the conscience. The publishing arm of the Maryknoll Fathers and Brothers, Orbis seeks to explore the global dimensions of the Christian faith and mission, to invite dialogue with diverse cultures and religious traditions, and to serve the cause of reconciliation and peace. The books published reflect the views of their authors and do not represent the official position of the Maryknoll Society. To learn more about Maryknoll and Orbis Books, please visit our website at www.maryknoll.org.

Cover: Photograph by Roland and Sabrina Michaud of Mashad Mosque of Gohard Shad (Iran). The mosque dates to the fifteenth century. See their book *Design and Color in Islamic Architecture: Eight Centuries of the Tile-Maker's Art* (London: Thames and Hudson, 1996). Used with permission.

Manufactured in the United States of America

Library of Congress Cataloging-in-Publication Data

Van Gorder, A. Christian.
    No God but God : a path to Muslim-Christian dialogue on God's nature /
A. Christian van Gorder.
        p.   cm. – (Faith meets faith)
    Includes bibliographical references and indexes.
    ISBN 1-57075-464-0 (pbk.)
    1. God (Islam) 2. God – Biblical teaching. 3. God – Comparative studies.
4. Jesus Christ – Islamic interpretations. 5. Islam – Relations – Christianity.
6. Christianity and other religions – Islam. I. Title. II. Series.
BP166.2 .V35 2003
297.2'11 – dc21

                                                    2002014780

Contents

Acknowledgments

James MacCormack at the Queen's University of Belfast, Ireland, and Kenneth Cragg at Oxford University were invaluable in assisting in the writing of this book. I also want to thank my dear friends who supported me as I wrote, especially Brendan and Angela McCauley (and their fourteen children!) in Downpatrick, Co. Down; Father Neil Carlin in Co. Doire and Willie and Gemma Burke in Clondalkin, Dublin 14. Thanks also to my colleagues in Open Doors, International, in the Netherlands and in the United Kingdom who were so supportive of this effort. I have also appreciated the warm support and consistent encouragement that I have received from Bill Burrows, Catherine Costello, John Eagleson, and the editorial staff at Orbis Books. Finally, I am very grateful to many Muslim friends of many years, Dr. Arif Shaykh, Arshad Khan, Nathaniel Hasan, Ali Datee, and Saif Siddiqi.

The brutal editorializing of my two most diligent critics: my beloved mother, now in heaven, Erika Helena Lutsch, and my wife, Stephanie, were most appreciated. I hope that my children, Patrick Xavier, Brendan Daniel, Keegan, and Sean Michael — robbed of many hours of football and walks along the Irish Sea by this research — will some day take a few hours to read this and argue with their father about how best to talk with Muslims about Christian understandings of God.

Special thanks goes to A. H. Mathias Zahniser, who changed my life while I was his student at Asbury Theological Seminary. In mosque and classroom, I have been challenged by Matt's sincere engagement with Muslims and by his inexhaustible enjoyment of both Islam and his faith in Christ. It is to this teacher, writer, and friend that this book is dedicated.

Introduction

Coffee in the Shadows

Bukhara, Uzbekistan. The dark pall of a moonless night chokes the air of the hotel coffee bar where I am talking with Yusuf. Over the thick glue that Uzbeks call coffee we are talking about God. Yusuf tells of Christians who have tried to explain to him the Trinity, the Incarnation, and the atoning work of Christ: the "Lamb of God." When Yusuf discussed this with the Imam, he was shown from the Qur'an that God could not have a son. "How could I believe," he asks me, "that God could become a man? How could I believe that Jesus would claim to be God? God would not be like that!"

"God would not be like that." Over and over again I have heard Muslims in Malay kampongs, Tajik teahouses, Jordanian bazaars, or in mosques in Africa, Indonesia, India, and China echo variations on this refrain. This book is born from the gracious sincerity of their questioning. I hope that my intended readership, Christians among Muslims, will move future interactions with their Muslim friends beyond misconceptions into a concerted exchange on the nature of God.

CENTRAL QUESTIONS

Since the tragic events of September 11, 2001, many Christians have become interested for the first time in gaining a fuller understanding of how Muslims understand the nature of God. Part of this interest comes from what has been written in the media or expressed in churches about the nature of Islam. Important questions begged to be addressed: How should Christians talk to Muslims about God? What is the orthodox Islamic concept of God? How do Islamic devotional sources describe Jesus, and how is this portrait of Jesus formed by Muslim views about the nature of God? What are the implications for relating an idea, such as the Incarnation of Christ, to a Muslim who finds such an idea about God to be reprehensible?

These are daunting questions and my intent is more to generate discussion and further inquiry than to attempt to arrive at any sense of conclusive theological resolution. I will begin by exploring ideas of how Christians should approach Muslims.

I began this study in the pedestrian tradition of comparing and contrasting Islamic and Christian theology. In this process, however, I discovered that the nature of God (which many of us assume at the outset is similar in the two traditions) is actually a very helpful paradigm for meaningful interfaith understanding. God in Christ is a participating (koinoneatic) God who does not send revelation but comes and lives among humanity. God in the Qur'an transcends the happenstance of the physical world while providing practical guidance and clear understanding. Therefore, the nature of God and the purpose of God are the fulcrum on which this theocentric discussion turns. It must always be remembered that specific communities and persons dealing with each other in their own unique situations will ultimately determine what is the meaningful applicability of these ideas. The people that we meet and the unique convictions that they hold, and not some theoretical model, must serve as the "foreground" for all interfaith discussions.

I need to state that when I say "Christian" in the pages that follow, I am not trying to say that *every* Christian will subscribe to the construal of Christian doctrine and practice that I refer to. Instead, I am quite aware that the construal of Christian identity I portray is that of fairly conservative Christians, roughly those who, in the American context, are considered and call themselves "Evangelicals" or Catholics who are happy to identify themselves with the teachings of Pope John Paul II in *Redemptoris Missio* (the pope's 1990 encyclical letter on mission).

In chapter 2, Muslim views about God will be discussed: How do Muslims understand God's unity and how does God's oneness relate to His other attributes? How is it that nothing can be said about God's nature while at the same time something of God's characteristics can be known? How is God's holiness or His mercy seen distinctly by Christians? How do Muslims view God's transcendence, and how does God's transcendence relate to the reception of revelation or to the Christian belief that God was in Christ?

This last question is crucial. Is revelation understood in the same way in both faiths? Is the revelation described in the Qur'an preexistent as it is in Christianity? If so, is the revelation of God also a self-disclosure or is it only the explanation of His will?

Christians believe that revelation takes shape in the Incarnation. But how can a Christian meaningfully talk with a Muslim about the Incarnation without first knowing how Muslims perceive Jesus? Islam paints a picture of Jesus, but it is a different portrait than the one that is seen in the New Testament. How does this portrait of Jesus change as Muslims encounter Christians? Can it be said that the likeness of Muhammad becomes increasingly "christic" as Islam interacts with Christianity? Why is there no mention made of Christ's moral nature until tenth-century Islamic devotional literature?

How do these questions relate to how Christians can best explain to Muslims the Christian doctrine of God? This will be the focus of our last three chapters. We will examine the doctrines of the Incarnation, Christ's divinity, God's Triune nature, and the revelation of God in covenant with Christ as mediator.

RETHINKING MUSLIM-CHRISTIAN RELATIONS

After hundreds of years, one would think that there were already enough books seeking to explain Christianity to Muslims. The problem is not that Christian theology has yet to be recounted to Muslims. The problem is that Christianity has often been introduced independent from the Islamic concept of God and the Muslim perception of Jesus. Few Muslims have heard an unclouded presentation of who God is according to Christianity. Instead, Muslims have been subjected to explanations of the Trinity and the redeeming power of Christ without reference to the foundational question, "Who is God?"

Tangential approaches emphasizing soteriology, divorced from an exposition of God's nature, litter the horizon of Muslim-Christian encounters. Some Muslim apologists attack the reliability of the Bible. Some Christians probe Islam for glimmers of consideration of atonement for sin. Some are careful to delineate the different roles of Muhammad and Jesus. Muslims can easily dismiss many Christian discussions of God as flawed, because they ignore the oneness (*tauhid*) of God. Some Christians counter by claiming that "Allah" and "Elohim" are one. Muslims who agree are often quick to add that most Christian views of God are distorted.

Comparisons of belief are often made without a qualitative search into the "kerygmatic" concern of how the Islamic view of God affects their understanding of Jesus. Christians should begin with the foundational concept of God in the Qur'an, their view of Jesus, and then relate these views with what the New Testament claims about Jesus.

STARTING POINTS FOR DISCUSSION

As a Christian, I make the basic assumption that the coming of Jesus provides a unique presentation of God's nature and His relation to the world. Obviously, there is no "one" Christian faith. My own faith journey has been primarily informed by Wesleyan pentecostalism and Anabaptism. I am now a member of a liberationist African-American church. Nor am I trying to define for Muslims the nature of "their Islam" but only to discuss what Islam has been for most Muslims. There are a host of "Islams." It is possible, however, to "stake out" what is a classical or standard version of Islamic faith garnered from written sources and to respond to that Islam with that which might broadly be called Christian orthodoxy. When I use the term "Christian" and "Muslim" I recognize my inability to define either tradition for their respective adherents. I will be responding as a Christian to an Islamic "Christology." Islam is not a rigid monolith but a living faith cherished by well over one billion people. I will focus on the primary sources used within orthodox Islam: the Qur'an, and the Hadith (which interprets the meaning of the Qur'an). Scant attention to the Hadith by Christians has resulted in a host of onerous miscastings of Christian ideas to Muslims. Formative Islamic devotional and theological perspectives will also be introduced because they are widely accepted by Muslims as an ideal source to shed light on how the Qur'anic portrait of 'Isa (Jesus) is to be understood.

For purposes of definition, "formative Islam" refers to the period between the first revelations of the Qur'an and the fall of the Abbasid dynasty in A.D. 1258. This date marks the end of an era; afterwards few scholars were patronized by the emerging Mongol and Seljuk powers, and travel was greatly inhibited as Seljuk militarism frowned upon creative theological inquiry.

As a non-Muslim, I am concerned that I am able to interpret Islamic source material in a way that is consistent with Muslim interpretation. Muslims and Christians believe that they have received authoritative revelation. Historic Christianity teaches that Christ is one with God. Islam rejects this by explaining that God is one without a second and has not "begotten" a Son. It is here that interaction must begin and not conclude.

A fuller appreciation of Islam will help Christians to better discuss their faith with their Muslim friends. The opportunity to interact with followers of the world's second-largest faith about the nature of God may be difficult but can also be quite rewarding. My prayer in this book echoes Moses' cry in the Qur'an: "O Lord! Relieve my mind and ease my task for me; and loose a knot from my tongue that they may understand my saying" (Surah 20:25–28, Pickthall).*

---

*In using Arabic terms, I have sought to be consistent and use widely accepted spellings. Citations from the Qur'an have been taken from the translation of A. Yusuf Ali. When Mohammed Marmaduke Pickthall's *Meaning of the Glorious Koran* has been quoted, that translator's name follows the citation. There is occasionally a variation in the numeration of verses among different Qur'anic translations. When this occurs, one should read the verses immediately surrounding the citation.

1

Reinvigorating the Muslim-Christian Encounter

FOUNDATIONS FOR INTERACTION

One legend conjectures that if a Muslim touches a copy of the Bible insanity or paralysis might ensue. I hope to underscore, instead, the madness of theological intransigence and show that the paralysis of doctrinaire self-assertion has no place in discussing Christian faith with Muslims. We should go beyond stubborn refutations of Islam and haranguing affirmations of Christian dogma.

First, Christians could begin by seeking to gain a comprehensive knowledge of Islam, including a familiarity with the history of the Muslim-Christian encounter. Our attitude in this is best consistent with the humility and patience of Jesus. The language we will use must be reevaluated with a focus on clarity. Finally, we need to seek "bridges" to Muslims that may serve as starting points for discussions about the nature of God.

The Bible teaches that humanity, created in God's image, is capable of receiving revelation. In addition to what God has revealed in scripture, humanity's spiritual pursuit has repeatedly fashioned observations that have provided a wealth of insight. There is, no doubt, something of truth and the true God known in all humanity and in all religions. There is also the possibility that people will say more about God than has been imparted to them, or will recast God in images of their own design.

When Christians have interacted with Muslims, many of these presuppositions have been set aside. Many Christians have made little effort to apprehend the nuances of centuries of Islamic theological thought. Unfortunately, careful Muslim students of Christianity are also rare. For too long, both Christian and Muslim have relied on time-worn, dismissive arguments instead of heeding the advice of the great teacher al-Ghazali:

To refute a system before understanding it and becoming acquainted
with its depths is to act blindly. Man cannot grasp what is defective in
any science unless he has so complete a grasp of that science in question
that he equals its most learned exponents.[1]

Christians cannot proceed in isolation from thorough knowledge of Islam.
At a recent conference between Muslims and Christians, this fact was
illustrated by one Muslim's response to inaccurate observations made by
Hans Küng:

What good would it do if a person like Hans Küng were to spend the
next ten years of his efforts trying to develop a model for dialogue with
Islam which does *not* [his emphasis] correspond to any reality on the
Muslim side?[2]

The first task is to begin by listening to Muslims. The effort to comprehend
leads to the ability to be understood. Polemic monologue is not effective
interfaith communication. Mutual participation advances naturally to unifying sympathy, if not complete agreement. Toleration is appropriate because
humanity is cast in the image of God and not in the image of evil. Openness
is logical as well as expedient. The incarnation of Jesus among humanity is
about the patient exposition of truth. Christ was consistently sensitive to the
perspectives (accurate or inaccurate) of His audience. He seemed deftly able
to understand and address the concerns of those to whom He spoke. Because
of this, the way of Christ can serve as a "bridge" across which interaction
can best proceed between individuals.

Beginning to listen to Muslims calls for Christians to first gain a
"self-understanding" of Islam before explanations will become constructive.
Individuals naturally feel an instinctive reserve toward those who do not
empathize with them. St. Paul taught that "perfect love casts out fear." Not
taking the effort to be knowledgeable of one's audience is an expression of
lovelessness. As one West African proverb laments, "If your brother does not
understand you, perhaps it is because you do not love him."[3] Often, Muslims and Christians have been neighbors in ignorance rather than partners in
comprehension.

The biblical revelation about the nature of God can be presented as a
message that is "receivable" to Muslims. Christianity explained to Muslims
will need to be presented in the forms, syntax, and cultural language of the
listeners. Unfamiliarity has also often typified many Muslim responses to
Christians. There are few detailed expositions by Muslim authors of Christian faith in all of its diversity. Muslims have usually been content to respond
to Christian denunciations with blasts of their own. Islam has seen its association with Christianity primarily as an obligation to rid the Christian "heresy"

from error. Many Muslims would not readily think that religious truth could be garnered from Christianity's theological aberrations. With these presuppositions firmly fastened in Muslim minds, the task of meaningful interaction is daunting.

Christians interacting with Muslims can vigorously challenge this lack of interest. We can say to Muslims that, although they may not agree with us, they should at least try to appreciate what they are rejecting. Some Muslims summarize Christianity as an exercise in mysticism. Cynical skepticism can frequently combine with a lack of cognizance to create a dangerous mixture of vague disparagement and militant castigation. Unsympathetic interpreters parody what Christ actually taught, or they dismiss vital historic Christian doctrines with sarcastic compliments such as:

> It is indeed difficult to avoid being impressed by the peculiar content and sheer incredibleness of some Christian creedal claims. It may be fairly said, at the risk of sounding polemical and unsympathetic, that among monotheistic creeds, the embrace of Christianity requires assent to the largest collection of highly implausible beliefs requiring at times what a Tertullian or Kierkegaard would welcome: an unusually dramatic suspension of critical powers.[4]

Unfortunately, Christians often rehash doctrinal formulas that they themselves do not understand. The task of effective communication calls for comprehension from both messenger and receiver. To explain Christian ideas about God's nature is a gradual process, because important ideas need to be restated in fresh forms without altering the truth that is shared. Even a cursory glance at Christian interaction with Muslims shows that familiarity with the Islamic concept of God is not usually the first concern. All too often, more energy has been expended in refuting terminology than in grasping its significance for those who believe. Christians must eschew this tone of disengagement. Our posture in interaction should be free of presumption. This approach is expedient because Christian theology, forged from centuries of reflection, is not immune to error. St. Paul reminds us that we look "through a glass darkly" at that which is beyond the frail dimensions of the everyday. In this spirit of humility, Christians approach Muslims free from strident judgmentalism. In His life, Jesus displayed a heart of love even for His detractors. The historical relationship between Islam and most of Christendom, however, little resembles the meek example of Jesus.

Dynamic interaction presupposes common ground. Certainly, there are many shared factors between Muslims and Christians. Generally, what is parallel between the two religions are those elements that are not specifically Christian, but are universal to the broader spiritual venture of humanity. Both religions declare to have revelation from God. Common themes such as worship, forgiveness, submission, and God's greatness are apparent. Both traditions reject that God is many or that He is subordinate to the created order. To come into right relation with the Creator, both religions advocate submission to the divine will.

What elements of Christian teaching are readily accessible to Muslims? Biblical teachings on prayer, fasting, divorce, adultery, and revenge parallel Muslim convictions. Faith might be reexamined for its communal, as well as its individual, ramifications. Eschatology, as an element of soteriology, could receive greater consideration. A quest for applicability would also place more emphasis on community or morality and ethics than it has in the more individualized European *Sitz im Leben.*

Theology is a process of communication as well as proclamation. It is an expression of finite attempts to relate to an infinite being who is under no constraint to use terminology or forms imposed by human explanation. Interfaith interaction demands constant recasting whenever new questions about God arise. The topic addressed here will be described in a way that addresses Islamic assumptions. In Singapore, a Muslim once asked me what bearing the death of Jesus twenty centuries past had for him. He felt if God forgave sin, there was no need for anyone else's assistance. This man was not asking if the message of Jesus was true; he was wondering how it was applicable. The problem for him was not the truth of the claim but its relatedness to his life.

A grappling with relevance will lead to the development of a distinct vocabulary for interaction. For too many Muslims, Christianity is defiant of reason (cf. 1 Corinthians 1:21–25). The language used to express Christian views is best built around an accurate analysis of how Muslims comprehend what is presented. Even cherished phrases need to be reexamined to see if continued usage among Muslims conveys what Christians believe these ideas to mean. It is heartening to remember that the rhetoric of Jesus was thoroughly rooted in the world of His hearers. Christ spoke to farmers, fishermen, and zealots with a common vocabulary. An example of care in terminology is His use of the term "Son of Man," which helped His listeners perceive His mission in a new light. Jesus saw the fruit of effective communication: first understanding, then receptivity. His use of language said much about the nature of the God that He announced.

A conscientious approach to form will also facilitate meaningful discussions. Islam holds that truth should be able to be explained simply and succinctly. There is no room for obfuscation. After hearing one explanation of Christianity, one Muslim retorted, "Complexity is one thing, incoherence another. Paradox is one thing but nonsense is something else."[5] Without apology, Christianity is filled with mystery. In reference to the atonement, Charles Wesley eulogized, "The Immortal dies! Who can explore his strange design?" Yet, effort must be made to communicate logically what that mystery means to us. Theological paradoxes need to be framed in the specific context of Muslim perception.

It is not the responsibility of the receiver to receive but the work of the communicator to communicate in an appropriate way. The resistance of Muslims to Christianity is as much an indictment of our own misconceptions about God's nature as it is of Muslims' inability to accept Christian ideas. If Christianity is not intelligible to Muslims, it may be distorted in its presentation. If the message is garbled, it is no longer the "good news" but in some way our own distorted message. High Jericho walls of division will tumble, not with shouts of defiance, but with the clear resonance of a message explained in such a way that invites a response.

Christians relating to Muslims can adapt their language, attitude, and form issues to their audience. Particular attention could be given to the way in which the Christian understanding of God interacts with Muslim views of God. To do this, one might look at the barriers inherent in the Muslim claim to be "beyond" dialogue with Christianity. Christians can respond to this seeming lack of openness to theological discussion by looking at how God called St. Peter to look past his own confidence in possessing truth to bring insight to non-Christians. Christians should be willing to enter with Muslims into an encounter that promises both genuine dialogue and faithful witness.

In interfaith relations few ideas are more frayed or shopworn than the notion of "dialogue." The term is now so hopelessly loaded with frustrated expectations that it has effectively lost any ability to convey the reality of what ideally might happen between Muslims and Christians. This process can be the meeting together of people in mutual respect and sincerity. Instead, Muslims often suspect the ulterior motives of the Christians that they meet. Many Christians have concluded that talking to Muslims about the nature of God is futile because of Islamic convictions that Christian views are beyond discussion.

Christians themselves must grapple with certain fears that many have concerning dialogue with Muslims. Many dread compromise, but Christian interaction with Muslims need not end in syncretism. Because Christian theology teaches that Christ is divine, there can be no "negotiated compromise" in the process of discussion. Faith convictions cannot be the sum of consensus distilled from cross-theological reference. Claims of truth, however, should lead to a posture of humility and not arrogance. It must be truth that is, by definition, "intolerant." The danger comes when truth that has been given and truths that are extrapolated are revered with the same degree of authority.

Meaningful interfaith discussions are capable of moving beyond simplistic commonality into accurate explanations of differences. Without this focus, the

Muslim-Christian encounter becomes merely the sharing of personal experiences and opinions. Encouraging exchanges often provide only a mutual willingness to cooperate on specific social concerns, or the relatively inconsequential agreement that both traditions affirm God's greatness and role as Creator. The goal, instead, must be to communicate what is principal in faith.

Many Muslims whom I have met look askance at "dialogue" and feel that it is primarily a subterfuge to conceal ulterior, often evangelistic, motives. But what is the orthodox posture of Islam in conversation with other faiths? The Qur'an seems to offer the hopeful prospect for an attitude of openness:

> And dispute ye not with the People of the Book, except with means better (than mere disputation), unless it be those who inflict wrong: But say, "We believe in the Revelation which has come down to us and in that which has come down to you; Our God and your God are One: and it is to Him we bow." (Surah 29:46)

Surah 10:95 (Pickthall) reads, "And if thou art in doubt concerning that which We reveal unto thee, then question those who read the Scripture before thee." Perhaps few Muslims have heeded these injunctions because they are without doubts. It seems more likely that questions about God's nature are not often asked of Christians because many Muslims do not believe that what Christians know about God can be trusted as accurate or comprehensible.

Islam claims to be *al-din al-hanif,* the primordial religion of universal truth. It is the final revelation, the summary and synthesis of knowable truth. Those in other religions face no compulsion from Islam (Surah 2:256) and are responsible for the consequences of their own beliefs. As Muhammad says, "Unto you, your religion and unto me, my religion" (Surah 109:6, Pickthall). Toleration, and not dialogue, seems to be the guiding principle in the Qur'anic response to Christians. A history between the two faiths, characterized by the blood-drenched memories of the Crusades, has dulled even hopes of forbearance. Muhammad Talabi warned fellow Muslims, "Interaction with Christianity will either lull faith to sleep or sustain us in a perpetual posture of *ijtihad* (variously translated independent judgement or cautious reflection)."[6]

I have experienced little readiness from most Muslims to enter into a genuine interaction about the claims of Christian faith. In speaking to Muslims in Asia and Africa, the first barrier to dialogue is often an understandable wariness about underlying motives. To many Muslims, discussions must first vault walls of suspicion before effective communication can proceed. "Dialogue" is sometimes seen as an enemy that might eventually lead to a betrayal of cherished traditions.

Confident people of faith, however, are able to initiate and foster an attitude of openness and mutual respect. If Christians or Muslims claim to be the guardians of eternal truth, as is claimed, then another religious claim will pose no threat to its impact. Christians are "of all men most to be pitied" (1 Corinthians 15:19) if they are deceived. Jesus told His followers that not even the "gates of hell" could prevail against what He would build. St. Paul announced that the day would come when every other view would acquiesce, not to the claims of Christianity *per se,* but to Christ (Philippians 2:10–11).

In relating to Muslims, Christians can be open as St. Peter was in meeting Cornelius (Acts 10:28–48), not only to present a message but also to receive in a spirit of teachability. Peter's encounter with Cornelius broadened his vision of God's love (Acts 10:34). Truth is often only partially grasped and is never something exhausted or comprehensively owned. Further, the Hebrew conception of truth is relational and is experienced in contrast to a Greek understanding of truth as a conception and as a category. Like Peter, we can be amenable to receive from anyone, including "non-Christians." What the Christian hopes for is more than polite *savoir-faire;* we seek a present-tense revelation of God's presence from the encounter. Diplomacy, in fact, often inhibits the potential for genuine insight.

The clearest example of how the New Testament views interfaith dialogue is found in St. Paul's discourse in Athens. As Paul walked around the city (Acts 17:16), he became "greatly distressed" (*paroksuno*) because he saw that the metropolis was abrim with idols. As a person with stout convictions about humanity's future in heaven and hell, he was overcome with concern in such an idolatrous atmosphere. It is notable that he chose not to translate his disdain into condescending, castigating diatribe. Instead, Paul reasoned with patient exposition (Acts 17:17) on how God had revealed Himself in Christ. Paul's observations spurred him into the kind of dialogue (*dialegomai*) in which Christians should be involved. Paul persisted with the Athenians in the hopes that he could surmount the gap between his view of God and their polytheism.

The contemporary engagement of Christians with Muslims can be equally dynamic because the Bible is not a systematic, didactic handbook intent on defining God. Christians believe that God used human language and human experience (Jesus) to reveal divine truth. Christian doctrine emerges through time to answer questions that are raised. This process is once again taking place as Muslims and Christians jostle with each other in the marketplace and teashop. Theology is more than a science to codify orthodoxy; it is also a tool to explain afresh cherished ideas in new situations and in response to new questions.

The reinvigoration of the Muslim-Christian encounter will go well beyond the molding of a peaceful truce. It will be about the quest for truth. Christians are able to enter into the process of interaction available to the prospect of God's using Muslims to bring insight just as He used Cornelius to direct Peter

into deeper dimensions of truth. This posture of willingness to learn underscores the Christian's confidence. When introduced into the Muslim-Christian
encounter, this note of teachability often engenders a similar response from
Muslims. The Bible admonishes Christians to be willing to enter into every
person's world with a posture of participation. When Christians meet Muslims the goal is the same as that of Jesus, who explained on the Emmaus road
the reality that the villagers needed to apprehend. Christian doctrine teaches
that truth from God brings freedom from misconceptions about the Divine
nature.

UNDERSTANDING THE MUSLIM DOCTRINE OF GOD

When Christians have not understood the Muslim concept of God, the
result has been murky presentations of Christianity. Until Muslims are able
to appreciate what Christians mean by "God," all other doctrinal issues are
secondary. Why should Christians expect Muslims to fathom the concept
of the atonement, or the Holy Spirit, if they cannot first comprehend the
Christian revelation of God's nature?

It is too simplistic to frame the debate in terms of the question, "Do we
serve the same God?" It is more helpful to ask, "What kind of God is revealed
in Christianity and in Islam?" Both traditions agree that God is one, but there
is no concord on how that unity is to be expressed. This fact is vital for
Muslims. Any explanation, then, of the role of Jesus that does not take into
account the Muslim view of God risks being dismissed as incomprehensible.

At the heart of this discussion is a divergent concept of God. In Islam, God
is the giver of guidance (*huda*) and inspiration (*wahy*). In Christianity, God
gives Himself in incarnational revelation. The relation that Christians have
toward God is based on the concept of God as "our Father," an appellation
rarely heard in nonmystical Islam. If God can be seen in this uniquely Christian way, then the Incarnation would no longer be viewed as a blasphemous
absurdity but the summation of God's Fatherhood. Jesus asked His disciples,
"Who do you say that I am?" The Christian view of God is best presented
with such clarity that it becomes conceivable for Muslims to understand how
the disciples came to respond, "You are the Christ, the Son of the Living
God" (Matthew 16:16).

An inaccurate grasp of the Muslim view of God will impede meaningful interfaith communication. Christians, eager to declare to Muslims the
promise of relational intimacy with God, should realize that in nonmystical
Islam, humanity's distance from God is often described as a positive force
that maintains and defines creation. God's "separateness" is the magnificent
distinction of Islamic theology. I once spoke with a Muslim about intimacy
with God only to hear him respond that he was glad that God was distant

and uninvolved with the sinful details of his life. For him, bridging the gap between God and man was seen as undesirable as well as impossible.

To see how one should begin with another's concept of God before proceeding, it is instructive to consider the interfaith experience of St. Paul. In Paul's exposition at Lystra (Acts 14:15–17), he began by affirming God's existence as Creator before anything else. At this stage, Paul was dealing with Lystrian misconceptions about God's nature, based on their presuppositions about Zeus and Hermes. In Athens (Acts 17:24–29), Paul centered initially on the characteristics of God that applied both to the Athenian legend of Zeus and the revelation of the supreme God. He first explained God as Creator (v. 24), self-sufficient (vv. 24–25), the unifying factor in all human experience (v. 26), and sovereign over all. By starting with natural theology, Paul affirmed elements of truth that his audience already possessed. He then described humanity's search for God (v. 27) and the need to repent in preparation for the final judgment (vv. 30–31). In so doing, he demonstrated how the Greek philosophical conception of God remained open for further engagement with the Christian revelation. Only after the concept of God is articulated did Paul allude to Christ's resurrection as proof of divine authority (v. 30).

For St. Paul, the unresolved tensions between the concept of God that he was outlining and the view of the Athenians did not stop him from proceeding. Paul did not defend his view of God but simply declared it and was content to leave the results to God, the Holy Spirit. The concept of God's nature as compassion moved Paul beyond iconoclasm and negativism. He lived for the opportunity to explain his view of God in the expectation that the message itself would disarm any apprehension. Was Paul's approach successful? There is only one further reference to Lystra in the Bible (Acts 16:1), and Athens did not figure in Paul's third missionary journey. What is apparent is that in Athens, Paul's audience asked to hear more about God (v. 33). Later, some of these inquirers became Christians (v. 34).

In the tradition of Paul, Christians are able to point Muslims to that within the Islamic view of God which is consistent with Christianity. It is central to know how Muslims comprehend the meaning of the term "God" before the Christian view of God revealed in Christ can be set forth with penetrability.

THE HISTORICAL DIMENSIONS
OF THE MUSLIM-CHRISTIAN ENCOUNTER

The historical dimensions of the Muslim-Christian encounter have had a tremendous impact on contemporary interfaith relations. Both Islam and Christianity are considered "historical" religions, claiming to have received divine revelation in history. Both share a common heritage as Semitic, mono-theistic traditions. The history of both traditions has been greatly influenced by Greek rationalism. For the Muslim polemic, it is also important that Islam is the "last" disclosure of truth from God to humanity.

More than six hundred years after Jesus, the Prophet Muhammad emerged in Arabia. The originally "Christianized" lands of the Middle East and North Africa were quickly conquered in the first hundred years of Islamic military progress. Christianity in these nations was no match for advancing Muslim armies. By the eighth century, much of Spain was under the sway of Islam. By the ninth century, Muslim-occupied territory rivaled in its breadth the area under Christian influence.

What kind of Christianity did Islam initially encounter? Two of the largest groups of Afro-Asiatic (Middle-Eastern) Christians, the Modalists and the Assyrian Church of the East, were beyond the pale of orthodoxy. Modal-ists argued that Jesus was not a distinct person from God the Father. The Assyrian Church, which largely flourished in Persia and Iraq, believed that Christ had dual (human and divine) natures which coexisted. Emphasis on the humanity of Christ by Assyrian Christians (sometimes known as "Nestori-ans," a term they reject) probably helped validate the tenet of early Islam that Jesus was merely a prophet. Aside from these two groups, there were other strands of Christianity resident in the seventh-century Afro-Asiatic world. Certain groups of Christians reworked Greek philosophy with Christianized nomenclature. Controversy and doctrinal division characterized Near Eastern Christian communities in the seventh century, and there was so much chaos within the church that when Islam first appeared, some, like John of Damas-cus, assumed that it was an expression of "bastard Christianity."[7] The results of this bickering invariably led to confusion among observers of Christianity.

The major theological discussions of the seventh century revolved around the nature of Christ. By this time, however, the doctrine of the Trinity was widely perceived to mean what it does today. Much has been made of the fact that early Muslims may have developed their unusual interpretation of the Trinity from the Collyridians. What is more likely is that their tritheistic view came from a misinterpretation of orthodox Christian doctrine.

At the time of the Prophet Muhammad there was no really vital Christian community in Arabia. It is known that Christian services in the Arabian peninsula in the seventh century were held in Aramaic and not Arabic and did not use an Arabic translation of the Bible.[8] Any familiarity with Christian dogma would have come from traders returning from Mesopotamia, Syria, or Abyssinia in the West. Small clusters of Christians lived in the coastal cities of Yemen. Abyssinian mission stations in southern Arabia existed from the fourth century, but many of the converts returned to Abyssinia when political fortunes shifted in the sixth century. The wilderness areas between Syria and

Arabia were frequently used as places of monastic retreat, and it might have been possible for Arabs to meet individual Christians in that region.

The meteoric rise of Islam was linked with the weakness of viable Christianity in the Middle East. Islam, however, does not accept any attempts to "historicize" the origin of its faith, just as some Christians might bristle at theories that Christianity sprang from the militant Essene communities of Qumran. Muslims maintain that they subscribe to the "first religion," present at creation and beyond the confines of time. The primary motives of Islamic historiography have been either to authenticate claims of political power or to authorize the sources of religious traditions.

The steady advance of Islam toward Europe came to an abrupt conclusion at the battle of Tours in A.D. 732. Turning to Asia, Muslim traders carried their faith as far as China and the Philippines, as well as to the extreme edges of Africa. Venetian merchants interacted with Muslims. Europeans also did business with Arabs in the context of the emerging slave trade. Christian clergy in the eighth and ninth centuries began to caricature Islam as a religion of concupiscent debauchery but still saw it primarily in terms of its being a military and political threat. Two centuries of Crusader invasions worked irrevocable damage on subsequent attempts for interaction between Muslims and Christians. In medieval Europe, a negative picture of Islam continued to emerge which left no doubt that Islam was a perversion of the truth, spread by the sword, and fostered by licentiousness.

In this era, there were only a few bright lights from the standpoint of Christian interaction with Muslims. One of these was the pilgrimage of St. Francis of Assisi to meet the caliph Salahu d-Din (Saladin) in A.D. 1218. The first translation of the Bible into Arabic was completed by Peter the Venerable in A.D. 1156. Raymond Lull was another pioneering Christian who worked in Algeria before his long-desired martyrdom there in A.D. 1315.

During the Crusades, Christian Europe heard almost nothing about Islamic theology. The most notable Muslim theologians of this period were Ibn Rushd (Averroës) and Abu Hamid Muhammad al-Ghazali of Persia (478–505 A.H./A.D. 1058–1111). Ibn Rushd developed a dialectic that helped diffuse some of the earlier misconceptions about Islam. Al-Ghazali is best known for his extensive apologetic material, which confidently refuted all philosophies (including Christianity) that Islam encountered. However, Persia was the brightest spot for theological interaction between Muslims and Christians.

The centuries after these wars saw little interaction between Islam and Christianity. Historical events are seen by some Muslims as the stage where God exculpates the righteous; thus, the Crusades showed the superiority of Islam over Christianity. After this, the predominant place where Muslims and Christians interacted with each other was in Spain and, to a lesser degree, in Asia, Egypt, the Balkan states, Turkey, and Ottoman-controlled Armenia.

The roots of European Islamic study did not gain impetus until the era of colonialism (*isti'mar*). This correspondence is not lost on contemporary Muslim apologists. During the colonial occupation, ruling powers sought to learn something about the people that their superior military technology had subjugated. Unfortunately, these pioneer European Orientalists usually passed on ancient stereotypes and did little study of the Qur'an.[9] Hadith and early theological interpretation were even less accessible. A notable exception to this was the scholarship of Nöldeke and Goldziher. Nevertheless colonialism seemed to foster in even these scholars a paternalistic arrogance that some Muslims argue remains the emblematic flaw of European civilization.

During the period of colonialism, Islam began to encounter Christian missionaries. Colonialism and mission remain inseparably linked in the popular Muslim mind. In addition, early mission efforts were characterized by inadequate perceptions of Islamic theology. As a result, Christianity was often viewed as "foreign." In spite of concentrated effort, these early missionaries saw few Muslims choosing to become Christians.

And what is the present relationship between Islam and Christianity? Regrettably, the distance between the Christian message and Muslim views has not diminished over time and, in many cases, greater intransigence has taken root. Recently, the century-old practice of demonizing Islam has revived with the spotlight on notorious characters such as Osama bin-Laden, Saddam Hussein, Mu'ammar al-Qadhdhafi, Yasser Arafat, and the Ayatollahs of Iran. Brash terrorism, suicidal fanaticism, and a host of other unflattering images dominate European and American media-generated pasquinades of Islam. This trend is also evidenced among Christians. Few have bothered to nurture a deep and studied appreciation for Islamic art, music, poetry, and literature. Economic and political issues of injustice, in such places as Palestine, Kashmir, and Kurdistan, are championed by some Christian service organizations. Heartening exceptions to this trend include recent statements by Pope John Paul II and the United States Conference of Catholic Bishops calling for a clear commitment to the cause of justice for oppressed Palestinian peoples.

In conclusion, the historical relationship between Muslims and Christians has passed to the present generation a host of unenviable preconceptions that cannot be sidestepped. I experienced one such barrier in India when I was told by a Muslim that being a "Christian" meant nothing more than that you ate pork, drank wine, and tolerated profligacy. Christians should be cognizant of historical tensions in order to be sensitive to their role in the present Muslim-Christian encounter. There is no justification for continued ignorance and defamation. Yet, the two factors that most characterize the present relationship between Muslims and Christians remain the polar stances of passivity and aggression. Given a chronicled legacy of distortion, falsification, and politicized bias, it is not difficult to understand the voices decrying the feasibility of genuine interfaith communications. It is also perplexing to see why greater effort is not made to overcome these blockades and strive for increased clarity in interfaith discussions.

UNDERSTANDING ISLAMIC WORSHIP

At first appearances, Islam is a religion filled with arabesques of devotion. For most Muslims, ritual is the central normative function and the inner sustaining force of life. The day begins in the mosque with the first touches of the sun against walls filled with rivers of calligraphy which explain the world. Elements of the day, month, and year are infused with ritual meaning, reinforcing the creeds of Islam. It is no wonder that there is a universal confidence held by Muslims that, in Islam, they are sustained in the absolute truth about God.

Muslims express their hunger for God in countless devotional practices. Devotional liturgies frame that quest. The exercised observance of Islam is meaningful to those who have entered into the gates of its potential. Five times daily and thirty times within those sessions, Muslims touch their forehead to the ground in contrition. The wayward influences of society — filled with evil spirits — are mitigated by habitual prayer (*salat*). The poetic symbolism of each aspect of worship aids in experiencing ablution (*wudu'*) from the grime of this world. Rituals often try to capture the "soul" of an idea. Worship, without avenues of ceremony to explore the dramas of human life, descends into tedium and brings a sense of void. Ritual is seen as a form of revelation and a gift from God. That is why St. Martin observed that rituals are the best possible translation of divine revelation.

Does an emphasis on ritual make Islam a religion of externals? Islam does not teach (as some Christian apologists suggest) that outward ceremonial observance can replace the primacy of proper inward motivation. Some Protestant missionaries, such as Samuel Zwemer, have condescended that Islam is a "religion without song," caught up in cold, lifeless diffidence, void of meaning even to its adherents. Such castigations hinder Christian discussions because they question the intense conviction of Muslims. These views also betray a lack of effort in appreciating the dimensions of Islamic ritual as worship directed toward God.

Stephen Neill observed that when one enters a mosque one should always come with bared feet. Christians should approach what others consider holy with honor. Islam will never fully be appreciated unless it is approached with "barefooted" reverence. Christians should examine forms of Islamic ritual and devotional literature, both to appreciate the experience of Islam and to see if there is a possible bridge of explanation within those forms to convey something of the Christian understanding of God's nature. For example, when confronted with Muslim reticence to enter Christian halls of worship, Christians in West Africa ventured to adapt their facilities to make them more approachable. One observed that "curious and inquisitive Muslims will come near a congregation at worship if they hear worship forms that are intriguing and familiar."[10] Attempts to contextualize Christian worship in a Muslim setting are not devoid of problems and can be easily dismissed because of instances when contextualization has been unwisely applied to settings where "imitating" Islamic forms is dismissed as heretical subterfuge. Nonetheless, devotional practices have the potential to become viable ways to explain new ideas. All too often, Muslims who become Christians are culturally disenfranchised from their original community. These Christians should be protected from developing a cultural "split personality" (*izdiwaj*). An example of adaptation might be the question of how the sacrament of baptism is approached. Baptisms could be performed in family groups (Acts 16:33) instead of individually. Other Christians in a Muslim context have chosen to abstain from cultural stumbling blocks such as clothing issues, using pork or wine, or publicly flouting the fast during the month of Ramadan.

The nomenclature of ritual also merits theological consideration. In some Muslim contexts, Christians have chosen to avoid the nuance-laden term "Christian," choosing instead to be called "followers of Isa." The New Testament does not insist upon the use of a particular collective noun, and this kind of adaptation might serve to mitigate unnecessary alienation. Attempts along these lines may be fiercely opposed by guardians of Islamic orthodoxy. In Malaysia, government agencies tried to prohibit the use of the Arabic terms *Allah, iman, rasul,* and *injil* when speaking about Christianity. In spite of resistance, the process of explaining Christianity in forms that are less "threatening" to Muslims should not be abandoned.

In conclusion, externalized forms of worship can be analyzed in the process of explaining Christian faith to Muslims. Islamic ritual forms should not be dismissed simply because they are different. Zwemer's disparagement of Islam's "lack of song" to convey the spiritual aspirations of Muslims overlooks the reality that these are satisfactorily conveyed by other means. Representing Christian views on the nature of God using indigenous symbolism may assist the process of understanding. Rituals predominant in European cultures can be reexpressed when Christians worship in Muslim contexts. Familiar forms can provide an excellent forum for relating unfamiliar ideas.

CULTURE AND WORLDVIEW

Christians need to become increasingly aware of how the Islamic worldview affects Muslim receptivity to Christian faith. The worldview of a community is defined as that which people understand to be real about the world around them (their presuppositions). This system of values is usually accumulated over centuries. It defines what is prized as significant and explains how people cope with the world. Examples of how one's worldview affects communications can be found in the lives of Jesus and Paul.

E. Stanley Jones alleged that the conclusive commentary on the New Testament could not be written until his beloved India had "been Christianized."[11] God created humans to develop as social beings. God is above culture and not confined or opposed to any one culture. Furthermore, God's revelation comes within the framework of culture in order to be fathomed. As Jones's observations on India suggest, the fulfilling of each society's unique heritage will only come when the particulars of that culture are surrendered to the Creator. Only then can the multifaceted implications of God's multicovenantal (many cite at least six covenants in the Bible) relations with humanity be fully appreciated.

Cross-cultural interaction lies at the heart of Christianity. The mandate of Matthew 28 is that Christ's followers should take His message into every cultural expression of humanity (*panta ta ethne*). Jesus led a life of constant cross-cultural communication. His genealogy reminds us that He hailed from an interethnic Afro-Asiatic ancestry. At birth, Jesus was greeted by Persian magi and then fled the Roman Empire as a refugee into Africa. In His preaching, Jesus spoke to Romans, Syrians, Aramaeans, Samaritans, and Canaanites. In each case Christ modified His approach. Contrast, for example, His dealings with Nicodemus (John 3:1–21) with interactions with the woman of Samaria (John 4:7–26). Christianity holds that Christ's life and death are applicable to every culture and that the ministry of Jesus is as much for the people who call themselves Muslims as it is for other peoples.

St. Paul was also born in one culture but called to share his faith to another. He reminded fellow Christians that God is the God of both Hebrews and Gentiles (Romans 3:29). In Christ, cultural and gender barricades were destroyed (1 Corinthians 12:13; Galatians 3:28; Colossians 3:11). His preaching strove "to become all things to all people so, that by all possible means" he might reach some (1 Corinthians 9:22). Even when Paul had reason to be critical of culture he usually remained courteous. In Ephesus, a town rife with immorality, Paul was obliging to such a degree that even the town clerk found nothing in his language that degraded the guardian deity Artemis (Acts 19:37). In Pisidian Antioch (Acts 13:16–41), his preaching stressed biblical history. Among Gentile audiences (e.g., Acts 14:14–17), he made no mention of the scriptures. At Mars Hill (Acts 17:1–4), Paul included elements of biology (v. 25), history, and geography (v. 26), and quoted Greek literature (v. 28). His communication style is what Kenneth Pike calls an *"emic"* approach,[12] where one enters into the thought-patterns of one's audience and borrows freely from their worldview in order to communicate.

Proclamation sensitive to distinctive worldview issues has not been the norm in Christian interaction among Muslims. Muslims are often required to disentangle the significance of Christianity from a distinctly European or American presentation. One Muslim despaired, "This Jesus is a Western Deity who resembles a movie-star, rather than an Israeli prophet, blonde with blue eyes and fair skin."[13] Christians are called to share the Christian message that "God was in Christ" without also exporting culture. Listen to the advice given in 1659 by Pope Alexander VII (1655–67) to Jesuits in China:

> Do not regard it as your task and do not bring any pressure to bear on the peoples, to change their manners, customs and uses, unless they are evidently contrary to religion and sound morals. What could be more absurd than to transport France, Spain, Italy, or some other European country to China? Do not introduce all that to them, but only faith, which does not despise or destroy the manners and customs of any people, always supposing that they are not evil, but rather wish to see them preserved unharmed. It is the nature of men to love and treasure above everything else their own country and that which belongs to it; in consequence there is no stronger cause for alienation and hate than an attack on local customs, especially when these go back to a venerable antiquity. This is more especially the case, when an attempt is made to introduce the customs of another people in the place of those which have been abolished. Do not draw invidious contrasts between the customs of the peoples and those of Europe; do your utmost to adapt to them.[14]

Sensitivity to a Muslim's worldview demands effort on the part of the Christian who is called to "reclothe" the teaching of Jesus in Arab, Malay, or Kazakh robes. As an idea is expressed, the Christian should ask, "If I were a Muslim, how would I respond to this?" This cross-cultural sensitivity will go a long way toward neutralizing deeply held reservations. The reclothing of the message will also, in Michael Nazir-Ali's words, "evangelize the evangelist as he discovers what aspects of the Gospel are highlighted by the particular situation in which enculturation is taking place."[15] The task of effectively communicating a Christian understanding of God's nature will free it from sexist, classist, racist, and cultural elements so that it can be applied to the "new wineskins" required by the Muslim context.

An overview of how Islamic theology affects the worldview of Muslims would include a number of considerations. Islam describes existence in two dimensions: this world (*al-dunya*) and the next life (*al-akhirah,* literally "the last," as in the "last abode"). The cosmos is permeated with legions of angels, devils, and saints who are involved in the elaborate dance of life orchestrated by God. The doctrine of fate (*qismah*) often results in a posture of calm equanimity in spite of adversity. The course of the world is established by God (Surah 54:49–50). Every person's character is predetermined, as is each person's final destiny. Other recurring motifs include a love for unity, the desire for harmony in the family, a disdain for hypocrisy in matters of religious life, and a "sociocentric" pride in Islam.

In addition, various regions within the "house of Islam" are characterized by distinctive cultural norms. Bedouin Arabs are renowned for their hospitality, strictness toward children, and respect for courage. Muslims of the Malay Peninsula place a high priority on dignity and "saving face" (*wajh*). They also seem deftly able to find a remarkable amount of time and money for frequent feasts and festivals, celebrated with flamboyant generosity.

An important factor in the development of one's worldview is the social pressure levied on the individual. The Muslim worldview, an example of what Emile Durkheim terms the "manifestations of the collective spirit,"[16] is often founded on religious traditions that have been filtered through cultural identity and have passed from one generation to the next. Ideological orthodoxy may be open to theoretical discussions about similarities in Islamic and Christian theology. On the level of cultural commitment, however, I have experienced little latitude from Muslims in defying the pervasive social expectations that weigh heavily on individuals. For many the declaration "Allah akbar!" seems synonymous with the shout "Islam akbar!"

In conclusion, the Islamic worldview asserts that the "gospel" of Islam is that God can help humanity because He is "all powerful" and beyond human limitations. Because there is within God nothing of finite pain, sin, or human suffering, He can provide salvation. The mission of every Muslim is to fight against the idea that God is "humanized" in any way that compromises His grandeur. One's worldview also affects the perception that one has about how to respond to God. Humanity is not inherently "fallen" in Islam and, as a result, individuals do not need a savior from some generalized notion of original sin. The Muslim worldview prides itself on being a perception rooted in knowledge, not mystical sentimentalism. The intellect (*al-'aql*), which is a gift from God, leads individuals into truth: "Islam is a religion based on knowledge — and not on love, as is for example Christianity — a knowledge in which the intellect itself plays the positive role in leading men to the Divine."[17]

The Islamic worldview is not neutral toward Christianity but predisposes to reject it because it "humanizes" God. Central to the Muslim worldview is a theme within Islam: God is great because He is far above the chaotic fray of human experience and vulnerability.

RELATIONAL DYNAMICS AND
THE MUSLIM-CHRISTIAN ENCOUNTER

What are the relational dynamics that are important between Muslims and Christians? Christians should learn from, and affirm, what is best in Islam, and begin with what is correspondent between the two views of God. This does not mean that Christians can or should replicate an Islamic *modus operandi* in terms of relational dynamics. Throughout the effort to communicate the doctrine of God, Christians should follow the humble, patient example of Christ in the nature of that proclamation.

A retrospective of the relationship between Islam and Christianity uncovers a state of *jihad* existing between the two traditions. Any currency of goodwill evidenced in the Qur'an has long since evaporated in the face of aggressively opinionated polemic. Instead of a reasoned exposition of the Christian understanding of God, Christians have often chosen to malign the Muslim view of God and demonize the Prophet Muhammad. A history of stultifying negative attacks against Islam has brought about, to no one's reasoned surprise, the galvanization of Muslims against Christianity, quenching any curiosity in the Christian revelation of God as Father. The climate between Muslims and Christians has often been marked by volcanic tension steaming below a thin veneer of polite courtesy.

Islam makes no apology for a militant posture which protects God's honor. The Qur'an instructs, "Therefore when you meet the Unbelievers, smite at their necks; at length when you have thoroughly subdued them, bind a bond firmly (on them)" (Surah 47:4), and, "When the forbidden months are passed, then fight and slay the Pagans (*al-mushrikun,* the 'associanists') wherever you find them, and seize them, beleaguer them, and lie in wait for them in every stratagem (of war)" (Surah 9:5). It is the duty of Muslims to defend the faith and to keep other Muslims from becoming "pagans."

When Christ was asked, "Should we strike with the sword?" (Luke 22:49), His response was that militant stridency was not the prudent course. The "more excellent way" of Christian persuasion is love (1 Corinthians 12:31; Romans 5:8). A tone of tolerance and respect joins with an understanding that God is "not willing" for Muslims to perish (1 Timothy 2:4), although it would seem that many Christians are not so unwilling that Muslims "perish" from them theologically or relationally. Jesus was "filled with compassion" (Luke 15:20), not didactic dismissiveness. The example of the Incarnation affirms that the transforming power of love is the basis and motive for Christian interaction with Muslims.

There is no room for the vituperative language of warfare and the caustic methodologies and ethics of battle. It is unusual for an individual at war to appreciate and embrace those numbered among the enemy. The task of the opponent, instead, is to look for the worst in the enemy and to expose weaknesses. It is relatively easy to parade the "darker side" of another's tradition and then broadcast the brightness of one's own faith in high-definition contrast. As Sydney Cave mused, "The power of a religion lies not in its falsehood but in its truth."[18]

Denigration of cherished hopes and ideals is not in keeping with the nature of God as Love.[19] When Muslims hear the Christian proclamation of love wrapped in the cloak of angry polemics, it becomes an alien threat instead of divine revelation. Crusading missionary "jihad" against Islam should be replaced by a seasoned exposition of the Christian faith. If it is true, as Jomier says, that "A man's estimate of another is a revelation of himself,"[20] Christians have estimated Muslims with sparse compassion and abundant simplistic fanaticism. Too often Christians have followed less the tone of Jesus and more the Qur'anic stance: "O Ye who believe! Take not the Jews and Christians for your friends and protectors... verily God guideth not a people unjust" (Surah 5:51).

The process of helping Muslims gain a sharper awareness of Christian teaching is a progressive one that requires love expressed in equanimity. An understanding of Christian faith often comes incrementally for Muslims as difficult distinctions between the Muslim and Christian understanding of God are addressed. Christian teaching in its multifacetedness demands a step-by-step, systematic presentation which avoids contentiousness (2 Timothy 2:14). Jesus' expositional narrative approach began by addressing misconceptions and then gently leading people into truth. The parables, for example, moved His followers to a more comprehensive picture of God's nature. The forbearance that Jesus showed Bartimaeus, Nicodemus, the disciples, and the woman of Samaria meant that He listened to people in spite of their preconceived misconceptions.

The revelation that "God is Love" cannot be "proven," but it is easily discredited by strident advocacy. Pride and prejudice do not facilitate an open reception to new ideas over entrenched dogma. Before God could use Peter among the Gentiles, He had to root out the fisherman's arrogant bias (Acts 10:1–48). In His ascension, Jesus told His followers to go to "Jerusalem, Judea, and Samaria" (Acts 1:7–8), confronting their ethnocentric resistance not to work among people similar to themselves. The work of the Holy Spirit at Pentecost (Acts 2:5–11) slashed dramatically across cultural and religious boundaries. Before proceeding in meaningful dialogue, Muslims might first ask their Christian counterparts the question that Jehu asked of Jehonadab: "Is your heart true to me as mine is to yours? If it is, then give me your hand" (2 Kings 10:15). Trust fosters openness.

Daily lives combine with rhetoric to communicate what is believed. A dedication to effectual interfaith witness will be expensive. Christ was crucified and St. Paul was "poured out as a drink offering" (2 Timothy 4:6–7) as exposition met opposition. To become relevant, the communicator is first required to get close enough to listen. Christians among Muslims should begin by asking themselves, "How can I serve and honor these people?" In my experiences in Asia and Africa it has been the relational dynamic of genuine compassion, more than anything else, that has drawn Muslims to consider the Christian declaration that God can be known as a loving Father.

NOTES

1. W. Montgomery Watt, *The Faith and Practise of Al-Ghazali* (London: Allen and Unwin, 1953), 21.

2. Seyyed Hossein Nasr, "Responding to the Article by Hans Küng," *Muslim World* 77, no. 1 (January 1987): 203.

3. Jacques Jomier, *How to Understand Islam* (London: SCM Press, 1988), 134.

4. Shabbir Akhtar, *A Faith for All Seasons* (London: Loewellew, 1990), 175.

5. Ibid., 178.

6. Cited by Kenneth Cragg in an article, "The Art of Theology," in *Islam: Past Influence and Present Challenge,* ed. Alford T. Welch and Pierre Cachia (Albany: State University of New York Press, 1979), 293.

7. Richard Bell, *The Origin of Islam in Its Christian Environment* (London: Frank Cass, 1968), 4.

8. Ibid., 17. This idea, Bell says, is confirmed by Harnack. Irfan Shahid claims, in his history of Arabia during the Roman period, that there may well have been an Arabic translation of the Bible before Muhammad.

9. This is not to say that Nöldeke, Goldziher, and other scholars did not do some excellent pioneering work in Qur'anic and Hadith studies but that their work was ultimately done with a sense of superiority and in a paternalistic spirit.

10. Larry G. Lenning, *Blessing in Mosque and Mission* (Pasadena, Calif.: William Carey Library, 1980), 126.

11. E. Stanley Jones, *The Christ of the Indian Road* (New York: Abingdon Press, 1925), 200.

12. Cited in George J. Jennings, *All Things, All Men, All Means — to Save Some* (Le Mars, Iowa: Middle East Missions Research, 1984), 5.

13. Ali Shariati, *Man and Islam,* trans. Fatallah Marjani (Houston: FILINC, 1974), 88.

14. Stephen Neill, *The History of Christian Missions* (Baltimore: Penguin Books, 1964 ed.), 179.

15. Michael Nazir-Ali, *Frontiers in the Muslim-Christian Encounter* (Oxford: Regnum Books, 1987), 12.

16. Emile Durkheim quoted in ibid., 89.

17. Seyyed Hossein Nasr, *Islamic Life and Thought* (Albany: State University of New York Press, 1981), 56.

18. Sydney Cave, *Redemption: Hindu and Christian* (London: Oxford University Press, 1919), 144.

19. Ibid., 20.

20. Jomier, *How to Understand Islam,* 134.

2

The Concept of God
in Islam and Christianity

ISLAMIC THEOLOGICAL HISTORY

"Let God be God!" could be the cry of both Muslims and Christians. For Islam, the unequivocal declaration of God's oneness and greatness is something of a "protective shield" around all other statements of doctrine. The constant repetition of the truth "There is no God but God" in many respects defines Islam. God's revelation is crystal clear and impossible to misunderstand.

The name *Allah* is used by both Muslims and Arab Christians to describe the one, supreme Being. "Allah" closely parallels the Hebrew term *eloah* and probably originates from the Arabic *al-ilah* meaning "the God." Centuries before the Qur'an was revealed in Arabia, "Allah" was a term used in Arabic to describe God. An indication of its early use is that Muhammad's father was known as *'abd-Allah*. Other Muslims provide a less historiographic view of its advent. One tradition ventures that the name is an eternal combination of Arabic letters inscribed on the throne of heaven.

Unfortunately, some Christians have taken the position that the name "Allah" cannot be used to communicate a Christian understanding of God's nature. Militant semantics are undergirded by decades of Protestant missionaries such as Samuel Zwemer (and others) who have described "Allah" with such gruesome caricatures as, "white-hot Omnipotence and white-hot Uniqueness, whose personality evaporates and vanishes in the burning heat of His aspects."[1] Such presentations force an artificial wedge between "Allah" and "God," with "Allah" seen as an alien demonic force. This is lamentable because the Muslim concept of God is the very foundation for the Islamic approach to holiness, justice, philosophy, and the ontology of the Muslim worldview. Without even the initial acknowledgment that the Arabic term "Allah" is not, in itself, a barrier, theological communication between Muslims and Christians is muddled at the outset.

Islamic theology was not codified in the early stages of the faith. The prophet Muhammad initially discouraged any speculation about the nature of God. Only what God had revealed about His unbounded nature could be ascertained. Suspicion was rife toward academics who, by argument, could construe falsehood as truth and cast truth as error. Early Muslims were skeptical of any attempts to construct a theological framework that might "demystify" God. They looked askance at theology as an attempt to evaluate or encapsulate God. Instead, God should be the focus of worship.

If talking about God in theological terms opened the door for intellectual idolatry, how could early Muslims convey an Islamic doctrine of God? Muslims began the theological interpretive process cautiously, not by describing who God is, but by defining what, or who, God is not. Negation became the accepted way to express something about the divine nature. It was established, for example, that God has no relation, no pain, and no limits to His power. He was in no way human or finite.

Once the beachhead of interpretive possibility was established, "the science of theology" (*'ilm al-kalam*) blossomed in the Islamic community. The term *kalam* literally means "speech," or "discourse with someone." This usage springs from the fact that early Islamic theology was accepted by the larger community to fulfill a primarily apologetic and defensive role. *Kalam* was fashioned to witness to revealed truth, solve dogmatic problems, and protect the community from heresy. Early Muslim theologians observed that the Prophet's first assignment was to war against those who associated anything with God or who said that there were parallels between Him and the other pagan deities. *Kalam,* seen in this prophetic tradition, came to be defined as a science of iconoclastic clarification.

The next period of Islamic theological development added to the early apologetic focus on external "enemies" (such as Jews and Christians). This phase dealt with doctrinal tensions within Islam. God needed no defense, but the community needed authoritative elucidation. Faith required definition. In this context, early Muslim theologians taught against departing from the God of worship in the worship of God — an error seen as rife among non-Muslims.

The first positive theological definitions within Islam were raised as bulwarks of protection around the doctrine of God's unity. In contrast to the *Mu'tazilite* sect,[2] orthodoxy affirmed the oneness of God as a truth consistent with the revelation of His attributes. Muslims largely rejected rationalistic argumentation (*qiyas,* literally "to compare") in discussing God's nature and attributes as idolatrous. It was felt that such an approach relied too heavily on analogies, which are invariably imperfect when describing God. This conclusion is important to Christians seeking to discuss their faith with Muslims.

Far too much Christian literature for Muslims (for example, discussions about the Trinity) unwittingly follows this discredited method. Instead, Christians would do well to rely on the straightforward retelling of biblical narratives.

After the initial stage of independent interpretation, Islamic theology fell into a posture of retrenchment. Subsequent generations of Muslim theologians (*mutakallim,* literally "a speaker") no longer formulated theology but simply applied what had already been revealed to specific cases. With the passing of independent interpretation, what Christians know as "theology" was supplanted by textual commentary (*tafsir*). The maintenance of traditional interpretation replaced creative theological paraphrase, exegesis, and explication.

A lack of familiarity with Islamic theological procedures has doomed numerous ill-advised exchanges between Christians and Muslims. Some Christians, for example, have unwittingly encouraged Muslims to embark on a process of dialogue that is tantamount to the early practice of "independent interpretation," or *ijtihad,* (literally "independent effort"). This course is problematic because *ijtihad,* relating to issues of jurisprudence, does not mean complete freedom from theological judgment (*kalam*). More accurately, *ijtihad* is the process of exerting one's self in the confirmation of legal and social orthodoxy. Any operation of autonomous exploration, free from the constraints of other interpretations, is usually held to be no longer possible (culminating, it is often held, in the eleventh century, with the *ijtihad* of al-Ghazali). Since the late nineteenth century the notion that *ijtihad* can no longer be initiated has been dramatically contested by liberal, reformist Muslim scholars. The argument of these scholars is that the widespread reliance on *taqlid* (uncritical acceptance of tradition) and the imitation of such medieval legal authorities as al-Ghazali invariably stifle the Islamic community's ability to address contemporary legal and social issues. This question relates to issues of Islamic theological interpretation (*kalam*), but it is safe to say that there is far less willingness among most orthodox Muslims to open the doors of theological discussion and interpretation (*kalam*), and it is this intransigence that is not helpful to interfaith discussions. One cannot say something "new" about the Prophet and the inspiration of the Qur'an and other foundational Islamic pillars of faith. Muslims are interested in questions about Islamic order but are not very open to new ideas about theological inquiry.

Christians meeting Muslims in discussion should seek to present their views within the framework of the accepted patterns of Islamic theology. Christians should familiarize themselves with the literature, structures, and assumptions of Islamic theology. This will result in Christians' not relying solely on Islamic source material (such as the Qur'an), which is not subject to other interpretation. Instead, Christians should point to orthodox precedents when framing responses to specific textual questions.

THE ISLAMIC DOCTRINE OF GOD'S ATTRIBUTES

In Muslim doctrine, God's attributes (*sifat*) describe His will and not His nature. This distinction is important for Christians who claim that Jesus is an expression of the nature of God. Before the Incarnation and divinity of Christ can be discussed, it is important to grasp how the Muslim and Christian views of this question are dissimilar. Once this is done, the implications of this variance for an understanding of revelation (and the related question of soteriology) can be articulated.

Mystics disclosed that there are 100 names of God but only 99 of these have been revealed. European Islamicists have culled as many as 550 different references to God from various Islamic sources.[3] Most Muslims, however, since childhood have recited the ninety-nine "beautiful" names of God (*al-asma' al-husna*). These speak of what God does and say nothing about His divine nature. The conclusion of early Muslim theologians was that "descriptions of Allah must be, at the best, inadequate and misleading, and, at the worst, impossible."[4]

Christians can ask Muslims, "Is it possible to know God?" The answer of Islamic orthodoxy has been that God is beyond knowledge. An individual can "know" his or her proper relationship with God, but this "knowledge" protects God's nature from being examined or evaluated as if theology were some branch of the modern sciences. Only God's attributes can be observed as they are expressed in the life of the world. If God can be known, orthodoxy contends, then God also becomes, to some degree, accessible and thus subordinate to humanity. The Islamic doctrine of God converges on the attributes that are essential to God's being and on the characteristics which prove His being. Islamic theology addresses the issue of what God does but does not answer the question, "Who is God?" This is because God is free from personality, perceived to be a quality of limitation. Islam insists that God, devoid of personality, is imbued with a luminous "simplicity." This also means that God is beyond any human capacity to commune with His nature. To think otherwise is to be misled.

How do Muslims perceive God's attributes? The monotheism of Islam underscores that there is no greater evil than the blasphemy of "associating" (*shirk*) anything with the divine nature (Surah 4:116). God's attributes are fundamentally that He is infinite, impersonal, and eternal: "neither is He a body or a spirit and neither does He exist in anything or does anything exist in Him."[5] The numerous anthropomorphic references to God in the Qur'an (for example, His "eyes" in Surah 11:37; 20:39; 23:27) are deciphered as symbolic and not seen to impugn God's difference (*mukhalafah*) from all created beings. Within the Muslim view of God there can be no "differentiation" that could lead to something like the doctrine of the Trinity. Since the *sifat* of

God speaks of His will but not of His character, Christians can ask Muslims to explain the relationship between God's will and His divine essence.

An introduction to the Muslim concept of God is aided by an awareness of His attributes as they are described in the Qur'an. God, in His omnipotence (*kuhrah*), is also omnipresent and "close" to every creature (Surah 34:50, 50:16). God is the compassionate (*al-rahim*), the forgiving (Surah 5:98), and the merciful (*al-rahman*). He is known as the powerful (*al-qadir,* Surah 2:20), and mighty (*al-'aziz,* Surah 60:7); without any equal. Another truth about God is that He is the eternal one (*al-samad*), unbegotten, and without children. God is the just[6] and the holy (*al-quddus,* Surah 59:23), the "all-compelling" (*al-jabbar*) motive behind all actions and "the one who decides" (*al-fattah,* Surah 34:26). God is depicted as He who is "subtle" in His actions (*al-latif,* Surah 6:103), and who is all-wise and all-knowing (*al-'alim,* Surah 2:261) in His dealings. He is "He who lives" (*al-hayy,* Surah 25:58) and dies not. God is self-subsistent (*al-qaiyyum,* Surah 2:255), the "wonderful engineer" (*al-badi,* literally "He who originates," Surah 6:101) of life. The work of God is perfect (Surah 67:3), and He provides for all (Surah 15:20). He never changes (Surah 48:23). God is the "evident and the hidden" (Surah 57:3).

The two most recurrent names for God in the Qur'an could provide opportunities for interfaith discussions about the nature of God. They are that God is "the merciful" (*al-rahman*) and the "Lord of all" (*al-rabb*). The reminder of God's mercy begins all but one of the chapters of the Qur'an. The thirty references to God as "Lord" closely parallels the New Testament usage of the term (*kyrios*). Both Muslims and Christians could be asked to explain what this Lordship means in terms of their relation to God. Muslims and Christians could relate how they have received divine mercy and how it affects their lives of faith and their understanding of God.

Christians can ascertain other areas of agreement with the Muslim concept of God. God is described in the Hebrew Bible as being omnipresent (1 Kings 8:27; Psalms 139:7–10); eternal (Habakkuk 1:12; Jeremiah 23:24); omniscient (Psalms 139:2–5; Psalms 147:5); and unchanging (Malachi 3:6; James 1:7). God is good (Psalms 145:9), merciful, and long-suffering (Exodus 34:6; Psalms 51:1; Micah 7:18).

Some of the designations of God revered by Muslims, however, seem difficult for Christians to reconcile with the New Testament. These include descriptions of God as the "proud one," the "one who leads astray," the "avenger," the "abaser," and, the "one who harms." It cannot be said in Christianity that God is "the one who leadeth to stray whom He will" (Surah 13:27; see also 35:8), or "the one who deceives both the good and the bad" (Surah 14:4, 27). The Hebrew Bible describes God as "jealous" (e.g., Deuteronomy 4:24) and the one who creates both light and darkness (Isaiah 45:7); He who is "vengeful" (Isaiah 47:3) and one who "repents of evil" (Jonah 3:10). God's jealousy and vengeance are not capricious in any respect. The holiness of God means that He cannot Himself do what He condemns or instructs His creation not to do. The Christian doctrine of God's holiness, defined in moral terms, claims that the perfect nature of God excludes the possibility of divine imperfection. The biblical view of God's holiness (Isaiah 6:3; Exodus 19:1) shows God as "too pure to look on evil" (Habakkuk 1:13) and intolerant of wrongdoing.

How does Christianity express the relationship between God's nature and His attributes? Christians believe that the New Testament is a revelation that emerges in a progressive, historical process of divine self-disclosure. The intent of classical Christian theism has been to strike a balance between an evaluation of the individual attributes of God and what can be known about His essence. The foundational doctrine of God's Triune nature confirms that the acts of God are always ancillary to His character and are unerringly consistent in explaining that character. Christian theology, unlike Islam, becomes a systematic exposition of God's nature as well as His attributes.

An instance of this different view of the relation between God's nature and His attributes is seen in the understanding that God is the one who forgives (*al-ghaffar*). In Christianity, unlike Islam, the forgiveness that humanity receives is both the work of God and a revelation of the divine personality. God in Islam must be excluded from any participation in suffering. The torment in Gethsemane (Matthew 26:36–42) and Golgotha (Matthew 27:33–50) "wins" forgiveness for humanity while embracing anguish. It is in suffering that God expresses His nature as loving and participant within humanity. Although some Christians have espoused an Aristotelian concept where God is defined in terms of pure causality, such a depiction does not take into account the primacy of the crucifixion and the extent of the Incarnation. God expressed in Christ is active in the pain of the cross and the unconditioned extent of His humanity. It is God's nature as love, and not some demand on the part of God for the shedding of "holy blood," that establishes covenants between the Creator and the creation.

In conclusion, the distinction in Islam that God's nature is not revealed by His attributes is a principal starting point in discussions about the Christian and Muslim understanding of God. The Muslim concept of God declares that He cannot be known in personality because His essential quality is beyond comprehension. The descriptions of God in the Qur'an announce what God does, and what His will is toward humanity, but do not describe the nature of the divine essence. The revelation of the Bible, while relating what God does, is intent on providing an answer to the more fundamental question of "who is God?" The uniquely Christian answer to that question takes form in the person of Christ.

ISLAM: "GOD IS ONE!"

In the silence a voice thundered far above their heads: "I bear witness that there is no God but God!" It was the mullah proclaiming the Oneness of God in the city of the Million Manifestations. The call rang across the sleeping city and far over the river and be sure that the mullah abated nothing of the defiance of his cry for that he looked down upon a sea of temples and smelt the incense of a hundred Hindu shrines.[7]

On the eve of Islam, the *ka'bah* in Mecca was ringed by as many as 360 idols of the Arabian tribes. The war against polytheism which the revolutionary Prophet inaugurated rattled the religious status quo. The earliest Islamic theological declarations reverberated that "God is One" and railed against the idolatrous falsehoods of a God construed in the image of humanity.

Islam exists to protect the truth of God's unity. What Islam castigates about Christianity is that divine unity is denied in the claim of the Trinity and the Incarnation. A consciousness of this treasured emphasis will steer the Christian into a more careful retelling of the doctrine of God which affirms God's unity and explains how this unity is upheld.

The words of the creed, "There is no God but God and Muhammad is the Messenger of God" (*la ilaha illah Allah, wa Muhammad rasul Allah*), are probably recited more than any other words in the world. The Qur'an came to Muhammad because previous generations of Arabs had not correctly esteemed God's unity (Surah 6:89; 22:74; 39:67). The doctrine of divine unity (*tauhid*) is the theological eye of the needle through which every other Islamic statement of faith (*iman*) must pass. God is one in essence without any distinctions, multiplicity of powers, or plurality of will. This unwavering affirmation of divine unity works with powerful simplicity to banish mythological confusion about God's essence.

In Islam, the greatness of God flows from the oneness of God. The *shahadah,* the incessant affirmation of God's unity, confirms that this unity is the basis for divine sovereignty (see Surah 2:163; 6:19; 16:22; 23:91–92; 37:1–5; 112:1–4). Because God is one, the message and messengers are also unified and provide a singular revelation of guidance — namely, Islam. The unity of God defines the transcendence of God. This truth cannot be explicated but must be taken by faith "without asking how" (*bi-la kayf*).

Christians recognize in Islam a theological tension between the affirmation of God's unity and the perception of His transcendence. This fissure unlocks a type of "practical deism" that opens the possibility of pantheism and mysticism. The notion that everything will ultimately be annihilated and "swallowed up in God" is centered on one reference in the Qur'an: "And call not, besides God on another God, there is no God but He. Everything (that exists) will perish except His own face" (Surah 28:88). The unalterable Islamic concept of God's unity as a mathematical singularity sets the stage for the depersonalization of humanity. Humanity travels from stage to stage of existence (Surah 84:19), but its final destiny is to "return to God" (Surah 6:60, 72; 10:45–46). In some sense it could be argued that humankind waits to be erased in the indivisibility of the Creator, the only reality.

A categorical defense of God's unity at the expense of any sense of personality within the divine nature invariably leads into conflict with Christian doctrine. In Islam, it is not possible to say that humanity is made in God's image because there would then be something of God beside Himself. Through the centuries, Muslims have chided Christians for saying that God took a wife (Mary) and had a child (Jesus). This is the basis for the Muslim accusation that Christians are polytheists. Even today, some children shake their fists at foreigners and scowl, "God is One! Jesus is not the Son of God!" (*"Allah wahid! 'Isa mush ibn Allah"*).

Muslims can be shown that the tenet of God's oneness is also foundational to Christianity. It is firmly anchored in the *shema Israel* of Deuteronomy 6:4: "Hear O Israel, the Lord our God, the Lord is one God!" Jesus avowed the oneness of God without any partnership (Mark 12:29–30). Christians might ask Muslims to explain if the oneness of God must be defined as a mathematical unity or if it could also be expressed as a complex unity. The biblical revelation of God's nature need not automatically be labeled polytheistic merely because the divine nature cannot be characterized as a monistic unity. Muslims could be shown that this idea is also found in other traditions besides Christianity. One Jewish writer, Rabbi Solomon Ibn Gabirol, intoned, "Thou art One, O Lord, but not as one that is counted or owned. For number . . . cannot reach thee."[8]

In church history, Unitarianism most closely approximates the Islamic view of God's unity. For the Muslim, God's essence has no second and His attributes are insusceptible to division (Surah 2:255; 4:171; 7:191; 16:51; 27:59). One can say "God is just and merciful," but such a declaration is only an asseveration about divine action. Only in this way does a discussion of God's attributes not compromise His freedom from any differentiation.

In conclusion, Islam, like the modalism of early Christianity, seeks to safeguard God's unity by rejecting the doctrine that Jesus could be fully divine. Islam condemns the Christian doctrine of God's unity in trinity. But for Christians God cannot be understood apart from the relationships of Father, Son, and Spirit. God is not a remote, metaphysical, force. God cannot be obligated to fit into the straightjacket of monism. By contrast, the Christian conception of God's unity invites the Muslim to reexamine axioms about God's nature. Muslims might consider the Christian claim that the "personality" of God is revealed in Christ Jesus. Muslims might be asked to deliberate on how the biblical portrayal of unity means more than mathematical singularity.[9]

CHRISTIANITY: "GOD IS LOVE!"

The central revelation of Christian faith is that "God is Love!" This claim is both an impediment and an avenue for Christians in their discussions with Muslims about the nature of God. This is because the love of God is not a conceptual abstraction to be debated but a relational truth that has been vividly imparted in Christ and is accessible through the revelatory power of the Holy Spirit. In this section, the Muslim idea that God is loving is contrasted with the Christian view of God's nature being described as Love. Finally, this section will note the implications of this distinction and how this can be clarified to Muslims.

In Christianity, divine love is the motive for all revelation and, ultimately, the source of salvation. The God revealed in the Bible cannot be described as distant, remote, or apathetic. Jesus disclosed the love of God with such a tremendous degree of intensity that John was able to pen one of the most intrepid theological definitions imaginable: "God is Love" (1 John 4:8). This *agape* love

> does not seek value, it creates value or gives value; it does not desire to get but to give; it is not attracted by some lovable quality but it is poured out on those who are worthless and degraded.[10]

The preeminence given to the theme of covenant in the Hebrew Bible prefaces the New Testament's articulation that God's essence and power are expressible as Love. The pronouncement that "God is Love" provides an indication of God's intention toward creation. God cannot be solitary if He is loving. This idea of God in communion with humanity brings with it a view that is beyond monism, because God Himself exists in interrelationship. Islamic unitarianism echoes the Aristotelian concept of an "Unmoved Mover" who is necessarily free from need, vulnerability, and passion.

This self-revelation of God as Love is conclusively more than a postulate about one of His attributes. The Jewish scholar Abraham Heschel spoke of a "theology of divine pathos"[11] in which God is to be worshiped as loving because He allows Himself to "suffer" as participant in the midst of human experience and uncertainty. The generous nature of God is so completely expressed in the New Testament that Jesus was described by early Christians as God's "suffering servant," as described by the prophet Isaiah. Both suffering and servanthood, concepts with no inherent majestic dignity, are embraced by Christ.

This participatory love of God invites a response. It penetrates human life with the possibility of communion with God. God calls humanity to love Him as an expression of obedience, and enables His invitation to be realizable by being the one who "first loves." The command to relate to God with all of one's "heart and mind and soul" (Matthew 22:37) is capable of being fulfilled only because God has first loved with all of His "heart" and "mind" and "soul" in sending Christ.

Does the Qur'an invite Muslims to this kind of "intimacy" with God? Al-Ghazali asserts that the reference in the Qur'an which characterizes God as the "best of those who show mercy" (Surah 23:109, 118) does not suggest that God manifests emotional involvement, or vulnerability, toward humanity. If God were to hold such sentiments, it would be an expression of weakness and not of divine power. God exhibits mercy to people and is compassionate, but God cannot "feel" anything in His divine essence beyond Himself. Islamic "intimacy" with God cannot include God's vulnerability to humanity.

In Islam, God is "the merciful," which illustrates His divine will and not His divine being. God extends mercy to those who are meritorious (Surah 4:97–100). Mercy (not *agape* love) is the impartation of divine favor. The Almighty decides to be clement (Surah 10:107; 29:21) and "grants mercy to whom He pleaseth" (Surah 9:27). God, as interpreted in Islam, is not "obligated" to love. It is His prerogative to dispense mercy to some and withhold it from others. By His choice, God is lenient and forbearing (*al-subur;* Surah 3:155) and offers the conditions whereby sins can be easily annulled. His love cannot be described as universal or unconditional toward humanity. God is "full of kindness to those who love Him but loveth not those who reject faith" (Surah 3:30–32; see also verse 45). God rewards the good (Surah 3:134, 140) and those who put their trust in Him (Surah 3:155) with His love. The love that God has for believers is more accurately seen as a result of submission or as a magnanimous response to those who are obedient to His will.

God does not love sinners. This fact is repeated twenty-four times in the Qur'an. He does not love evildoers (Surah 3:57) or the deceitful (Surah 4:107). It would be unbecoming, according to Islam, to represent God as a "shepherd who would leave the ninety-nine" to rescue one lost sheep (Luke 15:2–7). It would be incomprehensible to say, "God commended His love to us, in that while we were yet sinners..." (Romans 5:7–8). How does this inconceivability affect the way that Christians talk to Muslims about the nature of God? Perhaps it would be helpful to explain God's love as His greatness to destroy evil through Christ's submission to the divine will and plan of salvation.

In Islam, the mercy that God bestows is primarily the wisdom of the imparted divine law. Humanity must return the gift of God's guidance, not with "love" in a Christian sense, but with devoted service (*kunu 'ibadan li*). A person surrenders to God to merit the acquittal of sins. This is not a straightforward "business transaction," because God always reserves the right to do as He wills. The love that God calls humanity to is actually love for themselves in self-protection from the divine wrath that is to be poured out on the rebellious. From obedience to God, individuals garner the possibility of receiving mercy in the judgment and the hoped-for reward of deliverance from eternal punishment.

Islamic doctrine professes that God has no need for humanity and has chosen to remain aloof from the vile imperfections of this world. It is asserted that "If all the infidels became believers, God would gain no advantage; if all believers became infidels, God would suffer no loss."[12] Islam announces that God is loving and merciful, but it does so in a way that implies that the two words are synonymous. Yet, in the Qur'an, while God is called "the loving one" on two occasions (Surah 11:90; 85:14), He is referred to as "the merciful" over two hundred times. Muslims whom I have encountered are much more comfortable referring to the provision of "God's mercy" than the more ontological "love of God."

Christians must probe the implications of this view. Certainly, one approach would be to focus on the relationship between mercy and love and explain how love (*agape*) is unlimited and intrinsic in the act of creation. God's love is universal. The condonation of God, in Islam, flows from His will. In Christianity, the will of God originates in His nature as a God who, in *agape* love, gives of Himself without seeking remuneration.

The Incarnation is considered by Christians to be the fullest enunciation of divine love. The Bible shows that, since the time of Abraham, the truest test of commitment is love expressed in the willingness to give that which is most cherished. On a greater scale than Abraham's readiness to sacrifice his son, God has "poured out His love" (Romans 5:5) on creation. As St. Paul announced: "He who did not spare His only Son but freely gave Him up, how shall He not with Him freely give us all things" (Romans 8:32). This concept of God as Love is revolutionary. Emil Brunner remarked:

> The message that God is Love is something wholly new in the world. We perceive this if we try to apply the statement to the divinities of the various religions of the world: Wotan is Love, Zeus, Jupiter, Brahma, Ahura Mazda, Vishnu, Allah is Love. All these combinations are obviously wholly impossible.[13]

One of Christ's disciples exclaimed, "Herein is love, not that we loved God but that He loved us and sent His Son as propitiation for our sins" (1 John

4:10). The atoning work of God in Christ is an expression of the divine nature before it is a statement about human depravity or the need for surrender to God. Divine immanence and transcendence meet in the love of God at the cross of Jesus.

When I have asked Muslims, "In what way has God shown His love to you?" I have received a number of responses. I have never heard a Muslim answer, "God gave Himself." As imaged in the cross of Jesus, God gives Himself. The revelation that "God is Love" shows the heart of God, not merely the prerogative of His will. If one could hypothetically pose to God the question whether or not He could love, the revelation of Christ would reveal that God would have no choice! In hermeneutic terms, in other words, what I am saying is that a major focal image of the divine nature as self-giving love is different from the central focal image of God as portrayed in Islam.

Christians are called to walk in love without restriction, obligation, or hope for reciprocation. Christ bids His disciples to take up "crosses" of self-denial, service, and humility to share with others what they have freely received. The love expressed in Christ wars against pride, suffering, and evil, with the greatest power known in creation: the power of God. This potency is most clearly witnessed to, not in strength or wealth, but in poverty and weakness. Even the Qur'an testifies to this; in referring to Christians in seventh-century Arabia, it noticed,

> Strongest among men in enmity to the Believers wilt thou find the Jews and the Pagans; and nearest among them *in love* to the Believers wilt thou find those who say, "We are Christians": Because amongst these are men devoted to learning and men who have renounced the world, *and they are not arrogant.* (Surah 5:82; emphasis is mine. In Pickthall it reads: "They are not proud.")

The Christian's commission is to communicate that "God is Love" with such clarity that Muslims are able to accept that love and, in so doing, add to their comprehension of God's nature. Muslims can be encouraged to the point where intimacy with God is not seen as contradictory to a view of God that accentuates His majestic power. Christian revelation explains that these coexist in the Incarnation.

GOD'S TRANSCENDENCE

The orthodox view of God's transcendence in Islam claims that God is utterly unfathomable and nothing about His nature can be known. How is this transcendence bridged? Intimacy with God cannot be grasped and is not sought. All too often, interaction with Muslims does not take this into account.

Before Muslims should be invited to communion with God they will need to be shown that communion is desirable, and then that it is possible. To lay a foundation for this effort, the Islamic concept of transcendence will be discussed and suggestions will be made as to how interfaith discussion can respond to this perspective. It will be noted that the reality of most Muslims is that they live their daily lives as if God is immanent, and not distant, from their experience. This seeming contradiction does not seem to need clarification in either the Qur'an or Islamic theology. It may, however, underscore an intrinsic phenomenological need within humanity to intimately relate with their Creator.

Divine transcendence in Islam (*tanzil*) is closely related to God's unity (*tauhid*). There is an utter difference (*mukhalafah*) between God and His creation. The supereminence of God means that He cannot be "touched" in any way by humanity. Any "compassion" that God shows is not to be confused with human parallels because that would "humanize" God. Because God is completely recondite, nothing can be said about Him that is not in the Qur'an. Even the words of the Qur'an do not describe God because His essence is beyond description. By definition, God is one who is eternally shrouded and unknown. This "distance" of the divine is a gift from God in that it protects humanity from idolatry.

How does this emphasis on transcendence correlate with the idea that God gives revelation? The supereminence of God in Islam establishes that humanity is completely dependent on One who is beyond any dependence. The stress is placed on the distance between the divine and the human with the allowance that God has chosen to communicate something of His hiddenness. The world is given moral principles and some knowledge of God's attributes in order to worship Him more accurately. The Muslim would argue that this does not compromise the contrast between God and the isolated individual, a gap that is qualitatively infinite. To the Muslim, God's omnipotence means that He remains forever concealed from the purview of human estimation. The very existence of the Qur'an, however, seems to conflict with this position. The signs (*ayat*) that God gives, and the miracle of the Qur'an, stand in contrast to a deistic view of God.

In transcendence, God is beyond recognition. In Islam, God is said to be above knowledge and even removed from the concept of being. This elaboration seems to come close to the extreme transcendence of Plotinus or the divine "void" set out by Plato. Islamic theology seems intent on thrusting God further from humanity in order to avoid any hint of idolatry. In the process, however, the view of God can come to resemble a "pantheism of force"[14] in which God is inside and outside of everything and still one in substance. He is the power behind all phenomena but is not Himself affected.

The question arises: If God exists in unequivocal isolation from humanity, is He not in a real sense "irrelevant" (at least in terms of covenantal relationship) to humanity?

This cognizance of transcendence affects other areas of the Islamic view of God. The concept of transcendence must correlate with the belief that God is omnipresent (Surah 50:15; 57:4) and active in the world.[15] God orchestrates every event, even the "steps of a black ant on a black rock in a dark night."[16] Is God so completely indefinite that nothing can be known about Him, while at the same time every shard of information reveals something about His will and attributes? How does Islam reconcile the categorical separateness of God from His complete involvement where whatever occurs is done by Him? One medieval theological tome, the *Risaleh* of Barkhawi, claims:

> Not only can He do anything. He actually is the only one who does anything. When a man writes with a pen and piece of paper, actually it is God who has created in his mind the will to write. God at the same time gives him the paper to write, then brings about the motion of the hand and the pen and the appearance of the paper. All other beings are passive. God alone is active, the only motor, the sole energy in the Universe.[17]

According to Islam, the mystery of who God is can never be divulged. Christianity, by contrast, claims that God is not limited by the fact of His transcendence or bound in a prison of indifference toward humanity. God initiates covenants with humanity and is interested in individuals. He not only creates the world but is also able to participate within it. In the genesis of life, God's "spirit moved over the face of the waters" (Genesis 1:2). He does not remain vaguely perceived but is boldly called the "God of Abraham." The architect of the universe is willing to enter into covenant relationship with one man, Abraham (Genesis 15) and with all humanity after the flood of Noah (Genesis 9:8–17).

The Bible animates the idea that God has chosen to limit the prerogative of His transcendence. God is revealed as a personal being who is not made finite by having personality. The divine is not human, but is also more than simply unlike humanity as Islam portrays. "God, in Christ" is not "apprehended," nor is He completely knowable. He is more than absolute simplicity, and divine transcendence means more than that God is isolated and distinct.

Islam renounces the postulate that God can be explained as a personality. He is not "substantial" (defined by Islam as that which has extension). Islam insists that Christianity views God as a substance ("one of three," Surah 5:73) and as a Spirit, notions that are shunned by Muslims. The latter is because Islam warrants that spirits are created and thus defined in a very limited way. God is lacking spirit or personality and, in His essence, is simply "one."

The Qur'an, however, does not avoid anthropomorphisms to represent divine action among creation. It describes God as being corporal and resident on a heavenly throne. References are made to the face of God (Surah 6:52; 18:28) and His hands, feet, and eyes. The first Islamic theologians confirmed that God had these features, but they were not parallel with human qualities. Later, it was clarified that God had none of these; Qur'anic references were only symbolic metaphors to describe spiritual attributes. Finally, it was canonized in Islamic theology that God's essence was absolutely simple and without any multiplicity or characteristics.

The Muslim view of transcendence is that God is forced outside the realm of comprehension — a problem that it has in common with Christian theology. In this stress on God's "differentness," Islam becomes prone to a host of contradictory statements about God's nature. God is not in a place. He is not an object; He is not a person. His transcendence means "God is not a spatial infinity,"[18] nor is He limited. Muslims worship a God who is neither personal nor impersonal. God is not impersonal because something can be known of His attributes through His actions. These attributes can be named and accepted as reliable revelation. God is not personal because He is beyond passion, participation, emotion, or any other quality that approximates personality. Revelation and the giving of names for God are not a self-revelation. If they were, then God would be distinguishable and could then be understood. The doctrine of divine transcendence concludes that all efforts to comprehend God are idle exercises in futility.

It is important to remember that most Muslims, however, live their lives as if God's immanence, and not divine transcendence, is His most important attribute. The doctrine of transcendence may preserve the unity of God from philosophical idolatry, but it does not sate the worshiper in daily religious practice. The experience of God that most Muslims maintain through their faith, far from being distant, rules the eating, sleeping, living, and dying of their existence. The name "Allah" is the most commonly spoken word in the Muslim world. Yet, the Islamic doctrine of transcendence leaves little to be said about analogies in our experience to help us understand the word's meaning after the singular, clear truth that "God is One" has been said.

In conclusion, the Islamic view of transcendence means that God cannot be known. On the one hand, God is beyond comprehension, but on the other, it is asserted that He is relevant to every action and thought in life. Christianity claims that the cross of Jesus in history "solidifies" God's relatability. Christ suffered and died, not for Himself, but for humanity. The love of God holds within the divine nature the desire to overcome dimensions of preeminence that separate Creator from creation. Islam attests that God is both omnipresent and detached from human experience. This is not feasible from a Christian perspective. In the Incarnation, God chooses to eclipse any degree of intangibility and enters into physical space and historic time.

In terms of focal images of the Muslim and Christian worldviews, Islamic theology, without a doctrine of the Incarnation, cannot easily reconcile the parallel assertions that God is both transcendent and immanent. Muslims affirm His distance but function with a definite sense of divine immanence. This dichotomy exposes the problem in the insistence within Islam that God is beyond knowing. It also illustrates the need that individuals have to circumvent a view of God that is remote. In Christianity, though it has many of the same problems of articulating God's relation to the world of our experience, any drift toward abstract transcendence is dialectically countered by the doctrine of the Incarnation. God in Christ is motivated by love and chooses involvement and participation. Ultimately the image of God suffering wins out in the Christian imagination over the impenetrable security and isolation of distance.

GOD AS CREATOR

A notable divergence between the Muslim and Christian doctrines of God is in the question of His activity in creation. The implications of this are significant because of the biblical revelation that God has created humanity in His image. Inherent in this belief is the potentiality for individuals to experience a degree of communion with God. This provides an ideal starting point in dialogue because it would seem that the Islamic view that God is transcendent and, at the same time, Creator seems untenable. Muslims do not believe that humanity is crafted in God's "image." The lack of this perspective, I believe, makes it difficult for Muslims to conceive how it is possible for individuals to enter into covenant intimacy with the Creator as imaged in the New Testament.

Directly related to the question of His transcendence is the revelation of God as Creator.[19] In Islam, God fashions humanity but He in no way participates within it. He initiates everything but He is completely separate from all that He has made. Muslim theologians explain that, because God is continuously creating: "There are no stable natures in the universe."[20] Everything that exists is being constantly re-created moment by moment. Humanity is uncreative and has no capacity to fashion anything separate from God. Orthodox Islam condemned the *Qadariyya,* the only sect in Muslim theological history who held that individuals had some power to innovate. If humanity is creative in any way, then there would be other "Creators." This is impossible within the framework of Islamic theology.

Why, according to Islam, did God author the world? This work is an act of God's immense power and a result of His will. This view is compatible with orthodox Judeo-Christian cosmology. In the Bible, creation is the act of an infinite, personal God who generates, not out of His essence as an extension of His being, but *ex nihilo*. In Judaism and Christianity, however, there is the desire to be creative inherent in the nature of love which motivates God. God created humans for relationship with Himself and generated the world for His pleasure. There is no suggestion in Judaism or Christianity that God spawned the world in order to satisfy some unfulfilled potential within Himself, or out of some unachieved need to "manifest" divine love. The numerous covenants that God offers to humanity show His expansive, progressive nature, and not some ineffectiveness on His part toward His creation. For Judaism and Christianity, the fact that individuals are made in God's likeness speaks of the potential for covenant. The Genesis account affirms God's capacity for intimacy. Humanity crafted in God's image is seen as the height of creation, gifted with imagination, choice, and a sense of morality.

There are other implications of this view of creation for the Muslim-Christian encounter. The biblical exposition of humanity made in God's image belies human potentiality to know God. The generation of individuals in God's image shows the intention of the invisible God to be recognized. It can never be said of the God revealed in creation that He is silent because, in Judaism and Christianity, even the design of humanity is an act of self-revelation. This foreshadows the Incarnation, as the infinite God is expressed in a way that is comprehensible to finite beings. As God creates humanity in His own image, one can even say that a degree of self-humiliation is initiated between the Creator toward His creation. This "vulnerability" of God finds its truest expression in Jesus' description of God as "our Father" and the promise of covenant relationship in which individuals become God's "children."

For Judaism and Christianity, creation explains the hope of salvation and the nature of the world. God did not intend individuals to be without the potential to create and exert a degree of autonomy. He is not afraid of "competition"; rather, He seeks cooperation. In Eden, God is the Creator, but He is imaged as seeking Adam's participation in naming the animals and husbanding the garden. It is the love of God that imparts this ability to create and be free. In His grace, God invests within His creation something of Himself. The Jewish and Christian perspective of creation is a statement about the divine desire to establish relationship (*koinonia*) with humanity fashioned in His image. Christ saves humanity, made in the image of God, by being both fully human and fully divine. This sets forward the prospect of re-creation and the penultimate rectification of the problem of evil.

THE ABSOLUTE WILL OF GOD

No religious community, including Islam, holds an uncontested, mono-lithic set of beliefs. For most Muslims, however, it is widely accepted that everything that occurs in the world is a direct result of God's will. Because most Muslims reject the predominant Christian view that humans exercise "free will," the question arises of how individuals are accountable to God, if they are ultimately not responsible for their actions. Christian faith teaches that God in Christ does not impose His will with the demands of an enforced tyranny. Humans are invested with choice and are thus free from determin-ism. Individuals are able to blossom into relation with God but must also take responsibility for their own actions.

For most Muslims, every decision in life proceeds conditionally with the caution, "God willing!" (*insha'Allah!*). The Islamic worldview is largely col-ored by the unassailable inevitability of the divine will. This is illustrated in a tradition about the Prophet Muhammad's view on the destiny of each person:

> It is related that 'Aisha said: The prophet was invited to the funeral of a little child. And I said, "O Apostle of God, Blessed be this little bird of the birds of Paradise, it has not yet done evil nor been overtaken by evil."
>
> "Not so 'Aisha," said the Apostle, "Verily God created a people for Paradise and they were still in their father's loins, and a people for the fire and they were yet in their father's loins."[21]

The doctrine of God's predetermination of fate (*qismah*) is not detailed in the Qur'an, but it characterizes Islamic theology. An individual's personal destiny (*qadar,* from the Arabic, "to measure") is preordained and there is no question of one's independence from God. Although numerous Muslim theo-logians have wrestled with the implications of this, the underlying premise of determinism has remained predominant.

One theologian, al-Ash'ari, affirmed that while God was the sole Creator, His decrees work within the will of the human doer. In this sense there is a degree of "acquisition" (*kasb,* or the related term *iktisab*) of the action per-formed. Because a person holds the "acquisition" of a deed, it was regarded as "saving his moral responsibility and accountability."[22] In the creation of every person's deeds, be they sinful or righteous, God is glorified. Theolo-gian Abu Hanifa explains, "Even though God is responsible for creating evil which is done by permission, it is not His good pleasure."[23] The result of this is that the evildoer made corrupt by God becomes the object of God's wrath. God puts evil, as well as love, into people's hearts for Himself and for others (Surah 30:20).

Because God is the "unmoved Mover," He alone has power to act (Surah 54:50). The exercise of an individual's free will is preposterous because it essentially establishes an authority outside of God. The Qur'an seems to imply that individuals have a degree of autonomy (e.g., Surah 7:178–82; 13:29; 42:15). This status, however, is clearly dependent upon the overarching will of God (Surah 10:99–100; 81:29; 82:7–8). Because God's supremacy knows no limit, humanity has no autonomous authority. Humanity must strive to do God's will, but in striving or not in striving, God's pleasure (*rida*) is accomplished. The issue is not what a person should do, but rather what God intends to do through divine command (*amr*).

For Muslim theologians, God's action is not an expression of His moral nature but of His divine prerogative. The view of God as absolute will is a concept that would seem to contradict any idea of free moral agency. It is the assumption of Christianity that, in a real sense, unless one is able to withhold something, one is not free to give it. Where there is no volition on the part of the individual, there can be no genuine submission to another. Spencer writes that, within Islam, there is no area (external or internal) where an individual exercises freedom: "In the process of human thought, Allah's creation is discontinuous in itself and dependent for its existence on the immediate impulse of Allah's will."[24]

It is interesting that one of the ninety-nine beautiful names of God is the "deceiver" or "misleader" (*al-mudill*). God, "the best of Schemers" (Surah 4:143), is presented in a manner analogous with the role that Satan plays in the book of Genesis. In the Qur'an, Satan (*Iblis*) is made of fire (Surah 7:12) and directed by God to perform a host of malevolent deceptions (Surah 4:76). The fact that God allows deception, carried to its theoretical conclusion, would seem to call into question how a Muslim can be "certain" that any received revelation, including the Qur'an, might not also be a work of God-ordained deception. In actual fact, there is no such doubt among Muslims who are completely confident that God will not deceive them. This confidence speaks of the Muslim assurance that individuals are promised by God the capability of ascertaining divine truth.

It is often noted that the Qur'an attests, "God will not mislead a people after He hath guided them" (Surah 9:115). This, however, it could be argued, refers specifically to the accuracy of revelation given to the prophet Abraham. Twenty times in the Qur'an, God is said to lead people astray. God is responsible for human disunity (Surah 5:48), ignorance (Surah 6:35), idolatry (Surah 6:137), unbelief (Surah 10:99), and even the sin of "association" (*shirk*, Surah 16:35–36) leveled against His own honor. The Qur'an tenders the idea that humanity holds the "dignity of accountability."[25] At the same time it proclaims that God is completely responsible. As theologian Muhammad al-Barqawi explained,

He willeth also the unbelief of the unbeliever and the irreligion of the wicked and without that will there be neither unbelief or irreligion. All that we do, we do by His will, and what He willeth not does not come to pass.[26]

Islam contends that it is reprehensible to say that God does evil. But what does this mean in light of the fact that God is above morality and responsible for all that takes place, including evil? How is the fact that God creates "evil" in any way construed as moral? Is it that God permits wickedness so that some greater good might transpire, or is it that any gift which He gives to humanity is given in the knowledge that it will be abused and later removed? It is God who "wills" the unbelief of unbelievers and who is morally responsible for the evil of humanity. It is God who condemns to hell but who is incapable of experiencing anything of an individual's wretchedness within hell.

Humanity is under perpetual compulsion (*majbur*) in every situation to the fixed decrees of God. The intent of God is imposed without compromise, and humans are impotent to superimpose any will against divine power. There is no need for God to initiate any subsidiary manifestation of Himself as meekness, humility, gentleness, or love. If God chose to express Himself in these ways, it would only advance His inevitably orchestrated purposes.

The Bible proclaims that God "sits enthroned in Zion" (Psalms 9:11) and takes delight in human worship (Psalms 149:4) and great sorrow in rebellion (Isaiah 63:10). Christianity portrays humanity as free and shows that freedom in humanity and divinity are not mutually exclusive. Freedom is unstintingly given in creation (only two initial restrictions are established). This is because liberty and trust are expressions of love. Human history exists, a Christian believes, because individuals are free. Because humanity misuses that sovereignty, history has become a tragedy. Humans not only long for God, but God also longs for humanity. The yearning of the human heart is not the aspiration of a slave disabled beneath the weight of capricious predetermination; it is the expectation of one enabled by divine love and is a reflection of the divine nature.

In conclusion, Christians might consider exploring the Muslim understanding of God's absolute will and how God's authority may or may not lead to a strict determinism that would crush any significance of individuality. This also raises questions of how history is to be viewed as anything but static if it is said that God is ultimately the author of all that transpires. Can a person initiate any action apart from God if everything that happens is inevitable and the outworking of divine greatness? Under the weight of such predetermination, are individuals only temporary and without any intrinsic worth apart from their role as a component in God's great design?

This relates to Muslim and Christian understandings of salvation. Christians must recognize that Muslims feel no need for a savior because God has predestined whether or not salvation is allotted to them. God is responsible for all actions, be they good or evil. He demands obedience whether this is rewarded with Paradise or hell. With these presuppositions, individuals foster little sense of God's love in the face of His unquestioned power. Concurrent with the view of transcendence, there is no concept of intimate and relational communion with God in orthodox Islam except among some Sufi Muslims. Most Muslims find satisfaction in the joy that God is completely sovereign. Muslims who are not Sufi find their dignity in this dependence because, it is said, a slave to God need be a slave to none other. Christians could describe how a belief in free moral agency provides another way to explain the worth that God has invested within each individual. The dignity that God imparts is ontological and not based on one's performance of ritual or obligation to attain merit.

CONTRASTING VIEWS OF GOD'S POWER

The first exclamation from the muezzin in the call to prayer is "God is Great!" ("Allah akbar!"). It is an affirmation that there are no rival absolutes besides God. All other attempts to attribute power to someone is the sin of polytheism (*shirk*). God is the "Lord of Power" (Surah 61:58), without partnership (Surah 6:136–37). His power is steadfast and over all things (Surah 2:284; 3:29). God has "power to send calamities" (Surah 6:65) and all other events (Surah 16:77–87): "To Him go all questions and decisions" (Surah 3:109). The all-powerful majesty of God is the guiding principle that helps Muslims understand God's actions. His omnipotence is unmodified and His power is absolute.

How does Islam advocate that humanity should respond to God's greatness? The appropriate reply is the active acknowledgment of divine Lordship (*takbir*) in submission (*islam*). For this reason, the measure of one's obedience to God and knowledge of His power approximates the extent of one's godliness and wisdom. In the confession of God's oneness and in the understanding of that transcendence, a person focuses on that which is truth. The ritual repetition of the creed (*shahadah*) refreshes the worshiper with the reminder of divine greatness. God, in His mercy, extends to all the invitation to submit to His will and rest in His protection.

Christianity calls believers into "submission" as a response of love for God and a desire for communion. This synergy is possible with a holy God because His power is able to transcend the frailty of humanity — not by absolute decree, but by patient love and gentle invitation. Jesus calls to humanity, "Behold, I stand at the door and knock. If anyone hears my voice and opens the door I will come in and sup with him and he with me" (Revelation 3:20). God in Christ comes to humanity with an invitation and seeks a response.

This emphasis on love in the Christian doctrine of God does not exclude divine power. The Bible testifies that God is *El-Shaddai* (Genesis 17:1). This name is interesting because it relates to the Hebrew term "breast" (*shadd*), signifying that the power of God encompasses the idea of nurture, security, and most of all, intimacy. God is the Lord of Lords (Psalms 115:3), the only Lord (1 Timothy 6:15). He is majestic in His power (Exodus 15:6) and saves by that power (Jeremiah 27:5). God has power over everything in the universe (Deuteronomy 8:17) but chooses not to exercise that power. According to most Christian theological traditions, God has given humanity free moral agency and the latitude to act independent of His will.

How can Christians explain to Muslims the relationship between God's power and His love? The power of love, not the force of an autocratic and unyielding will, is the authority that God in Christ exercises. This might is evident at the cross. God never willed the defeat of humanity (Genesis 3:8–19); the crucifixion unfolds the intention of God to bring victory over disobedient human will, sin, suffering, and death. The cross provides God's power for salvation (1 Corinthians 1:18) because only God's love has the power to forgive and overlook the sins of humanity. Christian doctrine maintains that the only solution to the problem of evil occurs when God comes among humanity. Only God could provide the holiness that He requires for intimate relation with Himself.

The power of God in Christ not only overarches all other attempts to attain power, but also resolves the desire for individuals to grasp sovereignty which rightly belongs to God. The power of God in Christ establishes a covenant based on love and not force. Christ has been given "all authority in heaven and on the earth" (Matthew 28:18) and invites humanity to share in His dominion. This is a supremacy won by Christ, the servant. Because Jesus was

> Obedient to death, God has given Him a Name which is above every Name, that at the Name of Jesus, every knee shall bow and every tongue confess that Jesus Christ is Lord to the glory of God the Father. (Philippians 2:8–10)

Christians believe that God has chosen through the Incarnation to pursue the path of choice and love — not an autocratic imposition of His will. The strength of God in Christ on the cross reveals an entirely different conception of divine authority. It is a sovereignty that does not strip humanity of the ability to act autonomously. It is a potency that makes the act of human worship possible and genuine. Christ provides freedom to know God as a loving Father instead of only experiencing Him as divine formidability and responding to Him in submissive resignation. Muslims argue that Christians have distorted their original mandate to testify to God's greatness. Divine power in Christianity is not drawn along human conceptions of invincibility, but describes an authority that is inherent in love and without compulsion. This ability overcomes humanity's fallen condition and will ultimately negate all injustice. Christians disclose that God is not only great, but that His greatness is not a barrier to His love. "God is greater" because "God is Love."

GOD'S WILL AND GOD'S HOLINESS

Holiness in Christianity is linked with human moral rectitude; in Islam, it emphasizes God's differentiation from humanity and is the expression of His will. Muslims could be shown how the Christian idea relates to their own understanding of the need to be holy in order to please God.

Islamic theology is based on the guiding principle that the law of God is the foundation for discerning every aspect of life. Divine justice, however, cannot be paralleled to human standards of equitableness (Surah 4:40). If it were, the temptation would then arise to question the morality of certain acts of God's will (Surah 85:16). How could a child be born with a terrible disease? How could God allow the massacre of Muslim children in Palestine? Islam answers such inquiries by saying that the justice of God is without flaw but not always easily comprehendible. God is the one who is "best to decide" (Surah 10:109). Every enigma, however, will be answered on the final day of judgment (Surah 36:51–54). In the final analysis, we will discover God's wisdom in all circumstances and situations.

How is God's justice viewed in Islamic theology? Right is whatever God commands; wrong is that which is not His will. God is not bound by any law but He is law Himself (see Surah 21:47). One Hadith vividly exemplifies this truth: On the judgment day, two individuals, one devout and one profane, stand before God. God dispatches the pious person of almsgiving to hell while the blasphemer is lifted to Paradise. When God is questioned about this He replies: "Be silent! Have I not the right to do as I please with what is my own?"[27] The justice of God is the will of God.

Islam describes God as the "Holy One" (*al-quddus*). The holiness of God is comprehended, not in a human or moral sense, but by the fact of His "difference" from all that is human. God is beyond grieving or rejoicing over any human situation because He is holy. God is free from all needs or desires (Surah 31:26; 35:15) including any requirement to relate with His creation. The Christian idea that it is humanity's moral destiny to share in the holy nature of God is reprehensible to Muslims.

The conviction that God is morally holy is not repudiated in Islam. It is, however, seen as irrelevant because God supersedes creation. Any statement about God's probity is pointless because it is based on an imposition of human moral rectitude against the fact of God's sovereignty. In contrast, every variant Christian doctrine of atonement relates to God's moral holiness and the obligation that holiness places on divine action. The doctrine of creation revealing God's nature and likeness links together the relationship between human and divine morality. In Christian faith, God's moral holiness confirms His righteousness and the purity of God and expresses the moral authority for His will.

Holiness, in both Christianity and Islam, separates God from humanity. In Christianity, humans are rebellious; in Islam, humanity is unholy simply by definition (i.e., they are not divine). The Bible emphasizes that apart from Christ "no man can see God and live" (Exodus 33:20; Isaiah 6:5; 1 Timothy 6:16). Individuals approach God with fear and reverence. The New Testament disclosure of God as "Father" and Christ as "friend" does not contradict the Torah's revelation of God's holiness. What becomes clearer in Christianity is that God's holiness creates a gap that is bridged by Christ in reconciling humanity to the purity of God. God in Christ is more than simply the "wholly other." Holiness speaks of God's moral character in a way that is recognizable because of the revelation of the Torah. This holiness does not mean that God is distant from His creation. Neither does God's nearness mean that He is proud or sinful. Islam views a God who is both holy and near to sinful humanity as schizophrenic. For Christians, one cannot understand holiness apart from God's love.

The term "holy" (*quddus*) is used in the Qur'an but is not defined. The early Islamic theologian al-Baidawi insisted that it was "the complete absence of anything that would make Him less than He is."[28] In Islam, there is no requirement for God to be morally righteous because He is sovereign. His dominion is over everything (Surah 3:189; 4:126; 5:120); all that He allows cannot be judged to be either morally righteous or unrighteous. Christianity maintains that God's holiness is a moral blamelessness, presented to humanity in sharp distinction to its own fallen nature.

In conclusion, Christians cannot accept that the holiness of God can be exclusively defined as the will of God. Moral holiness characterizes the Christian valuation of God's transcendent purity. The distance between God and humanity is not insurmountable because God desires that individuals participate in His nature. People can be holy because this is God's intention in creation and provision in the New Covenant. An awareness of humanity's unholy moral condition and a corresponding appreciation of God's moral holiness are essential in the transmission of Christian soteriology. Can it be said that God's transcendent holiness in Islam makes Him infinitely inaccessible? For Christians, the Incarnation has forever resolved the separation between humanity's impurity and God's holy nature.

NOTES

1. Samuel Zwemer, "The Allah of Islam and the God Revealed in Jesus Christ," *Muslim World* 36, no. 4, n.d., 307.

2. In an article "al-Mu'tazilah," by H. S. Nyberg in *The Shorter Encyclopedia of Islam,* ed. H. A. R. Gibb and J. H. Kramers (Leiden: E. J. Brill, 1991), 421–27, there is an introduction to this movement in early Islam. It has been suggested by some that the conclusions of the *Mu'tazilah* could provide a helpful resource in Muslim-Christian interaction.

3. Kenneth Cragg, *The Dome and the Rock* (London: SPCK, 1964), 84. Cragg goes on to say on the same page (84–85): "The figure ninety-nine is traditional. About two-thirds of that number actually occur quranically. J. W. Redhouse in the *Journal of the Royal Asiatic Society* (1880, no. 12, new series, pp. 1–69) collected from various sources no less than five hundred and fifty-two. But ninety-nine is the devotional number, fixed in the beads of the *Subhah,* or Islamic rosary. It also makes the sum of the Arabic numerals (81) on the left-hand palm and (18) on the right-hand palm — a fact which passes into symbol when, in devotion, the outstretched, upturned hands are lifted to God in prayer."

4. Cited in an article "Sifa" by D. B. MacDonald in *The Shorter Encyclopedia of Islam,* 545.

5. Al-Ghazali quoted in Samuel Zwemer, *The Moslem Doctrine of God* (London: Oliphant, Anderson and Ferrier, 1905), 31.

6. The title "God, the Just" is not in the Qur'an, although the term "justice" is mentioned in the Qur'an on twelve occasions.

7. Quoted from a poem by Rudyard Kipling, "The Bride's Progress," and cited in Kenneth Cragg, *The Christ and the Faiths: Theology in Cross-Reference* (London: SPCK, 1986), 81. In describing Islam in contrast to Hinduism, Yusuf Ali's footnote (number 3421) to Surah 28:88, says, "We know then that what we call our own self has no meaning, for there is only one true self, and that is God. This is also the Advaita doctrine of Shri Shankara in his exposition of the Brihad-aranyaka Upanishad in Hindu Philosophy," p. 1027.

8. Attributed to Rabbi Solomon Ibn Gabirol's treatise *The Kingly Crown,* trans. Bernard Lewis (London, 1961). This quote appears on pages 28–29 of that text. Cited in Cragg, *The Christ and the Faiths,* 32. Cragg also notes that this writer is noteworthy because he was a Spanish Jew who wrote in Arabic. Also known by the Latin name "Avicebron," this rabbi lived from A.D. 1020 to 1070.

9. St. Gregory of Nyssa teaches that the immanence of God does not contradict His transcendence. In his *Catechetical Oratios* (cited in J. Windrow Sweetman's *Islam and Christian Theology: A Study of the Interpretation of Theological Ideas in the Two Religions* [London: Lutterworth Press, 1947], vol. 2, part 1, 42), he states: "The Divine nature has the property of penetrating all things without mixing them and of being itself impenetrable by anything else."

10. Emil Brunner, *The Christian Doctrine of God* (Philadelphia: Westminster Press, 1961), 186.

11. Abraham Heschel, *The Prophets* (New York: Harper, 1957), 221.

12. Attributed to the *"Risaleh-Barkhawi"* and cited in John Elder, *The Biblical Approach to the Muslim* (Fort Washington, Pa.: Worldwide Evangelization Crusade, 1978), 59.

13. Brunner, *The Christian Doctrine of God,* 183.

14. Kenneth Cragg, *Jesus and the Muslim* (London: Allen and Unwin, 1985), 287.

15. Historic Christianity has also struggled to explain the relationship between transcendence and divine disclosure. For most Christians, resolution is found in the Triune nature of God, where He is in communication with Himself, and in the covenant, where God relates with humanity made in the image of God.

16. Attributed to "Maqsad ul-Asna" and cited in Elder, *The Biblical Approach to the Muslim,* 53.

17. Attributed to Barkhawi and cited in ibid., 52. In this context Surah 3:159, "God has power over all things," is often quoted.

18. Muhammad Iqbal, *The Reconstruction of Religious Thought in Islam* (London: Oxford University Press, 1934), 61.

19. In Zwemer, *The Moslem Doctrine of God,* 71, there is an interesting citation about creation: "According to the table-talk of the Prophet (*Mishkat-al-Masabih,* 24:1, part 3) God created the earth on Saturday, the hills on Sunday, the trees on Monday, *all unpleasant things on Tuesday* (emphasis Zwemer's), the light on Wednesday, the beasts on Thursday, and Adam, who was the last creation, was created after the time of afternoon prayers on Friday."

20. H. Spencer, *Islam and the Gospel of God* (Delhi: SPCK Press, 1956), 6.

21. Cited in Zwemer, *The Moslem Doctrine of God,* 97.

22. Cragg, *The Dome and the Rock,* 163. The entire quote reads as follows: "But He [God] decreed it within the will of the human doer. The latter in turn acquires (hence *kasb*) the deed and this was regarded as saving his moral responsibility and accountability. The intellectual 'solution' really hands back the problem in the form of an answer — a device to which philosophers are liable to resort. Since God willed the deed in the will of the doer, he was undividedly sovereign and man was still accountable. But the core of the issue, namely whether or not man could will otherwise than what God willed on him, was left unfaced. The explanation of freedom in any event leaves it illusionary."

23. Spencer, *Islam and the Gospel of God,* 50.

24. Ibid., 65.

25. Cragg, *The Dome and the Rock,* 168.

26. Cited in J. N. D. Anderson, *Christianity and World Religions* (Downers Grove, Ill.: InterVarsity Press, 1984), 31.

27. Cited in Elder, *The Biblical Approach to the Muslim,* 51. One is reminded of how this contrasts with the view of God presented in Exodus 32:11–14 where Moses intercedes for Israel and where it is said that, "the Lord relented and did not bring on His people the disaster He had threatened" (Exodus 32:14).

28. Cited in ibid., 54.

3

Revelation and the Concept of God

REVELATION IN ISLAM

Once, while the Prophet Muhammad was praying, an angel appeared to him and told him, "Cry!" The prophet responded with the soul-stirring question: "What shall I cry?" What followed was the revelation of the Qur'an. The term *"Qur'an"* relates to the Arabic *qara'a* or *qira'ah* meaning "he reads" in the sense of reciting. The word "Qur'an" is a Syriac variant of this Arabic verb (the root letters are the same).

Islam is a faith rooted in revelation. The Qur'an is seen as God's definitive guidebook for life. God, in His compassion, has chosen to answer ignorance with the words of prophets and the voices of angels. Before the advent of the Qur'an, the voice of God was not silent. There were thousands of words given in various revelations. Further, each cultural grouping received revelation. Surah 13:36 declares, "Amongst every people a messenger." Only four of these more than 100,000 heavenly disclosures, however, are known to have survived through the centuries. These were the Law of Moses (*tawrat*), the Psalms of David (*zabur*), the Gospel of Jesus (*injil*), and the Qur'an. The Qur'an tells Muslims to appeal to the other scriptures (Surah 10:94; 6:114) because they are given by God (Surah 6:20–21; 43:43–45). The Qur'an (Surah 5:44) speaks of the excellencies of the Torah and the "clear proofs" of the Gospel (in Surah 2:47, 87; 3:3–4; 61:6). With the arrival of the Qur'an, these books were authoritatively superseded.

The composition of revelation in Islam sheds light on the Muslim concept of God. The Prophet Muhammad never presumed to have discovered truth. Nor did the Qur'an teach that the Arab people gradually came to fathom revelation within their collective consciousness. Truth belongs to God alone and has been bestowed since creation. Every individual is capable of some knowledge of God, even if it is only the truth that nature is a gift of His kindness (Surah 15:19–21).

The Qur'an plays in Islam the role that Christ retains in Christianity. Muslims allege that the Qur'an is the most widely read book in the world. For its adherents, it is the definitive authority on theology, politics, ethics, and social issues. It is God's revelation in its specific form and conclusively defined by its content. God has spoken to one person, Muslims say, and in so doing addresses millions of people throughout the centuries.

The origin of the Qur'an is said to predate the Prophet Muhammad; its eternality emphasizes its divine authorship. Although the Qur'an was bestowed six hundred years after Jesus, its content was said to be in an unblemished form before creation. Presently there exists, according to Muslims, an exact replica of the Qur'an preserved on golden tablets in heaven (Surah 43:3) guarded by angels (Surah 85:21–22). These were inscribed in Arabic even before the language was formulated on the earth. "The noble Qur'an in a book kept hidden" (Surah 56:77–78) is an eternal mystery. God's speech, as uncreated, parallels the Christian view of the coeternal Word of God (*logos*) in Jesus (John 1:1–18).

The debate in Islam as to whether the Qur'an is created or eternal has important implications that both Muslims and Christians should consider. If the Qur'an is without beginning, then there are two noncreated entities: God and His word. If this is the case, then the nature of God is differentiated and the Muslim interpretation of God's unity (as being free from all characteristics) is compromised. If, however, it is concluded that the Qur'an is created, how can it be said that the speech of God is not created? There can be no duality in the divine nature, nor can it be said that God creates His own speech. This preincarnate view of the Qur'an holds intriguing ramifications. Christians might consider asking Muslims to synthesize the relation between revelation with their view of God's transcendence.

This belief of an eternal Qur'an raises the puzzle of how a host of abrogated, "satanic" verses are to be construed. Surah 23:14, for example, proclaims, "Blessed be Allah, the best of Creators" (Pickthall).[1] Surah 53:19–21 alludes to earlier gods and goddesses adulated in Mecca: "Have ye thought upon al-Lat and al-Uzza and Manat, the third, the other? Are yours the males and His the females?" (Pickthall). These are a few of many passages that have undergone divine abrogation, or "cancellation" (*naskh*), even though they are included in a text that is sacred and without human participation. Christians should ask what their inclusion says about God and the nature of Islamic revelation.

The orthodox Muslim response is that, although Iblis (Satan) tried to confuse the Prophet (Surah 22:52), God cancelled his attempts but allowed these texts to remain as a poetical reminder and proof of divine victory. There are as many as forty other verses that are abrogated (*mansukh*), "forgotten" and "caused to disappear"[2] from the Qur'an. The question of how abrogated scriptures can be found in a flawless book, however, is one raised only by unbelievers and critics of the Qur'an. For the faithful, the explanation of the purpose and nature of these verses remains with God.

Whatever its origin, Muslims are convinced that the Qur'an is infallible. It is the truth through which every other fact must be filtered.[3] The Qur'an is the unforgeable, incomparable (*i'jaz*) word from God without equal (Surah 10:37–38). Islam intones that it is superior to all other revelation because (among other reasons) it does not condescend to focus on personalities, as does the Bible with its emphasis on Jesus and the apostles, prophets, and patriarchs. The focus of the Qur'an, rather, is on the greatness of God[4] and the need for humanity to submit to God's will. If something else is written which does not agree with the Qur'an, then that other source is incorrect. The corruption of other scriptures is offset by the fact that the Qur'an is infallible. What other books ought to contain is found in pellucidity in the Qur'an. It is this iron-clad cycle of reasoning that Muslims use to evaluate every other theological statement outside of the Qur'an.

At the heart of this certainty remains the unanswered problem of how the oneness of God and the eternal nature of the uncorrupted Qur'an (complete with abrogations) are to be reconciled. The logic of faith, however, silences all questions with the implicit confidence in the finality of the Qur'an as given to the Prophet. Humanity may not understand the Qur'an, but this is because there has not been an appropriate submission to its authority.

The Prophet Muhammad's function in the process of revelation is passive. He is merely the recipient of the Qur'an. It is not his formulation and contains nothing of his personality. Islam is not "founded" by the Prophet Muhammad. This distinct lack of "human-ness" in Islam is distinctly counter to the human role played in the transmission of biblical revelation. The general consensus in Islam is that the less "human" revelation is, then the more surely it is divine. The postulate that there is no human element in the Qur'an is a ringing affirmation of its trustworthiness. To underscore this point the Qur'an tells us that the Prophet Muhammad was the "unlettered prophet"; one who was completely illiterate (Surah 7:157–58).

Humans are recipients but not participants in the impartation of revelation. The Qur'an submits, "It is not fitting for a man that God should speak to him, except by inspiration, or from behind a veil, or by the sending of a messenger to reveal with God's permission what God wills" (Surah 42:51). Humanity is only a speck in God's universe and has no ability to comprehend the spiritual dimension. In His mercy, God gives inspiration (*wahy*) to individuals either by a thought "thrown"[5] into one's mind, or by the less common verbal and "recited" (*matlu*) revelation reserved for prophets.

These chosen prophets are the primary recipients of divine revelation. Islam believes that God is not indifferent to humanity, and this is verified by the fact He has sent prophets. They are proof of His mercy. There is, however, no relationship between the prophet and the God who sends them. An appreciation of the Muslim view of prophethood is noteworthy in light of the fact that Jesus is distinguished as a Muslim prophet.

What is the relation between the prophets and the God who sends them, and what does it mean that they are "sent"? God is active in that He "sent down" (*nazzala* which relates to *tanzil*, "sending"). The act of sending, however, does not imply that God seeks a response from humanity. What is "lowered" and what "comes down" is the truth about the will of God. The fact that God gave the Qur'an does not imply that God in His approach to humanity desires to disclose something about His divine nature. The emphasis is on revelation as inspiration and guidance, not as an unveiling of God's nature.

For Muslims, the search for knowledge through revelation is not a quest for individual understanding. Rather, it is the process of accepting what has already been given by God. Whatever can be known can be learned through the Qur'an, approved Hadith, the consensus of the Muslim community (*ijma'*), and "analogy" (*qiyas*). Orthodoxy concludes that God no longer speaks; the revelation that has been given is entire and absolute. The finality of the Qur'an, its elaboration in Hadith, and its interpretation in early Islam have forever sealed the process of divine revelation. Nothing else can ever be known about the nature and will of God.

In conclusion, there is no comparable human element in Islamic revelation. As a result, Muslims look askance at the Bible's anthropomorphizing. Biblical revelation, in the Islamic account of Christianity, has been given to a host of prophets reaching a finale in the ministry of the Prophet Muhammad. Christians could ask why, if there is no human element in revelation, is the way of the Prophet Muhammad (*sunnah*) a source of divine guidance second only to the Qur'an. The Qur'an is the "incarnation" of the will of God and is seen by Muslims as more immediate than their conception of the Christian view of Christ's presence. Revelation has ceased to come and is not an individual pursuit. Simply by opening the Qur'an, however, any individual can immediately enter into the presence of God's authoritative revelation to humanity.

REVELATION IN CHRISTIANITY

> Long ago God spoke to our ancestors in many and various ways by the prophets, but in these last days he has spoken to us by a Son.
>
> — Hebrews 1:1 (NRSV)

Christianity claims that there are numerous sources of revelation from God. He speaks through the splendor of creation, through the fabric of human experience, and through the prophets and monarchs of ancient history. God provides dreams and sends angels. Today, God speaks through the active inspiration of the Holy Spirit. His Spirit directed the authorship of the Bible.

Revelation is at the foundation of Christian doctrine. Theology is the expression of beliefs about God as He is revealed in the Bible. Most Christians accept the historical scriptures as a theological unity wherein God unfolds His nature and provides a record of His divine involvement (*koinonia*) with humanity. The various forms of revelation find their apogee in the Incarnation.

The Bible is a compendium of various kinds of texts that catalogue God's work across a span of centuries. Because the Bible is written by a number of authors and is not one book (like the Qur'an), Muslims complain that it lacks coherence. Muslims whom I have encountered often find in the Bible a bewildering number of styles and perspectives, which only seem to underscore their doubts about its reliability. It is the predictable tactic of cacophonous Muslim apologists to focus their attacks against the Bible and its trustworthiness. These charges reflect the prominence that the Qur'an plays in their own thinking and the significance that Muslims place on its inviolability.

Biblical revelation is historical. This emphasis on revelation proceeding through time is incidental to Islam but paramount to Christianity rooted in the Incarnation of God in a specific time and place. Whenever one mentions the name of Jesus, one is referring to an unrepeatable fact of history.[6] Jesus breaks through the surface of myth and history to disclose the divine nature. The historicity of the revelation is an indication of God's nature to participate within creation and His desire for its redemption.

Unlike Islamic revelation, the Bible, in Christian theology, is portrayed as disclosing God's nature. It announces that Christ is "the image of the invisible God" (Colossians 1:15). The revelation of God as personality in Christ brings a fusion between objective, impersonal truth and subjective, personal covenant between God and individuals as well as their communities. The revelation of a knowable God in Christ is so definitive that there is no room for an impartial debate about its demands. Because of the experiential nature of Incarnation, revelation has everlastingly become more than limited theological representations. Christians, as a result, need not be concerned about defending the content, historicity, or form of revelation with an Islamic insistence on technical, literal inerrancy. The issue of biblical revelation is not the analysis of religious experience; it is an analysis of faith about who God is and where individuals and their communities of faith stand in their relationship with Him. Christianity harmonizes with Islam in saying that there is no room for mortal judgments about divine proclamations.

Christians can encourage Muslims to study the Bible and need not adapt its content to suit Islamic presuppositions. The bold proclamations of the New Testament (such as Acts 4:12) announce that there is no salvation outside of Christ and no knowledge of God beyond Christ for the followers of Christ.

God's self-revelation speaks supremely of the Word of God Incarnate. Discussions need not degenerate into bickering about textual specificities but are able to center on God's nature as revealed in scripture.

The Bible asserts that the Word of God is "sharper than any two-edged sword, penetrating even to the dividing of soul and spirit, joints and marrow and judging the thoughts and attitudes of the heart" (Hebrew 4:12). Christians are called to rely on this supernatural authority, able to appeal directly to hearts. Christians would do well to regard the recommendation of the Qur'an (Surah 5:71):

> Say, O People of the Book, you have no ground to stand upon unless you stand fast by the Law, the Gospels, and all of the revelations that have come down to you from your Lord.

THE ROLE OF THE QUR'AN AND THE BIBLE IN MUSLIM-CHRISTIAN INTERACTION

How might Christians approach the Qur'an in interfaith discussions? Within the Qur'an are a host of theological claims that concur with Christianity. It is fundamental that the Qur'an be studied by Christians. An accurate consciousness of Islam will precede the ability to communicate theological ideas cogently with Muslims. There is no need to vilify the Qur'an or raise questions about its authority. In its use, however, care should be taken to subscribe to Islamic methodology of interpretation.

The Qur'an, in the rolling rhythm of poetic Arabic, deals with the Trinity, the scriptures, the Virgin Birth, miracles, death, and resurrection of Christ. The Qur'an announces that Christians and Muslims worship the same God (Surah 22:40), that Christians find salvation in their own religion (Surah 2:62), and that the Bible has been given by God (Surah 4:47). The Qur'an propounds Jesus to be the Messiah and "of the company of those nearest to Allah" (Surah 3:45). These titles for Jesus are ideal points of departure in the Muslim-Christian dialogue. Caution must be taken, however, in handling literature that is held to be divinely inspired. Those who seek to unearth a "Christian potential" in the Qur'an expose themselves to questions about why they are not willing to concede that it is also a divine revelation. In examining the Qur'an, Christians should be careful to read what it says and not what they hope that it would say.

Historically, few Christians have given weighty consideration to the Qur'an and even fewer strive at gaining an informed appreciation of it. The Christian community's view of the Qur'an has been predominantly negative except for an occasional commendation of the "refracted glory" of biblical parallels. There are definite discrepancies between the Bible and the Qur'anic account,[7] but these need not solely define the Christian's response to the text. It is important that the study of the Qur'an proceeds unencumbered from the inherited conclusions of the past. In so doing, Christians will be in a better position to encourage Muslims to reciprocate and take a fresh look at the biblical narrative.

It is important to know how most Muslims believe the Qur'an should be approached. Firstly, the Qur'an is above criticism. Research by some Islamicists which conjectures that the Qur'an was derived from Jewish and Christian sources is unequivocally dismissed by most Muslims. There can be no redaction criticism of the Qur'an. It cannot be viewed as the "sum of its parts." Although one Muslim writer, Fazlur Rahman, purports that the Qur'an is "the word of God and at the same time the word of a human prophet,"[8] most Muslims would vehemently disagree with the notion that it contains any human element. Its authenticity springs from its divine origin.

How might Christians interpret the Qur'an? A Christian hermeneutic of the Qur'an would probably be as problematic as would a Muslim hermeneutic of the Bible. Although the interpretation of another tradition's texts does not imply a commitment to the authority of those texts, it should be able to proceed in a manner that is not condescending or dismissive. When the Qur'an is used, it must be treated as most Muslims treat it: in the time-honored practice of cross-referencing within the Qur'an and in careful harmonization with tradition. Instead, it is often analyzed free from its moorings in centuries of interpretation. When this is done, a wedge is driven between the Qur'an and its historic meaning. A Qur'anic hermeneutic without reference to Islamic interpretation might seem logical to those Protestant exegetes whose forefathers chose to disregard centuries of Orthodox or Catholic tradition but it is reprehensible to most Muslims. Christians often respond to the Qur'an with irrational disparagement and are hesitant to embrace the idea that there is truth contained within it. When one reads the Qur'an, it is obvious that it is a treasury of insight into various aspects of the human experience in search of God. Free from judgmentalism, the reader can gain personal challenges to spiritual growth, as well as a more accurate insight into the Muslim understanding of God. One should be able to examine the Qur'an without feeling obligated to believe that it is inerrant. The biblical guideline is:

> Whatever is true, whatever is honourable, whatever is just, whatever is pure, whatever is lovely, whatever is gracious, if there is any excellence, if there is anything worthy of praise; Brethren, think about these things. (Philippians 4:8)

There are also elements in the Qur'an and traditional source material that Christians could encourage Muslims to study in greater detail. Christians can play a role in sensitively directing Muslims to facets of their own tradition that explain the Qur'anic portrait of Christ in a way which is less jaundiced than that of many modern Islamic apologists. The Qur'an, for example, announces that Jesus is the Messiah and a "Spirit from God." Early Islamic thinkers, like al-Ghazali, conducted earnest studies of the New Testament without questioning its authenticity. These points are not widely known by many Christians.

Beginning from the Qur'an, Muslims should be encouraged to investigate the Bible. Christians need not apologize for the Bible and should remember that Muslims expect them to rely on it. Inaccurate interpretations arise from false presuppositions. When the Bible is carefully explained, many Muslim misconceptions about Christianity will vanish. Christians are capable of affirming the high authority given to scriptures without becoming enslaved to a conception of inerrant revelation that is more Islamic than historically Christian. It should be stressed that the Bible is viewed very differently in Christianity than the Qur'an is within Islam. This can be explained in the context of the Islamic worldview. One Muslim whom I met in Morocco, for example, did not grasp the reason for there being four gospels instead of one, until I explained to him that, just as in a court of law, a host of witnesses is helpful to confirm the truth of any report.

The Qur'an contains a host of statements concurrent with Christian revelation. Christians who interact with Muslims need to be students of the Qur'an who garner truth, and not only points of disagreement, from its pages. Treatment of the Qur'an must be consistent with Muslim interpretation, even though this will inhibit the prevalent missiological use of the Qur'an independent of Islamic hermeneutics. This effort, however, will win the respect of Muslims and might encourage them to take a similar posture toward the Bible.

THE RELATIONSHIP BETWEEN
INTOLERANCE AND REVELATION

Because Islam and Christianity hold different conceptions of God, revelation is also held in a distinct light. Revelation from God cannot be negotiated or compromised, and no other alternative to these two options is often advanced. What is capable of occurring, however, is that mutual understanding be encouraged. This fosters a better climate for the proclamation of truth. The present belligerent posture of many Christians provides no such receptivity. It must be replaced by a sensitive appreciation of Islam combined with a relevant exposition of Christian beliefs.

Both religions teach that God is active in imparting truth. The concept of God in Christianity is of one who actively involves Himself in fellowship (*koinonia*) with humanity. This idea of God's numerous covenants with His creation is the compelling motive for faith and witness within Christianity. The doctrine of God in Islam places the accent on His sovereign will over a world brimming with evil and "stubborn humanity."[9] Do these different views mean that there are two distinct revelations of the same God? Is only one of these perceptions accurate and the other false, distorted, or incomplete? Or, as others suggest, are both portraits partial without the other?

What is Islam's attitude toward biblical revelation? Muslims believe that God has willed both religions to exist. They claim that Christianity emerged for a specific dispensation and is one with Islam in its opposition to atheism. The Qur'an does not forbid interaction with Christians but does prescribe how Muslims should deal with them (Surah 29:46). While respecting Christians, Muslims believe that Islam provides a superior, final revelation. Islam possesses its own revealed knowledge of the nature of Christianity in the Qur'an. Because of this, there is little inclination to seek out Christians to learn from them something of God's nature. Muslims conclude that these are invariably human misconceptions.

Neither Islam nor Christianity can set aside its scripture, or apostolic traditions, and remain integral. The dynamic affirmations of Islam and Christianity expressed in practice and principle are what is distinctive of the two faiths. The Christian community is committed to the conviction that Jesus is God's fullest revelation of His divine nature as love and participant in human history. For Muslims, it is impossible to accept this claim or to interpret certain passages of the Qur'an without rejecting the (at least present) validity of Christianity. An example of this would be Surah 9:30:

> The Christians call Christ the Son of God. That is the saying from their mouth; (in this) they but imitate what the unbelievers of old used to say. God's curse be on them: how they are deluded away from the Truth!

Another ingredient which contributes to a lack of mutual understanding between Muslims and Christians is that much of either European and American Islamic historic scholarship and Islamic criticism of Christianity have been based on sources that originate from within their own religious communities. These have often been laden with bias. Antagonism, not appreciation, colors much "objective" academic research. Examples within Christianity begin with John of Damascus and other Arab Christians who encountered early Islam. This trend has continued in the writings of Samuel Zwemer, C. G. Pfander, and William St. Clair-Tisdall. On the positive side, missiologists such as Kenneth Cragg, Stephen Neill, Lamin Sanneh, Mathias Zahniser, and Michael Nazir-Ali have recently advocated a far less adversarial approach.

What begins as a sympathetic encounter often ends in a fruitless "battle of the books." Both Christians and Muslims advance strident objections to the theological claims of each other's tradition that are often not actually held.

Approaches in interpreting another's revelation are often fraught with myopic interpolation. Examples of this include the Islamic exegesis of John 14:26 as a reference to the Prophet Muhammad, or the Christian rendering of Surah 4:171 as a confirmation of Christ's divinity. As a result of this morass, the conviction that interaction is frustrating and unfruitful often takes hold.

The adherence to divine revelation need not be correlative with a posture of intolerance. One can bear witness to one's own experience and convictions of faith without needing to diminish or attack other people's perspectives in faith. What is needed instead of caustic belligerence is patient sensitivity to comprehend the ideas of another's faith. Education and exposition, and not merely interaction, is the goal of interfaith discussions. This process needs to be modeled and framed in a context of teachable openness in order to have any effect. Intolerance can be overcome as individuals realize the importance of sharing their understanding of truth that they have received. With measured sympathy, each should contribute an exposition of their faith in a way that is understandable to adherents of the other religious tradition. In this way, fruitful interaction will replace intransigent contentiousness even if the end result is not a dramatic paradigm shift in the understanding of God's nature.

COMMON GROUND AND DISSIMILAR VIEWS
ABOUT REVELATION

Christianity views revelation as historical and gradual, relating to God's *koinonia* with His people, while in Islam, revelation is unchanging and devoid of any descriptive unfolding of the divine nature. In Christianity, God has chosen to disclose Himself in specific epochs of time which, in turn, speak to all humanity throughout time; in Islam, revelation is ahistorical.

It is important to note that nowhere in its pages does the Qur'an refute the authority of biblical revelation. The idea that other scriptures have been abrogated is not found in the Qur'an. Accusations about "corruptions" (*tahrif*) refer not to the scriptures themselves, but to those who misinterpret them; to those who deliberately or accidentally mispronounce the Arabic of the Qur'an; and to those who use them for their own aims (Surah 2:75; 4:46; 5:13; 5:41). The Qur'an is unqualified in its acceptance of the original biblical text: "We have without doubt, sent down the message and we will assuredly guard it" (Surah 15:9; see also Surah 6:114).[10] In light of this affirmation, Christians are able to remind Muslims that the Bible in its original languages was completely canonized well before the Qur'an. This will caution Muslims not to say more than what the Qur'an says about the reliability of the Bible.

Islam accepts numerous points of common ground with Christianity. Muslims deduce that the God revealed in the Bible and the God shown in the

Qur'an are identical. Revelation springs from the same source but to different people and with a different focus. God, both disclosed and hidden, meets humanity at its own level of cognizance. All that can be known about God is what has been revealed. God has provided inspiration (*wahy*) and overcomes the hindrance of human ignorance. God has announced His intention to show compassion.

Although the Qur'an does not reject the biblical narrative outright, it does not accurately represent its present content. Foundational to the interrelation of the two faiths is the unassailable problem that Islam identifies Christianity as it is shown in the Qur'an, and not as it is revealed in the Bible. It is not helpful to conjecture whether or not the Qur'anic view of Christianity is accurate because it is based on a completely distinct rendering of God; thus, what emerges does not correlate with Christian doctrine.

The issue that needs to be discussed with Muslims is how God reveals Himself. Does God send down truth, or does He come into the world and among His creation through the Incarnation? A related dilemma for Christians is that their own theological frameworks provide no accounting for the "need" of Islam. Christians ask the question: Why, six hundred years after the supernatural birth, life, death, and resurrection of Jesus, would God dispatch the angel Gabriel to Mecca and inform Muhammad that God had no Son, that Jesus was not crucified, and that He was not the Savior or the Son of God?

What is dissimilar about Islamic and Christian revelation is rooted in differing concepts of the divine nature. God's utter transcendence in Islam (*tanzil,* literally "to be stripped" of all characteristics) excludes any concept of God incarnate. Muslims reject the idea that revelation involves the self-disclosure of God's essential nature. Because God is transcendent, Muslims assert that God can never be known. If God's existence could be proved through logic (an idea also rejected by Christianity), then He would be finite. If God can be "known," it is only indirectly. The fact that humans are made finite (Surah 7:54; 10:4) raises the question of whether or not God wants them to know Him. For Jews and Christians, the idea that humanity is formed in God's image implies that He does intend such a relationship (Genesis 1:26–27). In Islam, any act of revelation from God is not about God, but about human conduct: "The God who reveals is not revealed."[11]

For Christians, the transcendence of God and revelation are filtered through a trinitarian concept of the divine nature. Ignatius of Antioch called Jesus "The Word in which God broke His silence."[12] This revelation is the setting in action of God's capability to restore humanity to covenant relationship. This *logos* truth flows from a self-revealing God who demonstrates His nature as well as His will. Jesus preached, "He who has seen me has seen the Father" (John 14:9). For Christians, God must be like Christ. In Islam, the word of

God has become a revelation of truth — the Qur'an; in Christianity, the truth has become flesh in Christ.

Muslims argue that God cannot vary in His essence or in His purposes. The Incarnation of Christ implies to a Muslim that God "changes" in submitting Himself to the boundaries of time and space. For Christians, the Incarnation is that which had been "hidden" but which has now come to light (Romans 16:25; Colossians 1:26; Ephesians 3:9). The revelation of God in Christ is a revelation among humanity that places nothing between Creator and creation. Muslims cherish the impartation of the Qur'an as the literal dictation by the angels to a man of a book that has neither the fingerprint of humanity or the effort of divinity. The Incarnation, by contrast, is both a revelation of divinity and a demonstration of purified humanity. The Incarnation of the eternal God into the particular frame of an individual is a paradox in the truest sense of something that is contrary to appearance and exceeds the capacities of reason. The Torah asserted that if one "looked upon God" they would die (Genesis 32:30; Exodus 33:20). In the New Testament humans not only look upon God in Christ but even crucify Him. What Karl Barth labeled the "all-transforming fact" of the Incarnation of God in Christ summons recipients of truth to move from knowledge of God into communion with God. As John stated, "Before the world was created, the Word already existed. He was with God and He was the same as God" (John 1:1; TEV).

The two representations of revelation in Islam and Christianity could be summarized by the question: Is the doctrine of the Incarnation an impossible heresy denigrating to the divine nature, or the revealed truth about God's nature as participant among humanity? God, in Christian faith, actively seeks and desires *koinonia* with that which He has created in His image. When Muslims receive an accurate portrayal of the Christian doctrine of God, they will understand that the role of revelation in Christianity serves as a revelation of the nature of God as participant.

NOTES

1. Yusuf Ali's translation of Surah 23:14 ends with, "Blessed be God, the Best to Create." Ali's footnote on this passage confirms the idea that God alone is responsible for everything which is created and that there are no other "creators" besides God.

2. Another example of this was the Prophet Muhammad's initial command that Muslims pray toward Jerusalem, which was later changed toward the direction of Mecca.

3. This image of "filtering" was used by Stephen Neill in *Salvation Tomorrow* (London: Lutterworth Press, 1976), 63.

4. This helps to explain why the Prophet Muhammad is usually referred to in the third-person in the Qur'an (although he is also referred to in the second-person). The facts that he is not a miracle worker and that he was illiterate are seen as further proofs of the Qur'an's veracity.

5. This is the term used in Yusuf Ali's footnote on this passage in the Qur'an to explain how God reveals knowledge to humanity without condescending to their level.

6. Michael Green, ed., *The Truth of God Incarnate* (London: Hodder and Stoughton, 1977), 71, underscores this emphasis of history in Christianity by noting that: "Pontius Pilate, the second-rate Governor of a second-rate Roman Province has become the second best known person in the whole of human history." This is because Pilate's name is often repeated in the creeds of Christian faith.

7. There are many examples of discrepancies between the Bible and the Qur'an. A few of these include Abraham being saved by Nimrod's father, details in the life of Joseph, and Abraham blessing Ishmael (and not Isaac). Of greatest importance are the differing details about the birth, miracles, death, and message of Jesus.

8. Cited in Hans Küng, "Christianity and World Religions: The Dialogue with Islam as One Model," in *Muslim World* 77, no. 1 (January 1987): 87. Since the Qur'an was manifested in Arabic, the Arabic of the Qur'an is an irreplaceable part of its message. This is why, to be appreciated, the Qur'an should be heard in recitation. Muslims maintain that the Arabic in the Qur'an is flawless and that the revelation contains no non-Arabic terms. In response to this, Western textual criticisms of the Qur'an have irreverently pointed to several non-Arabic terms. They also noted that Arabic vowel signs were not in place until the eighth century.

9. Shabbir Akhtar, *A Faith for All Seasons* (London: Loewellew, 1990), 175.

10. Some Muslims, beginning in about the twelfth century, argued that the Christian scriptures were not falsified in their pure form but misinterpreted in translation (*al-tahrif al-ma'ani*). In this issue of how to interpret the nature of revelation, Paul Varo Martinson in his book, *A Theology of World Religions* (Minneapolis: Augsburg Press, 1987), provides diagrams to explain the various ideas about revelation in Islam, Judaism, and Christianity (54).

11. Ibid., 68.

12. St. Ignatius is cited in Wolfhart Pannenberg, *Jesus, God and Man,* trans. Lewis L. Wilkins and Duane A. Priebe (London: SCM Press, 1968), 161. Pannenberg cites the source as "*Magn.* 8:2."

4

The Portrait of Jesus in Formative Islam (A.D. 622–1258)

JESUS IN THE QUR'AN

To Muslims, Jesus is not a divine revelation of God as Love because that is not consistent with God's singularity. Christ is not God's Son because God cannot be described as a "Father." Jesus cannot be a mediator between God and humanity because God is sovereign. The Incarnation of God in Christ is unthinkable because God is infinitely transcendent above frail and finite humanity.

In order to proceed with an exposition of the belief that God was in Christ, it is requisite to understand the Islamic perception of Christ's nature. This will be done by examining the portrait of Jesus in the Qur'an, the evolving portrayal of Christ in the Hadith, and the rendering of Christ in the theological and devotional literature of early Islam. Questions will be raised about those aspects in the Muslim portrait of Christ that are most discrepant from the biblical narrative. This chapter will conclude with a summary of the uniqueness of Christ in these formative sources. This uniqueness revolves around His role as a sinless prophet and His position as a forerunner to the Prophet Muhammad. According to Islamic orthodoxy, "The only valid picture of Jesus Christ is that which is to be found in the pages of the Qur'an."[1] The ambition of Muslims in relation to Christians is often to explain what they believe Jesus actually taught and, hence, what it truly means to be a "Christian." Muslims explain that Jesus was a "Muslim" and confer on Christ the honor that is befitting the greatest of the prophets before Muhammad. Christ is mentioned in fifteen chapters of the Qur'an in 93 verses. He is the "seal of the saints" and can only be understood after He is freed from the heretical, encumbering barnacles that have corroded an accurate appraisal of His true nature as a faithful prophet.

The Qur'an refers to Jesus as *'Isa ibn-Maryam*. This frequent mention of Mary emphasizes the humanity of Jesus while, at the same time, reminding the reader of the Virgin Birth.[2] This name has raised a number of questions for many Christians. Some consider *Isa* simply the Arabic form of the Syrian *Yeshu*. This is without linguistic authority. There has been speculation that it may relate to the Hebrew prophet Esau but this is also improbable. Unlike the term "Allah" for God, which is prevalent among Arab Christians, the appellation *"Isa"* for Jesus is far less widespread.

Arab Christians usually refer to Jesus as *Yesu* (Yasu) or, to avoid all confusion, *sayyidna al-masih* ("our Lord Christ") or *sayyidna al-fadi* ("our Lord Redeemer"). Christians with whom I have spoken in Morocco sense that the Qur'anic account is so corrupted that *"Isa"* and *"Yesu"* are not correlative. The change of a name alone, however, would not alter the doctrine of Islam about the divinity of Christ. The original name *Yeshua* in the Hebrew is far removed from a host of transcriptions of Christ's name in languages around the world. What is portentous is not what name is used but that an accurate understanding be held about Christ's nature.

THE ANNUNCIATION AND BIRTH OF JESUS

The annunciation and nativity of Jesus depicted in the Qur'an closely parallel narratives of the Syrian church from the seventh century. The primary emphasis in these stories is that, while Jesus is fully human, He is also filled with God's spirit. Born of Mary (Surah 3:30–50; 21:91; 66:12), Jesus is directly created by the word of God as was the first prophet, Adam (Surah 3:52).

In the Qur'an, the angel Gabriel (*Jibril*) visits Mary and announces that it is God's will that she be the vessel for the miraculous birth of a noble prophet. Generally, the account of the annunciation in the Qur'an (Surah 19) corresponds to Luke 1:26–38:

> She said (to Gabriel): Lo! I seek refuge in the Beneficent One from thee if thou art God fearing. He said, I am only a messenger of thy Lord, that I may bestow unto thee a faultless son. She said: How can I have a son when no mortal hath touched me, neither have I been unchaste? He said: So (it will be). Thy Lord saith: it is easy for me. And (it will be) that We may make of him a revelation for mankind and a mercy from Us, and it is a thing ordained. (Surah 19:18–21, Pickthall)

The Qur'anic account goes on to embellish the story with a host of unfamiliar details (which may originate in Syrian apocryphal literature). In the Qur'an, Mary gives birth to Jesus in great pain underneath a palm tree which lowers its branches to feed her (Surah 19:23–26). At this oasis, a spring of

water miraculously appears. Although the Qur'an claims that Mary had to
travel to a place far away from Nazareth, there is no mention of Bethlehem.

The Virgin Mary was selected because she was unusually righteous (Surah
3:37, 42), and the child that she bore was without sin. Christians have made
much of its teaching that, in contrast to the Prophet Muhammad who had
to pray for forgiveness (Surah 40:55; see also Surah 80:1–10), the God-man
Jesus never sinned. In Islam, however, the fact that Christ never sinned does
not mean that He was divine. For Muslims, the central point of His birth was
that He was exceptional among men. Invariably, the Qur'anic and biblical
reports of the birth of Christ do not correlate. The Islamic concept of God has
nothing to do with the birth of a human child in a poor family in Palestine. All
that is revealed in the life of Christ is a wonderful example of the faithfulness
of a prophet to the will of God. In Islam, Jesus is a "word from God" fashioned
by the power of God. Angels appear at His birth only to confirm His role as
a prophet. Every aspect in the Qur'anic account affirms Christ's uniqueness
as a prophet and denies His divinity.

THE WORK AND MINISTRY OF JESUS IN THE QUR'AN

> Behold! the angels said: O Mary! God giveth thee glad tidings of a
> Word from Him: His name will be Christ Jesus, the Son of Mary, held
> in honour in this world and the hereafter, and of (the company of those)
> nearest to God; He shall speak to the people in childhood and in maturity
> and he shall be of the righteous. . . . And God will teach him the Book
> and Wisdom, the Law and the Gospel and (appoint Him) an apostle to
> the Children of Israel (with this message): "I have come to you with a
> sign from the Lord, in that I make for you out of clay, as it were, the
> figure of a bird, and breathe into it, and it becomes a bird by God's
> leave: and I heal those born blind and the lepers, and I quicken the
> dead, by God's leave; and I declare what ye eat and what ye store in
> your houses. Surely therein is a sign for you if you did believe." (Surah
> 3:45–49)

Surah 3 provides the most self-evident rendering of Jesus in the Qur'an.
This passage alludes to some of the miracles cited in the New Testament, such
as the healing of the blind and the leprous, and the raising of the dead. The
other references to Jesus' talking from the cradle (Surah 19:27–34) or making
clay birds fly (Surah 3:49) can either be read poetically or seen as an echo
from the many accounts of bizarre marvels credited to Jesus in apocryphal
sources.[3] The supernatural is repeatedly emphasized in the Qur'anic portrait
of Christ. Jesus is recounted as one gifted to heal the sick (Surah 3:49; 5:110)
although no details of any specific miracles are provided. Other prophets,

such as Moses (Surah 2:87), are also given these powers. Muhammad, in contrast, is not a miracle-working prophet except for the singular fact that it was through him that the Qur'an was made known. Jesus' miracles underscore His prophetic message and serve as "signs" (*bayyinat*) for the skeptical (Surah 19:21; 23:50).

Why is the teaching ministry of Jesus not emphasized in the Qur'an? The answer seems uncertain. Although the Qur'an never calls Jesus a teacher, He is set apart as one who taught what God had given to Him. The words that Jesus received, however, have been twisted by those who have taken their truths and reworked them to suit their own interests (Surah 2:79; 3:78). God has commissioned the Prophet Muhammad to correct misguided Christians who have stumbled into heresy while still rejecting idolatry.[4]

The title for Jesus which is most appreciated by Muslims is that of prophet. He is one of a great line of twenty-eight prophets (*an-nabiyyin*) named in the Qur'an and is usually listed with the greatest of these (Abraham, Ishmael, Isaac, Moses, and Muhammad; Surah 2:136). Jesus is a man among men, like Adam, without preexistence. For this reason, Islam contends that Christianity has distorted His life by making Him the object of veneration.

Jesus is characterized as the "gentle prophet who lacked the robust activism"[5] of Muhammad. Born in "the artisan class of a subject people,"[6] He had no political influence. Like Muhammad, Jesus defied the status quo but, unlike the Prophet Muhammad, He did not immediately triumph. The prophetic office of Jesus sought to restore the core meaning of submission to God. Christ taught that individuals should be freed from the constraints of traditional religious practice (*rusum*) and "literalism" (*zawahir*). He called humanity to worship God with a pure heart.[7] Did Christ's ministry extend beyond the boundaries of Israel? Does the Qur'an propound that Jesus has a universal mission? The Qur'an announces that Christ is to be a "sign to all creatures" (Surah 21:91), with an evangel (*injil*) for all people (Surah 2:253). God called Jesus to be His mouthpiece, making intercession (*shaf'ah*) on behalf of the people, sharing ethical imperatives, and calling for repentance. With these themes, Jesus serves as one more piece of the puzzle in the Muslim version of God's revelation to humanity.

THE DEATH AND ASCENSION OF JESUS IN THE QUR'AN

Among the most consequential issues in the Qur'anic portrait of Jesus are the statements made about His death. Unfortunately, this is also one of the most ambiguous areas. Does the Qur'an agree with the Bible that Christ was crucified? Is His death assumed in the Qur'an with subsequent comments serving as explanation of events? Or was Jesus not actually crucified? Did God provide a substitute for Christ as a final vindication of His work?

In the Qur'an, the end of Jesus' life is shrouded in the same mystery that dramatized His birth. Based on Surah 4:157–58, it is contested that Jesus was not actually crucified:

That they said; "We killed Christ Jesus the Son of Mary, the Apostle of God." But they killed Him not, nor crucified Him, but so it was made to appear to them, and those who differ therein are full of doubts, with no knowledge, but only conjecture to follow, for of a surety they killed Him not: Nay, God raised him up unto Himself; and God is exalted in Power, Wise.

The Qur'an supplies no specific mention of an individual dying on the cross in the place of Jesus. Many Muslims believe, however, that this is exactly what happened. This inference was also held by certain early Christians.[8] If Christ did not die on the cross, then who did? Speculation is rampant. Some have proposed Judas, the betrayer. Others have advocated that it was Simon of Cyrene. It has even been submitted that Pontius Pilate was crucified![9]

The central textual question in this passage is the meaning of the phrase, "It was made to appear to them" (*shubbiha la-hum*). Of the countless interpretations of this text, the one that seems most credible is the view which also agrees with the Bible. It may have "appeared" to the Jews that they killed Jesus, for they undoubtedly bear some of the guilt (Acts 2:23), but the soldiers and the Roman government (Mark 15:25; John 19:15–16) also sponsored His execution. Beyond this, Christianity teaches that no person is answerable for His death because He laid His life down willingly (John 10:17–18). Muslims and Christians accede that if Jesus was crucified, then ultimately it would be the sovereign God, and not any individual, who would be responsible (John 19:11).

Linked to the interpretation of Surah 4:157–58 is an understanding of what is meant in Surah 3:55: "Behold! God said: O Jesus! I will take thee and raise thee to myself." The phrase, "take thee" (*mutawaffika*), has been translated "to complete your term" or "to cause you to die" and is a general euphemism in Arabic to describe death. The Qur'an is unmistakable that if God were so predisposed, He could allow the Messiah to be "destroyed" (Surah 5:17). In the Qur'an, it is not unknown for prophets (see Surah 2:61) to be harassed, suffer, and even to be slain.

The execution of Jesus cannot be seen as a debacle because God had "taken" (*mutawaffika*) Him from destruction (Surah 5:17) and enabled Him to conquer death. What greater vindication could be won than a prophet's rising in triumph from the grave? What greater surprise could be handed to His enemies? The Qur'an certifies that God is always "plotting." Although the "Jews" schemed to kill Jesus ("they plotted," *makaru*), "the best of the plotters is Allah" (*wa'llahu khayru l-makirin,* Surah 3:54).

The Qur'an observes that "the Jews" determined to kill Jesus and thought they had succeeded in their attempts. Who is chargeable for Christ's death? Islam confirms that Jesus will die (a fact necessary to their comprehension of His humanity): "So peace is on me the day I was born, the day that I die and the day that I shall be raised up to life!" (Surah 19:33). Muslims, however, often interpret this to mean that Jesus will eventually reappear on the earth and die. Muslims can find no other way to correlate this verse with the prevalent substitution theory about the cross of Christ.

The Islamic postulate that Christ was spared the cross is consistent with the idea that there is no salvation through sacrifice. A "Muslim cross" shows another dying in place of Jesus, instead of Jesus dying in place of a broken humanity. The "Muslim cross" affirms that justice conquers attempts of the evildoers but says nothing about the nature of God's love. Jesus presented in the Qur'an is already a substitution of Christ as revealed in the New Testament who went to the cross to empower humanity to return to proper relationship with God. The doctrine of God in Christ on the cross is about much more than scoffers' being deceived and then being humbled.

The ascension of Jesus is another ambiguous puzzle in the Qur'an. Is Jesus presently alive? Surah 4:158 insists, "But Allah raised him up to Himself." In Surah 3:55 God confirms that He is "gathering thee and causing thee to ascend unto me" (or, "raise you to myself," *rāfi 'uka illayya*). This parallels the idea of "rapture" as in the case of the prophet Elijah. Perhaps all prophets, and not just Jesus, are physically alive in heaven today. The Qur'an is silent on this question; only Jesus is mentioned as one who lives beyond death. Christ is now "raised alive" (*'ub'athu hayyan*, Surah 19:33), which suggests "resurrection." It is not clear in this passage for what purpose, or why He, among all the prophets, is given this unusual standing.

A LOOK AT THE TITLES GIVEN TO JESUS IN SURAH 4:171

O People of the Scripture! Do not exaggerate in your religion nor utter aught concerning Allah save the truth. The Messiah, Jesus son of Mary, was only a messenger of Allah, and His word which He conveyed unto Mary, and a spirit from Him. So believe in Allah and His messengers and say not "Three" Cease! (it is) better for you! Allah is only one God. Far is it removed from His transcendent majesty that He should have a Son. His is all that is in the heavens and all that is in the earth. And Allah is sufficient as defender. (Surah 4:171, Pickthall)

The designations attributed to Christ in Surah 4:171 provide a lucid picture of the Muslim view of His nature. The designation "Messiah" (*al-masih*) is used in this verse and eleven other times in the Qur'an, but it is not defined. This usage, without explanation, probably means that it is intended merely to identify Jesus, not to describe His nature. It cannot be discounted that the term might also have been used to provoke Jewish listeners who would have bristled at this form of address for Jesus. Others proffer that the term "Messiah" alludes to one who travels (*saha*) because Christ was a leader of a group of wandering disciples. Some Muslims have suggested that it relates to the Arabic term "to touch" or "anoint" (*masaha*) and refers to Jesus' propensity to work miracles by touching the sick. Indeed, the Gospel writers frequently reported that His touch was efficacious. Jesus healed a woman who touched Him (Matthew 9:21) and invited His friends after His resurrection to touch Him (Luke 24:39) as a way of being healed of their doubts. Mothers gave their babies to Jesus to have Him touch them (Luke 18:15).

It is important to realize that this epithet for Christ is not comparable to the Christian meaning of one who comes to save people from their sins. In Christianity, "Messiah" corresponds with the Greek term "Christ" and articulates His role as Savior. The Muslim "Messiah" is not a savior because God is beyond the need of any assistance in bringing salvation to humanity.[10] Jesus, the Messiah, is a prophet (see Surah 5:81) who was foretold and who, in His obedience, offers a way forward from ignorance to submission to God.

The passage describes Jesus as "a spirit from God." This is seized upon by Christians eager to manufacture parallels with Islamic theology. Here again, the phraseology is not defined. Islam teaches that all of Jesus' power came from God and that He held no authority of His own. The indication that Jesus is a spirit (*ruah*) speaks of His inspiration from God. It should also be remembered that the Muslim idea of "spirit" is incompatible with the Christian view.[11]

Jesus is a "word from God." This phrase causes difficulty for Muslims because of its affinity with the *logos* doctrine of John 1. For Islam, the Incarnation is not possible because there is a distinct difference between a word in creation and a word of revelation. In order to demarcate this passage from John 1:1, Muslims expound that Jesus is called a "word" because He came into existence by God's command without an earthly father. Jesus as a "word (*kalima*) from God" is a "statement of truth" (Surah 19:34). The Arabic term *kalima* is probably better translated by the more restrained Greek word *rhema* (rather than *logos*). As a *rhema* word from God, Christ came as a specific word from God to a precise situation. As a word from God, Jesus is simply one who is in agreement with the divine will. In Jesus, Muslims teach that the divine word is untouched by the finger of Iblis (Satan). As a word from God (*kalimatu 'llah*), Jesus is God's messenger to humanity.

Lastly, in Surah 4:171, Christ is described as an apostle or "sent one" (*rasul,* called a "messenger" in Pickthall). This echoes the description of Christ in John 8:16–29. According to the Qur'an: "To every people (was sent) an Apostle: when their apostle comes before them, the matter will be judged between them with justice and they will not be wronged" (Surah 10:47; see also Surah 61:6). According to Islam, the primary apostolic role of Jesus was to gather the disciples ("helpers," *ansar*) together, preach submission to God, and foretell the coming of the Prophet Muhammad.

Besides those listed in Surah 4:171, other designations given to Christ in the Qur'an merit scrutiny. In fact, more honorary titles are given to Jesus in the Qur'an than to any other prophet of Islam (many of these are also consigned to the Prophet Muhammad). These names enhance His position as one unique among humanity. Jesus is called the "blessed one" (*mubarak*) in Surah 19:31. He is favored because of His obedience to God's will. He is a "servant of God" (*'abd,* Surah 19:31, 43:59), which speaks of His humility. In four different passages, Jesus is called a "sign" from God (e.g., Surah 19:21) given to turn people from polytheism. Jesus is called a "vessel of mercy" (*rahmah*) from God (Surah 19:21). This points to His kindness, but also speaks of His role as final judge.

THE PORTRAIT OF JESUS IN THE HADITH

The Hadith literature of Islam is the corpus of tradition that offers guidance for daily living. The Arabic word *hadith* originally meant "something new" (or "conversation"), which illustrates the early function of Hadith as oral traditions. In their extant form, they are short, narrative records that recount what the Prophet Muhammad did, approved of, or said. They often deal with areas of information untouched by the Qur'an. The Hadith develop an elaborate cosmology and systematize a code for daily behavior in imitation of the example of the Prophet. From the veneration of his example in the Hadith, Muhammad emerges as the greatest of the prophets.

The Hadith have taken a place of influence second only to the Qur'an and are held in great esteem. A parallel can be drawn between the role of the Talmud to Mosaic law in Judaism and the relationship between the Qur'an and the Hadith. For Muslim orthodoxy, the Hadith is what interprets the Qur'an; the one cannot be appreciated without the other. In spite of this, the Hadith are often ignored by Christians. This may be because they are far less accessible than interpretations of the Qur'an. It is as difficult to justify this oversight as it is to overstate the importance of the Hadith in the establishment of Muslim life and thought throughout the centuries.

The earliest type of Hadith work, the *musnad,* offered a series of sayings of the Prophet, which were credited to various eyewitnesses. Each entry involved the saying imputed to the Prophet (*matn*) preceded by the chain of authorities (*isnad*) by which its authenticity could be discerned. In early Islam, there was no formal way of substantiating the validity of Hadith. By the end of the third Islamic century there were six primary collections of Hadith.[12] The ratification of this canon of Hadith put an end to the geometric increase of forgeries, duplications, and fabrications. Still, seven generations after Muhammad, scholar al-Bukhari examined some six hundred thousand potential traditions and verified that only a fraction (about seventy-four hundred) were trustworthy.[13]

Islamicists, such as Ignaz Goldziher and Alfred Guillaume, insist that the compilers of Hadith appropriated large portions of biblical and apocryphal sources for their portrait of Jesus. Some of this borrowing is applied, not only to Jesus, but also to the Prophet Muhammad. Hadith report that Muhammad feeds five thousand and provides water in the desert. He even prays a prayer almost identical to the "Lord's Prayer" (Luke 11:2–4).[14] The net result of these stories about the Prophet Muhammad illustrates for the Muslim that he is not inferior to Jesus (or to any other prophet). Guillaume argued,

> Weary of hearing of the acts of love and mercy, of the supernatural power of 'Isa ibn Maryam they have made Muhammad after his likeness. Not content with the picture of a courteous, kindly and able man framed as the possessor of all human virtues, the idol of his race [*sic*], if he was to compete with the Messiah they must represent him as a worker of miracles.[15]

JESUS AS AN ASCETIC IN THE HADITH

Most of the instances where Jesus is mentioned in Hadith confirm the caricature presented in the Qur'an. The function of Hadith is often to help interpret more oblique Qur'anic references. The honorific titles for Jesus (such as "Messiah" and "Spirit of God") are retained in Hadith as are mention of His miracles and His sinlessness. There are also areas treated in Hadith that are not touched upon in the Qur'an. These include the teaching of Jesus on the "new birth," the need to forgive enemies, and the nature and power of God's love. Many of the parables are also paraphrased (such as those in Matthew 13:3–12; 20:1–16; and 22:1–10).

Bukhari's tradition asserted that Jesus was the only child who was ever untouched by Satan at birth.[16] Other birth narratives emphasize that Jesus was born into poverty. This set the stage for one of the most interesting developments in the Muslim approach to Christ — that of a poor ascetic. One Hadith (attributed to Ka'ab al-Akbar) recounted:

Jesus used to walk barefoot and He took no adornment, or goods, or clothes, or provision except His day's food. Wherever the sun set, He arranged His feet in prayer till the morning came.... His head was disheveled and His face was small. He was an ascetic in this world longing for the next world and eager for the worship of Allah. He was a pilgrim in the earth until the Jews sought Him and desired to kill Him. Then Allah raised Him up to heaven and Allah knows best.[17]

Christ's supernatural powers even equipped Him to raise the dead. In one instance, He brings Shem, Noah's son, back from the grave to embellish some salient preaching point.[18] In another story, Jesus beckons a gazelle to Himself, cuts its throat, roasts it, and then raises it back to life to frolic away in freedom. On another occasion, Christ turned desert sand into gold and then poisoned some onlookers who attempted to steal it.[19] This supernatural potentiality that Jesus had to perform marvels was directly related to His renunciation of the present:

The disciples asked Jesus: "How is it that you can walk on water and we cannot?" He then asked them: "What do you think of the *dinar* and the *dirham* (units of currency)?" The disciples replied: "They are good!" Jesus said to them: "But they and mud are alike to me."[20]

According to Hadith, Jesus wandered through the world with only a comb and a jug for water. Christ threw even these away when He saw another sage drinking from a well and combing his beard with his hands. Jesus encouraged people to make their home in the mosque and view their dwellings only as places to sleep. He advocated a diet of water and vegetables. Christ told His followers to rely on the moon as their lamp at night and the sun for fire in winter. Jesus expounded that, in spite of His poverty, He was the richest man in creation. To be happy, one should live with circumspection:

The world consists of three days: yesterday which has passed, from which you have nothing in your hands; tomorrow of which you do not know whether you will reach or not; and today in which you are to avail yourself of it.... Whenever Jesus was asked, "How are you this morning?" He would answer: "Unable to forestall what I hope for or put off what I fear, bound by my works with all my good in another's hand. There is none poorer than I...." Jesus, Son of Mary, met a man and asked the man what he was doing. "I am devoting myself to God," the man replied. Jesus asked, "Who is giving you what you need?" The man said, "My brother." Jesus said, "He is more devoted to Allah than you."[21]

Jesus, as described in Hadith, is a man of destitution. He ambles alone as a burdened prophet. Even in His present abode in Paradise, Jesus still chooses to wear a tattered peasant garment (the *muraqqa'ah*) with over three hundred holes.[22] In His discourses He underscores that this life and the next, like two wives, are perpetually vying for loyalty. The "Gospel" which the Christ of Hadith preaches is that denial provides the pathway of deliverance from this struggle.

This abstemiousness of Jesus is even more pronounced because it is such a contrast to the wealth that the Prophet Muhammad enjoyed. Perhaps this emphasis of Jesus as an ascetic came to early Islam through the example of the world-renouncing monks, who lived in the Arabian desert and who claimed Christ as their inspiration. The ascetic Jesus is clearly a human prophet who struggles with His own weakness but who achieves holiness through effort.

THE PASSION AND RETURN OF CHRIST

Many Christians would conclude that the resurrection of Christ is the primary miracle in His life and a clear revelation of His divine nature. This idea is execrated by Muslims. The Hadith reveals that God has endowed Christ with a number of assurances that He would not die. Although the Qur'an seems open to a wide degree of interpretation, it is the Hadith that extrapolates, "Jesus did not die and He will return to you before the judgement day."[23] Although there are early reports of different substitutionary theories in Islamic devotional literature (such as in Tabari's commentaries), it is not until later that these views predominate. In any event, the Hadith unmistakably denies the death of Christ.[24]

The Hadith rationalize the taking of Jesus to heaven as a preface to His responsibilities as final Judge. In Christ's return to earth, Christians will be the prime recipients of His wrath. Bukhari explains that Christ will return to the white mosque in Damascus and begin to break crosses, kill swine, and abolish unfair taxes.[25] Jesus will explain to Christians that they should become faithful Muslims and renounce the notion that He is God Incarnate. Christ's first task will be to slay *al-dajjal,* the anti-Christ. His rule on the earth will be marked by seven years of peace where "there will be no hatred between any two people."[26] During this time, Christ will marry, father children, and reside for forty-five years before dying and being buried beside the Prophet Muhammad.[27]

The eschatological function of Jesus, which unfolds in the Hadith, helps Muslims grasp His place in Islam. The emphasis on Christ's second coming clarifies the reason for His ascension and decodes the thrust of His mission. The frequent references to His eventual death and burial make it obvious and evident that Jesus is not divine.

JESUS IN THE HADITH

It is in the Hadith that the contemporary interpretation of Jesus finds its apogee. The Hadith embroiders the initial portrait of Jesus in the Qur'an and brings to the fore His ascetic role and function as judge at the end of time. His miracles are confirmed but put into perspective by a new emphasis on the Prophet Muhammad's miraculous powers, a representation completely absent from the Qur'an.[28]

A portrait of Christ's nature is not a primary objective of Hadith literature. What is ascertainable is that Christ is first and foremost a prophet. His "metier" as prophet was to foreshadow Muhammad.[29] In one Hadith, Jesus waits with Abraham and Moses beneath the throne of God to welcome the Prophet Muhammad to heaven during the "night journey."[30] Christ is the last of the prophets in chronological order who foretells the coming of the "Arabian Prophet." One Hadith tells of a man, seeking salvation, who meets each of the prophets. Each of them is insufficient to assist the man and each refers him to their superior. Moses commends the man to "Jesus, the Servant of God, the Apostle of God, the Spirit of God, and the Word of God."[31] When the man meets Jesus, he is told to go to the Prophet Muhammad. Jesus declares:

> I am not the one for that (to forgive sin). I and my mother have been made two gods beside Allah, so I can be occupied today with none but myself.... Verily Muhammad is the one with whom the prophetic succession was sealed. He has come to this day in which Allah has forgiven his former and latter sins. Go to Him![32]

The Prophet Muhammad encapsulates this role for Jesus when he says in Hadith that he himself is "most akin to Jesus among the whole of mankind."[33] Throughout the three centuries of the Hadith's evolution, the Jesus of Islam becomes both more concise and more subservient to Muhammad, the "seal of the prophets." The portrait of Christ in the Hadith affirms the Muslim view that God is not a participant in the sordid details of human experience. The denial that He has any soteriological role is consistent with the view that God is powerful enough to save without any intermediation. Christ in the Hadith reveals nothing about God's nature, but only points to what God desires from those who would be obedient to His will.

JESUS IN FORMATIVE MUSLIM THEOLOGY (*KALAM*)

It has been shown (chapter 2) why it is incumbent upon Christians who interact with Muslims to study formative Islamic sources. To do this, the field of Islamic theology will be introduced with attention given to the most prominent of Islamic theologians and their analysis of Christ. Most of these comments are made in the context of refuting Christianity, a posture that is less discernible in the Qur'an and Hadith. As a result, an awareness of these positions helps the Christian to better understand the origin and priorities of contemporary Islamic apologetic material. From this vantage, some of the quicksand of argumentation, frequent in the Muslim-Christian encounter, can be avoided. In this way, a less contentious and more relevant discussion of Christian faith can emerge among Muslims.

What factors generated the inception of early Islamic theological science? Dogmatic theology in Islam arose step-by-step as the community of faith struggled to interpret and synthesize the prophetic messages. This investigation came to be called *"Kalam,"* the term used in the frequent formula for interpretation: "The *kalam* (statement, argument) on such and such a doctrine is.... "[34]

Interaction with the wider world greatly affected Islamic theology. Theologians during the Abbasid Caliphate began to deal with issues raised by Persian and Hellenistic philosophers. Muslims also began to have increasing interaction with Christians at this time. In the predominantly Christianized city of Damascus, for example, Muslims began to grapple with their relation to other "People of the Book." This compelled them to confront such issues as free will and the meaning of God's oneness. *Mutakallim* (those who do *kalam*) began to explain the doctrine of God's unity (*'ilm al-tauhid*) as the primary antidote to the Christian interpretation of the Trinity and the Incarnation (an emphasis that reached its apex in the writings of al-Ghazali[35]). Theologians dispelled lingering doubts about Christ's role by giving precedence to His human and prophetic nature.

Kalam in Islam has always served a function completely distinct from its function in Christianity.[36] This presents obvious problems for the hermeneutical question of how to talk about theological issues when theology is viewed so differently within these two traditions. Indeed, the entire issue of "interreligious hermeneutics" is an immensely important area for properly understanding the kinds of basic issues that arise *within* traditions and even more *between* traditions. I venture to say that it is differences in views on interconfessional and interreligious perspectives on Islam and Christianity as "wholes" that cause our most serious and often unconscious problems. Such construals of a tradition as a "whole" are necessary for the kind of discussions we are engaging in. They are also a primary source of disagreement for people who disagree with my or any other such construals.

What is called "theology" in Christianity would be dispersed into several separate areas of Islamic scholarship.[37] Standardization and institutionalization increasingly characterized Islamic theology. As the study of *kalam* increased, schools of thought emerged with well-defined methods of research which ensured that conservative interpretation and consensus were upheld.

This tight control of *kalam* relegated theology to what Ibn-Khaldun in his renowned *Muqaddimah* called

> the defence of the articles of faith and the refutation of innovators who deviate in their dogmas from the early Muslims and Muslim orthodoxy. The real core (*sirr*) of the articles of faith is the oneness of God.[38]

The intent here is to probe how the Muslim view of God informs the view of Christ expressed in formative Islamic theological sources, and second, how this affects the nature of Christian interreligious discussions with Muslims. Focus has been given to the writing of noted Ummayad era theologians Ibn Hazm and al-Tabari, and Abbasid theologians Shahrastani and al-Razi. The renowned theologian, al-Ghazali, merits separate consideration due to the distinct nature of his views and his eminent position in the esteem of Islamic theology.

IBN HAZM'S ATTACK AGAINST CHRISTIANITY

One of the most widely known early Islamic theologians, Ibn Hazm (Abu Muhammad 'Ali ibn Ahmad ibn Sa'id; 384–456 A.H./A.D. 994–1064), was an Andalusian writer who won renown as a strident traditionalist, sharply criticizing all who did not adhere to the strict authority of the Qur'an and Hadith. Ibn Hazm is best known by Christians for a devastating four-volume censure of the reliability of the Bible. This study[39] "endeavours to find out contradictions"[40] in Christianity. He inveighed against the assertion that Christ was divine and pronounced that the falsehood of this idea was apparent.

Ibn Hazm noted that originally the *Injil* was one but was subsequently divided into four separate books by unfaithful scribes. He then proceeded, with numbing meticulousness, to cite a score of discrepancies in the text (such as the variant genealogical lists of Jesus' birth). He asked Christians to explain why they do not obey Christ's words and cut out their eyes when these cause offense. He demanded to know why Jesus, described by Christians as divine, did not perceive the deceptive nature of Judas. He dismissed the accounts of Jesus' telling people to keep silent after His miracles and the story of the devil leading Jesus around the wilderness. Ibn Hazm also detailed scores of prophecies made by Jesus that were not fulfilled.[41] Finally, he decried that Christians had not kept to the locus of Jesus' ministry, "the lost sheep of the house of Israel."

Ibn Hazm reserves his greatest scorn for the conviction that Jesus is divine. How is it possible, he asks, for God to pray to Himself as Christ prays to God? How is it viable for one who admits that "no man can see God at any time" (John 1:18) to be God in the flesh? And how is this announcement compatible with the alleged statement of Jesus, "He who has seen me has seen the Father?" (John 14:8). Even Jesus confessed to be only a man (John 8:40) and finite when He said He did not know "the day or the hour" of His own return to earth. How can Jesus be God and yet not know everything? Ibn Hazm contended that the doctrine of the Incarnation was a "mockery of religion."[42] It is heresy to believe that Jesus is not only "equal" to God but also that He "enables" God, as Ibn Hazm puts it, in completing the divine work of salvation. Further, Ibn Hazm felt that the New Testament portrayal of God as Love was contradicted by the Torah's description of God sending floods, famines, plagues, slaughter, and death against humanity for their manifold errors.

In summary, Ibn Hazm placed his analytic emphasis on Christ's humanity and the flawed nature of the Bible. These two themes still resonate in the contemporary Islamic response to Christianity and reflect the Muslim view that God is beyond the self-revelation that is described in the Bible. Ibn Hazm is far less concerned than the Qur'an is to emphasize the good points of Jesus. He does faithfully uphold the Qur'anic record of Jesus and praises the Qur'anic account of the Virgin Birth. He then observes that the analogous biblical story reports "God as having a mother, uncle, aunt, cousin, step-father, sister and brother! Perish the wits of those who say God has a step-father, the husband of His mother!"[43]

The author concludes that scores of discrepancies in the texts of Christian scriptures are responsible for the rise of countless sects within Christianity. Christ was a righteous prophet who has been betrayed by those who claim that He was God. What matters most for those Christians interacting with Muslims is the widespread currency that these attacks have gained into the present day. The censorious vilifications of Ibn Hazm continue to be quoted by Muslims as helpful in their own attempts to discredit Christianity.[44] The benefit for the study of these initial arguments is to see the outcome of the Muslim view of God. With this vantage, Christians will be more prepared to "give a defense for the hope that is within us" (1 Peter 3:15), when these arguments are repeated again by Muslims.

JESUS IN AL-TABARI'S QUR'ANIC INTERPRETATION

Al-Tabari (Abu Ja'far Muhammad ibn Jarir; 224–310 A.H./A.D. 839–923) was a celebrated Arab theologian and historian. He is well known for his devotional material about the lives of the prophets and his commentary on the Qur'an (*Jami'al-bayan fi tafsir al-Qur'an*). This text has come to be held as a classic reference in Qur'anic exegesis because of its meticulous detailing of the traditions that relate to each reference.

In his remarks about Christ, al-Tabari (like Ibn Hazm) deduced that the original gospel of Jesus has been corrupted. His study of Christ, however, is far less vituperative than that of Ibn Hazm. Al-Tabari seemed especially engrossed in relating Hadith that present Jesus as a preacher advocating godliness through asceticism and a conjurer with miraculous powers. Christ was gifted by God with a special dispensation to cure the blind and leprous and even raise the dead. In spite of this, al-Tabari observes that Christ's powers are clearly inferior to those granted to the Prophet Muhammad, who has surpassed Christ in every dimension. An illustration of this is a story he tells which shows how Jesus has come to foretell the Prophet Muhammad. This account is also noteworthy in that it reflects a familiarity with Christian sources in certain details:

> Ibn Abbas said they (the disciples) were fishermen who were catching fish. Jesus passed them and said, "What are you doing?" They replied, "We are catching fish." He said to them, "Will you not come with me that you will catch men?" They replied, "How do you mean?" He said, "We will summon men to God." They replied, "And who are you?" He said, "I am Jesus, Son of Mary, God's Servant and Apostle." The disciples asked, "Are any of the prophets above you?" Jesus replied, "Yes, the Arabian Prophet." So they followed Him and believed on Him and set out with Him. And Sadi said, "They were sailors" and Ibn Arbat said, "They were fullers."[45]

Al-Tabari taught that Jesus was a rabbi who held that outward action must be congruent with inward motivation. Jesus, he explained, resisted conceit, self-promotion, and unforgiveness:

> Do not behold the sins of others with the eyes of masters, but consider your own sins with the eyes of slaves.... How many lamps has the wind blown out and how many worshipers have been spoiled by self-conceit?[46]

When al-Tabari dealt with Surah 3:54, "and God plotted, and God is the best of plotters," he wrote that God had confounded those who tried to crucify Jesus. Al-Tabari believed that, after the final meal with His disciples, Jesus cast His likeness upon every member of His following so that the authorities could not determine which was Jesus. As a result of this, Judas, and not Christ, was crucified.

The Christ which al-Tabari described is a man who, in both life and eventual death, was a steadfast and noble prophet. God had given Christ the Holy Spirit; it was this power which worked through Him and not His own ability. The incorruptible witness of Jesus, according to al-Tabari, always pointed to God and the Arabian Prophet who would follow Him. Most positive in his rendering of Christ was the emphasis given to Jesus' teaching ministry, rarely mentioned by other Muslim theologians. Negatively, al-Tabari was instrumental in canonizing the substitution theory of Christ's death and further popularizing the view that the Christian scriptures were marred beyond recognition.

PERSPECTIVES OF JESUS FROM OTHER EARLY ISLAMIC THEOLOGIANS

A number of other theologians in formative Islam present a portrait of Christ which generally agrees with the stances represented in Ibn Hazm and al-Tabari. A few sources, however, provide additional perspectives.

Al-Razi (Fakhr al-Din Abu 'Abd Allah Muhammad ibn 'Umar ibn al-Husain; 543–606 A.H./A.D. 1149–1209[47]) was a noted theologian and poet from Persia. Along with his contemporaries, al-Razi sought to integrate Greek and Persian philosophy into an Islamic framework. In his book *'Ilm al-Akhlaq,* al-Razi concentrated on Jesus as an admirable recluse who held that the best way to change the world was through the denial of its many-tentacled evils. Al-Razi was circumspect in not condemning the title "Son of God" for Jesus because it was seen as metaphorical and, as such, consistent with the Qur'anic view of Jesus. Christ was revealed as a prophet who was intimate with God, able to perform miracles.

Al-Razi felt it significant that God had desired Jesus to begin His ministry at the age of thirty and not at forty like the Prophet Muhammad. Jesus preached for three years, three months, and three days, and then was chosen by God to judge humanity because of His purity. According to al-Razi, the Prophet Muhammad met Jesus in heaven. Soon everyone will see Christ when He returns to slay the anti-Christ (*al-dajjal*). Most noticeable in al-Razi's portrait of Jesus is the stress that is laid upon His humanity and eventual death and burial in Arabia.

Another theologian, al-Baidawi ('Abd Allah ibn 'Umar; 613–685 A.H./A.D. 1226–1282) is deemed one of the most distinguished early theologians of Islam for his extensive Qur'anic interpretation. He commented upon the Qur'anic legend of Jesus' talking in His cradle as proof of His humanity because it immediately glorified the power of God. He also underlined that Christ's frequent injunction to renounce the world formed the central theme of His life. The message of the Galilean prophet, claimed al-Baidawi, was summed up in His advice, "Be in the midst (of the world) and yet walk on one side."[48]

Other theologians, in response to Christian preaching of the cross, began increasingly to affirm the substitution theory to explain the events at the end of Christ's ministry. But there are intriguing exceptions to this drift. Al-Tirmidhi (Abu 'Isa Muhammad ibn 'Isa ibn Sawra ibn Shaddad; died 279 A.H./A.D. 892) believed that Jesus was actually crucified on a Monday and buried three days later. Ibn 'Abbas ('Abd Allah al-'Abbas; died 32 A.H./A.D. 652), a cousin of the Prophet to whom many questionable traditions are attributed, held that the Christian and Qur'anic versions of the death of Christ were completely compatible. Al-Tha'labī (author of the *Qisas al-Anbiya'*) credited an earlier Hadith with saying that Jesus was crucified and then raised by God. God received Jesus and "clothed him with feathers, dressed him in light and removed from him his desire for food and drink."[49]

The creedal proclamation of al-Nasafi (Abu Hafs 'umar Nadj al-Din; died 537 A.H./A.D. 1142) affirms that Jesus will come again to vanquish the anti-Christ and vindicate the cause of Islam.[50] He will descend from heaven on a white horse, wielding a lance, and leading an army of recruits garnered throughout the ages. Christ will then begin forty years (eighty-four by a solar chronology) of just rule[51] based in Jerusalem. There He will pray to God in the Dome of the Rock before dying and being buried among other kings and prophets.

These writers lived within the context of increasing exposure to Christianity, but all of them unstintingly reaffirmed Christ's humanity. Few of these Muslim scholars indicate any glimmer of sympathetic interaction with Christian doctrine. It is notable to see how themes are repeated that advance Jesus as an ascetic and the returning judge. Interestingly, there is little attention in these sources to the idea that Jesus was a forerunner to the Prophet Muhammad. This may be because, as many Muslims became increasingly conversant with Christianity, they also became aware of the implausibility of this assertion.

JESUS IN THE WRITINGS OF AL-GHAZALI,
"THE GREAT IMAM"

Al-Ghazali (Abu Hamid Muhammad ibn Muhammad al-Tusi al-Shafi'i; 450–505 A.H./A.D. 1058–1111) was the "most original thinker Islam has produced and its greatest theologian."[52] In addition to mastering theological perplexities, al-Ghazali was a historian, jurist, writer, and the mystic most responsible for the legitimization of Sufism. In this sense, al-Ghazali defies the simple categories of "Sufi mystic" or "orthodox theologian." Nonetheless, it is his theological analysis, more than his devotional experience, that is his greatest legacy to Islamic theological history. He is the most substantive figure in both the intellectual and spiritual life of medieval Islam and, perhaps, in all Islamic history.[53]

Al-Ghazali opened a new era in Muslim spirituality by "closing" the previous one. With scholarly thoroughness he reinvigorated Muslim "theological, philosophical, devotional and sectarian thought."[54] Kenneth Cragg described al-Ghazali as "a man in whom a profound psychology of religion was achieved from within a biography of high intellectualism and mystical conversion."[55] Yet, as one reads his writing, one cannot help but decipher that al-Ghazali seems profoundly dissatisfied with every path which he pursues. One detects fascinating chords of resignation and discontentment in his writings.

One of the most consequential developments in Islamic theology is the conviction of al-Ghazali that the aspiration of spirituality is salvation through faith. Al-Ghazali teaches that one's knowledge of God is based on communion with God and active participation in the will and work of God. The path of moral discipline needs to merge with intuitive insight in order to overcome the inevitable despair born from the uncertainty of one's own standing with God. Inner experience and intellect, according to al-Ghazali, lead to a knowledge of God and a purity of soul. The goal for every Muslim is *kashf,* "discovery through illumination."

In light of this unprecedented emphasis, how did al-Ghazali describe Jesus? In *The Alchemy of Happiness* (*Kimiyat al-sa'dah*), he praised Christ's intense spirituality and His boundless love of God, expressed in His passionate resignation to the divine will.[56] Jesus' life of active participation in God's will and work is a pattern that others should seek to emulate. In al-Ghazali's estimation, this function of Christ as a role model makes His divinity unthinkable in that it isolates Him from the rest of humanity. To al-Ghazali, Jesus is less "honored" by Christians than He is by Muslims. His humanity is minimalized by the claim of His divinity. Christ is a *faqir* who is to be imitated in His world-renouncing zeal:

> O Preacher! Take Christ as your model for it is said that He had no purse, for twenty years wore the same shirt of wool and in His journeys earned nothing but a mug and a comb.[57]

Jesus invites individuals to pass through this world as if it were a bridge to travel across.[58] He preached that individuals should despise the world and prize divine love. Christ warned, "Those who by-pass beggars will have no angels to visit them for seven nights."[59] Outward behavior marks the integrity of one's life but is only validated by one's inward goodness, seen in love for God instead of a desire for possessions.

Regarding the claim that Christ is one with God, the Great Imam says this idea is to be interpreted metaphorically. Al-Ghazali does not dismiss the avowal of Jesus, "I and the Father are One," as a textual corruption, but as words used to describe Christ's intimate relationship with God. This would be the same as someone's saying, "I and my friends are one."[60] The result of this intimacy is that Jesus is now resident in the fifth of seven heavens.[61] Jesus cannot be God, however, because then there would be more than one God, and the Almighty would become, in al-Ghazali's words, "a god."

When al-Ghazali discussed the verse, "He who has seen me has seen the Father," he argued that this speaks of Jesus' complete unity with God's will. The theologian does not draw the next conclusion, held by Christians, that the will of God expressed in Jesus is an expression of the divine character. Al-Ghazali also theorized that Jesus did some works in His humanity and other works through the divine spirit. The question arises as to whether or not there is any Christian influence in this position, which abrogates the idea that all of Christ's actions were those of a human prophet.

For the esteemed Imam, much of the Bible should be read as metaphoric poetry. This is consistent with the fact that Jesus was a poet and a teller of parables. Al-Ghazali confirms this free use of language by noting that Christian priests are called "Fathers" and that Christians call themselves "sons of God" (John 1:12). Rationality alone, the theologian warned, will not shed light on the allegory of the Bible.

Al-Ghazali proposes a series of questions intending to dispute the doctrine of the Incarnation and affirm the humanity of Jesus. The story of Jesus' cursing a fig tree (Mark 11:12–13) reveals Christ's anger, as well as His attitude toward the Pharisees. Al-Ghazali questions the holiness of such emotions. Luke recounts that Jesus "grew" (Luke 1:40), which is a human attribute. He wonders how Jesus could be "God" and still pray to God. Considering the prayers of Jesus in Gethsemane (Matthew 26:39, 42), al-Ghazali judged,

> What God is He whose characteristic is to doubt His own ability to cause the cup to pass, who has lifted up His voice to enquire of His God who has left Him (His cry from the cross) and who differentiated between His own will and the will of His God, saying, "Not as my will but as thy will?"[62]

While al-Ghazali affirms that Jesus is unique among the prophets, he categorically denies that He could be divine. In an astonishing admission, al-Ghazali conjectures that it is a hypothetical possibility for a Muslim, in good conscience, to modify the standard creed of Islam and proclaim, "There is no God but God and Jesus is the messenger of God."[63] This statement is perfectly accurate with all criteria of Islamic revelation. Al-Ghazali cannot accept the Christian delusion that God is the third of three, Jesus is both fully human and fully divine, and the Christian denial of the prophetic status of Muhammad.

In al-Ghazali's inspection of the Gospel of John (*al-radd al-ilahiyat 'isa bi-sharh al-injil*),[64] the author sets out a thorough refutation of the divinity of Christ. Al-Ghazali contends that the feeble arguments of Christians about the nature of God are fraught with ambiguities causing them to rely on blind allegiance. He concentrates on discrediting the doctrine of the Incarnation. It is impossible, he assails, for there to be any fusion of the divine with the human. The idea that Jesus is both human and divine is "chameleon-like." The two natures must be mutually exclusive:

> Humanity is an attribute of man specifically as man: Divinity is an attribute of God specifically as God. Join Divinity and humanity together and both the specifications "as God" and "as man" no longer pertain. Therefore, Divinity and humanity together cannot be attributed to a third substance without losing both of these attributes, which is contradictory.[65]

One passage, which al-Ghazali knows for certain to be a corruption of the text, is found in John 17:22, "Thou hast given them the same glory which thou hast given me." He recounted that when he read these words he was reduced to tears: "Is it possible for divinity to be given?"[66] The answer for al-Ghazali is that divinity cannot be dispensed. Christ is a prophet who may turn children into pigs and clay into birds, but He is not divine and cannot transform humanity destined for hell into children of God.

Al-Ghazali claims that the clearest proof of Christ's humanity is the cross. How is it possible that God should bleed? How can God die? "No!" al-Ghazali concludes, "May God forgive the error of this foolish mob!"[67] The crucifixion narrative is followed by the even more implausible idea that God in Christ is buried: "By Allah! There is no stupidity to be found more foul, than of those people who believe that the God of the world has been buried. . . . Verily, the one whom God misleads has no right guide."[68]

The Muslim perception of God as one (*tauhid*) is the greatest foil to the divinity of Christ. According to al-Ghazali, Christians have woven around the person of Jesus webs of misleading perplexities that have blurred His nature as prophet. Christ can only be the "word made flesh" in a metonymous sense. He is a special "event" with a unique personality (*khususiyyah*), enabling Him to be described in theopathic language, which has only "metaphorical value."[69]

In conclusion, al-Ghazali's interpretations of Christ are remarkable for a number of reasons. Primary of these are his apparent acceptance of biblical material and his willingness to accept that statements about Christ as the "Son of God" and God as a "Father" need not be dismissed. Another emphasis, which echoes Christian doctrine, is the idea that salvation is gained through faith. The Muslim view of God, however, prohibits al-Ghazali from countenancing the possibility of the Incarnation. Because Christ is human, He merits emulation and not worship. Jesus was, according to al-Ghazali, a prophet who taught the importance of love, but no mention is made of Christ's revealing the nature of God as Love. In spite of this omission, the fact that Christ's teaching of love is mentioned at all is significant; it is a theme that is almost completely absent from every other source in orthodox Islam.

Al-Ghazali probes themes in Christianity with an openness that few Islamic theologians have exhibited. He approaches the Bible with respect, and Christian doctrinal claims with consideration instead of aloof dismissal. In spite of his indisputable rejection of Christ's divinity, al-Ghazali goes further than any other early Muslim theologian in relating with the Christian doctrine of God. For the first time, in al-Ghazali a Muslim theologian grapples with the issue of God's transcendence in relation to salvation. His conclusion, in agreement with Christianity, is that the goal of faith is a degree of intimacy with the Almighty that is both desirable and possible — a conclusion contrary to previous Islamic interpretations. In spite of this vital first step, the nature of God expressed in al-Ghazali is clearly Qur'anic; it is the primary obstacle that Christians must first address in interaction with his writings.

JESUS IN EARLY ISLAMIC DEVOTIONAL LITERATURE
(A.D. 640–1258)

To augment the practical theology of daily Islamic life, a wealth of popular devotional literature was spawned that adulated the saints and prophets. These writings were often punctuated by the reminder that Muhammad was the greatest of all the prophets. As a result, the picture of Jesus in this literature is often of one who serves as a divine crescendo before the advent of the Qur'an. While these narratives uphold the view of Jesus in the Qur'an and Hadith, they are remarkable for their apparent awareness of Christian tradition and their obvious borrowing from these sources. In this devotional literature a genuine process of dynamic interaction can be seen with Near-Eastern/West Asian Christianity.

The two sources from this field examined here are the *sirah* of Ibn Ishaq and the later *Qisas al-Anbiya'* of al-Tha'labī. This narrative material is far less critical of Christ than most Islamic theological sources; the opinion of Christ is less apologetic and more engaging. A chief accent in the devotional representation of Christ is His supernatural power and His example of renunciation. The well-liked nature of this material provides clues to the Christian of what a relevant depiction of Christ might look like in the Muslim context. In response to this assessment in devotional literature, Christians can present a biblical view of Christ's supernatural power and the renunciation of materialism.

IBN ISHAQ'S PORTRAYAL OF JESUS

Of Islamic devotional authors, one of the first who dealt with Jesus was Ibn Ishaq (Abu 'Abd Allah Muhammad, 87–150 A.H./A.D. 704–67).[70] The first division of his life story of Muhammad (*kitab al-mabda wa-qisas al-anbiya*) concentrated on the Prophet's spiritual ancestry, the line of prophets beginning with Ibrahim. In this portion, Ibn Ishaq discourses upon many of the controversial Christian doctrines that Muslims were just beginning to encounter. These include Christ's miraculous birth and the suggestion that Jesus had both an earthly and heavenly nature. Ibn Ishaq was probably the first to place the rise of Islam in a historical context, showing it to be the continuation of Judaism and Christianity. Christ's life was a preface to the life of Muhammad, and His message finds an unobstructed presentation in the Arabian Prophet.

Because of this emphasis, Ibn Ishaq accented the humanity of Jesus against the claims that He was the Son of God. According to Ibn Ishaq, Jesus came first as a prophet to the Jews, then fled to Yemen, where He died.[71] After His death, Jesus was stripped of His humanity and made into an angel, presumably so that He could live in heaven for the centuries before His return. Jesus will come again as the *mahdi* to rescue the righteous and judge the wicked.

JESUS IN THE *QISAS AL-ANBIYA'* OF AL-THA‘LABĪ

Al-Tha‘labī (Abu Ishaq ibn Muhammad ibn Ibrahim, died 437 A.H./A.D. 1036) wrote the memorable *Stories of the Prophets* (*Qisas al-Anbiya'*), which blends the Qur'an and the Bible with a host of apocryphal legends. Al-Tha‘labī commandeered substantial portions of his work from Ibn Ishaq's *World History* and wove this material together with individual Hadith to formulate a continuous narrative.

The *Stories of the Prophets* supplies a complete panorama of Jesus and reaffirms the clarion dominance of the Qur'an in Muslim perceptions of His life. The author begins with a genealogy of Jesus in which both He and His mother are said to be without sin. Before Christ's birth, Gabriel (Jibril) appeared to the Virgin Mary in the form of a "well proportioned man"[72] who gave her a son after she allowed him to breathe on her bosom. At Christ's birth, all of the idols of the earth were overturned and Satan called the demons of hell together to lament, "Never was there a prophet more dangerous to you and me than this one just born."[73]

A host of extrabiblical details which spring from apocryphal legends appear in the story of Jesus. Al-Tha‘labī submits that Jesus and Mary were abetted by a carpenter named "George," who later brought them to the synagogue and introduced them to Joseph. The angel Gabriel loomed over Joseph and admonished the "sweet tempered carpenter"[74] to transport the mother and child into Egypt. When Jesus began His schooling, He stunned the instructor with a discourse on the "true" meaning of the alphabet and the content of the lectures.[75] As a youth, Jesus animated clay birds. In another instance, Jesus went to call on some playmates. The parents, however, had misgivings about the boy's faculties of sorcery and lied that their children were not home. Jesus, sensing their artifice, transformed their toddlers into swine as punishment.[76] In another fable, Jesus threw a bundle of robes into one vat of dye to save time. All of the clothes miraculously emerged from the caldron tinctured in the colors that the supervisor had requested.

In the *Qisas al-Anbiya'* Jesus is described as a wise teacher. Some of these explications intimate a biblical origin. He instructed people to be "born twice." He reminded them that the "sick do not need a physician," and encouraged people to "take no thought for tomorrow." When He was asked how he gained such erudition He replied that he merely watched the "ignorance of ignorant men and avoided it."[77] A major theme in His teaching was that outward behavior should correspond with inner godliness:

> If one tells many lies, his beauty departs and if one quarrels his manliness falls to the ground, and if one has many cares he will become ill, and if one has bad manners, he punishes himself.[78]

> Learned men who are evil are like the pipe of a lavatory whose outside is plaster but whose inside is stench.[79]

> Of what use is a dark house having a lamp on its roof or a man having wisdom who does not act upon it.[80]

There are junctures in the *Qisas al-Anbiya'* where Jesus, sounding very much like a Muslim *mullah,* beckons individuals to adhere to external protocol and religious ritual. Such an emphasis has no origin in Christian apocryphal sources, nor is it accordant with Islamic Hadith about Jesus. This reveals the way in which Jesus had come to be utilized as an endorsement of specific points of argument. Al-Tha'labī attributed to Jesus such sayings as:

> Two characteristics of ignorance are laughter without anything extraordinary and sleeping in the morning without a (previous) vigil.[81]

> The steps of some slip only in regard to three things: smallness of thanks to God, fear of something other than God and hope in created things.[82]

To a much greater degree than Ibn Ishaq, but consistent with Islamic Hadith, al-Tha'labī's caricature of Christ reveals an impoverished ascetic with disheveled hair and a gaunt face. Jesus described the world as a field belonging to Satan. In it, He was a homeless drifter who often slept on dunghills among the dogs. Jesus calls humanity to "seek a great amount of what fire cannot burn";[83] namely, the pursuit of godliness. He was a barefooted pilgrim who shunned comfort: "Mud and gold were alike to Him."[84] When once asked if anything could be built with permanence from stone or brick, Christ replied, "A house built on the waves of the sea."[85]

Jesus is a man mired in combat against an onslaught of temptation and materialism. Al-Tha'labī told of one stormy night which forced Jesus to flee into a nearby tent only to discover a woman inside. Dashing next to a cave, He confronted a lion. In distress, Jesus cried out to God who reassured Him that luxuriant ease awaited Him in the world beyond. Until then, Christ must notify people that, to have any chance of seeing God, they first have to make their "livers hungry" and their "bodies naked."[86] Those who desire this world are like those who crave to drink water from the sea. The pleasures of this world, such as wealth and women, must be combated with fasting. The world is a toothless old prostitute bedecked in the jewels paid to her by the numerous husbands whom she has assassinated.

Another theme in the *Qisas al-Anbiya'* underscores the Hadith's estimation of Jesus as a prophet with extraordinary powers. Examples of this abound. In gratitude to one person's kindness Christ turned the rocks of a garden into emeralds. When the miracle of the loaves and fishes is retold, it adds that any diseased who ate were instantly healed. Jesus performed this particular miracle for forty consecutive nights. At one point, when the crowd was becoming complacent, Christ turned a broiled fish into a live one before transforming it again to its more edible state. The episode concludes by observing that throughout these days of feasting, everyone was "filled to satiety and belching"[87] and, subsequently, became loyal followers. Skeptics of His strength, on the other hand, were often transmuted into swine:

> While they were sleeping at night on their bed with their wives in their houses (they became pigs), so that when they woke in the morning they went about the roads to the rubbish heaps and eating the filth from the courtyard. And when the pigs saw Jesus they began to weep and circle around. Jesus called them by name one by one and when He did, they would weep, making signs with their heads but being unable to speak. They lived three days and then perished.[88]

None of these supernatural abilities imply that Christ is divine. In fact, many of the miracles in the *Qisas al-Anbiya'* confirm the opposite conclusion. When recounting the Qur'anic story where Jesus turned clay forms into live birds it adds that these fowl died without delay. This was to demarcate "the distinction between the work of a creature (Jesus) and that of Allah, and show that perfection belongs only with Allah."[89] When Jesus brought the dead to life, He always chanted the formula, "O Living, O Eternal One!"[90] making it unmistakable that God was responsible for the miracle.[91]

How does the *Qisas al-Anbiya'* describe the death and ascension of Jesus? Al-Tha'labī detailed that at the end of Christ's life, He began to sweat drops of blood. At the Last Supper, Christ washed the disciples' feet and prayed that death would be avoided. God granted this request and Judas was crucified.[92] Three hours after Judas was placed on the cross, God delivered Jesus into Paradise. Seven days later, Christ returned to the earth and spoke to Mary Magdalene, asking her to assemble the disciples. Jesus summoned them to go to the nations and gave each of them a different language to preach:

Go to the Kings of the earth and convey to them what I have charged you with and summon them to that which I have summoned you, and do not deceive them, for when I leave my humanity. . . . I shall be standing at the right hand of the throne of my Father and shall be with you wherever you go and shall strengthen you and help you with strength by the permission of my Father. Go, and summon them with gentleness and cure them and command them to be kind.[93]

The portrait of Jesus in al-Tha'labī concludes by pointing to His future influence as an eschatological figure. As is true in Hadith, Jesus resides in Paradise until the last days when He will return as God's appointed ruler (*khalifah*) over the Muslim community:

He will be a man symmetrical in stature of reddish-white complexion, lank hair as though his hair were dripping with perfume though it has not been moistened. He will come down in a greenish-yellow garment, will break crosses and kill swine. He will put an end to the poll-tax and will make wealth abound. He will . . . make war on behalf of Islam until, in his time, he will destroy all religions except that of Islam.[94]

At the terminus of His forty years on earth, Jesus purportedly dies and is then entombed beside Caliph 'Umar in Medina. From there He will await, with all other mortals, the final resurrection.

Jesus in Muslim devotional material is esteemed as a blameless prophet who worked miracles and advocated asceticism. Except for His dour countenance,[95] Christ is a prophet to be emulated — especially for His purity. There is never any doubt that Jesus is not completely subservient to the Prophet Muhammad. When asked if there are others like Himself, Jesus replies, "Yes, he whose talk is glorifying to God, he whose silence is meditation and he whose look is a tear, he is like me."[96] These writings affirm Jesus for His exemplary humanity; anyone who eschews materialism can mirror the saintliness of Christ.

THE UNIQUENESS OF JESUS IN FORMATIVE ISLAM

The presentation of Jesus in formative Islam shows that the Muslims' perception of God determines their view of Christ. In Islam, any affirmation about the exceptionalness of Jesus is invalid if it is not framed in the underlying context of God's unity and transcendence. Christ is presented as one who has an uncommon role in the furtherance of God's revelation. His supernatural birth, life, and destiny confirms that He is chosen by God. Al-Ghazali affirmed that God had imparted to Jesus a "special personhood" (*khususiyyah*), but this is premised on His humanity.

The problem of ascertaining exactly who Jesus is, according to Islam, is compounded by the fact that Christians have obscured His original missive. Muslims insist that Christ's prophecy has been preserved in the Qur'an independent of "corrupted" biblical sources. The fraudulent misrepresentation of Christ in the Bible is surmounted by the faithful account of the Qur'an. Since the Qur'an is perfect it is also definitive regarding the prophet Jesus. The Qur'an steers the Muslim between the complete rejection of Christ's role seen in Judaism and the deification of Christ in Christianity. Jesus never intended to launch a new religion. His singularity lay in His unerring loyalty to the truth of God (Islam). Islamicists have discerned evident traces of Arianism, Gnosticism, Nestorian dualism, and Monophysitism in these formative Islamic renderings of Jesus.

A principal point of agreement between the Muslim portrayal and the Bible is Christ's purity. Among all the prophets, Jesus alone was sinless. This is proof, according to al-Tabari, that Christ should be emulated. This clarity of Jesus as example led one Muslim to explain, "I have no doubt that I am one of the followers of Christ just as I am one of Muhammad's followers."[97] As a teacher, He delivered a message which, in Islamic literature, was summarized as one of renunciation. Christ lived to fulfill a divine commission:

> God told Him to come forth to the people and summon them to Allah; speaking to them in parables, curing the sick, the infirm, the blind and the mad, taming the devils, rebuking them and humbling them so that they used to die for fear of Him.[98]

The titles garlanded on Jesus in Islam affirm this authority. Christ is called, among other things, the "Messiah," the "Word of God," a "Messenger and Apostle of God," and a "Spirit from God." Invariably, Muslims ascribe similar, and often higher, honors to the Prophet Muhammad.

The picture of Christ in Islam differs in many key aspects from that in the Bible. Muslims often contend that Christ was not crucified; thus He cannot have been resurrected. There is no mention of Jesus' teaching about the kingdom of God or His beckoning individuals to service and sacrifice. There are only the thinnest of allusions to the Sermon on the Mount. Because God is unitary, transcendent, and unknowable, Jesus cannot be described as a "way" to God. As a man, Christ also needs deliverance from hell and death.

Christ's role cannot be understood independent of the Prophet Muhammad. Jesus is unique because He is the last prophet before Muhammad. As a prophet, His preaching exceeded all others who have preceded Him. The clarity of His prophetic life is to be honored. Jesus is significant to the destiny of every person as the judge on the final day. Jesus, alone among humanity, has not died; after twenty centuries He waits to return again to the earth.

Although Jesus is decidedly a figure of both fascination and frustration to the writers of early Islamic literature, it is evident that He is not their foremost preoccupation. Jesus is not mentioned in over 100 of the 114 Surahs of the Qur'an. He is an eminent prophet, the most portentous before Muhammad, but His role is marginalized by the advent of the Qur'an. If anything, His position in Islamic source material diminished after the Qur'an. The depiction of Jesus in the Hadith is relatively less emphasized and more "confined" than the Qur'an. In devotional literature, there is no known biography of Christ. By the time of al-Ghazali, the consciousness of Jesus seems to be primarily for illustrative purposes.

The efforts of Christians to familiarize themselves with the portrait of Jesus in Islam is appreciated by Muslims with whom I have spoken, as long as this does not become a manipulative tool in Muslim-Christian interaction. In spite of any skepticism (or a defensive posture) by Muslims, Christians should continue to analyze the import of the Islamic examination of Christ with accuracy in order to comprehend precisely what Muslims surmise about Jesus and how that understanding is based on the Muslim concept of God.

Can the Muslim portrait of Jesus be a link in the presentation of the Christian doctrine of God? By explaining the differences in the two views of God, Muslims can be shown the logic of the nature and the mission of Christ. The Muslim portrait of Christ can be shown to originate from the Islamic concept of God.

Christians in dialogue with Muslims best begin at the level of insight held by their audience. From this starting point, according to historic Christian pneumatology, each Muslim will need to be led by the Holy Spirit in the process of more clearly perceiving the nature of God in Christ. Jesus cannot be stranded in Galilee as a prophet of righteousness when He Himself refused to stay there but pressed on toward Jerusalem to be crucified. John tells of a Samaritan woman whom Jesus once met becoming increasingly aware of His divine nature. "Sir," she said, "I perceive that you are a Prophet." Rather than contradict this initial affirmation, Christ continued to speak with her until she could see that He was more than a prophet. Later she asked Him if He was the long-awaited Messiah. Jesus straightforwardly presented Himself to her: "I who speak to you am He" (John 4:26).

NOTES

1. Stephen Neill, *The Christian Faith and Other Faiths* (London: Oxford University Press, 1961), 64.

2. All but five of the references to Jesus are written in the Meccan period of Qur'anic revelation. Although Jesus is referred to as the "Son of Mary," no mention is made of Joseph in the Qur'an.

3. Many originate from the Christian community at Najran. Other accounts are called the Syrian and Arab "infancy Gospels."

4. A good example of this trend in Christianity is the development of monasticism. One Surah states, "Then we caused our messengers to follow in their footsteps; and we caused Jesus, Son of Mary, to follow and gave Him the Gospel and placed compassion and mercy in the hearts of those who followed Him — But monasticism [*rahbaniyya*] they invented. We ordained it not for them; only seeing Allah's pleasure, and they observed it not with right observance. So we give those of whom believe their reward, but many of them are evil-livers" (Surah 57:27, Pickthall).

5. Kenneth Cragg, *Jesus and the Muslim* (London: Allen and Unwin, 1985), 43. Jesus lived in meek openness before men and, as a result, faced continual opposition from corrupt religious authorities.

6. John Hick in an article, "Islam and Christian Monotheism," in *Islam in a World of Diverse Faiths,* ed. Daniel Cohn-Sherbok (New York: St. Martin's Press, 1991), 115.

7. Jane Dammen McAuliffe, *Qur'anic Christians: An Analysis of Classical and Modern Exegesis* (New York: Cambridge University Press, 1991), 143.

8. According to the footnote for Surah 4:157–58 in Yusuf Ali's translation (230): "The Basilidans believed that someone else was substituted for him. The Docetae held that Christ never had a real physical body, but only an apparent or phantom body, and that His crucifixion was only apparent, not real. The Marcionite Gospel (about A.D. 138) denied that Jesus was born and merely said that He appeared in human form. The Gospel of Barnabas supported the theory of the substitution on the Cross."

9. Geoffrey Parrinder, *Jesus in the Qur'an* (New York: Barnes and Noble, 1965), 111.

10. Perhaps the only mention of a sacrificial atonement of one for another in the Qur'an is the unique incident of Abraham's willingness to offer his son (Surah 61:64). The idea of sacrificing one's self for another has a clearer precedent in Shi'a Islam and among the veneration of certain saints within Sufi Islam.

11. A discussion of the difference between the Muslim and Christian view of the Holy Spirit and "spirit" is found beginning on p. 119.

12. These supported collections are:
      1. The *Sahih* of al-Bukhari (died 256 A.H./A.D. 870)
      2. The *Sahih* of Muslim (died 261 A.H./A.D. 875)
      3. The *Sunan* of Ibn-Maja (died 273 A.H./A.D. 887)
      4. The *Sunan* of Abu Dawud (died 275 A.H./A.D. 888)
      5. The *Jami'* of al-Tirmidhi (died 279 A.H./A.D. 892)
      6. The *Sunan* of An-Nasa'i (died 303 A.H./ A.D. 915)
The first of these, the *Jami' al-Sahih al-Musnad min Hadith Rasul Allah* by (Muhammad Ibn abd Allah ibn Ismail) al-Bukhari has 97 chapters and 3,460 subchapters. The *Sahih* of Muslim is, along with al-Bukhari, the most valued of these collections. In addition to these six widely accepted collections, some Sunni Muslims accept three other collections. Shi'a Islam has developed its own Hadith.

13. Muslims assert that the Hadith has "undergone the most scrupulous checking and verification (procedure) in the history of recorded scholarship." Muhammad Ataur-Rahim, *Jesus: A Prophet of Islam* (London: MWH, 1979), 221.

14. "Our Lord God, which art in heaven, hallowed be thy name: Thy kingdom is in Heaven and on Earth, as Thy mercy is in Heaven, so show Thy mercy on the Earth. Forgive us our debts and sins." Attributed to Muhammad in a Hadith according to L. Bevan Jones, *The People of the Mosque* (London: SCM Press, 1932), 82.

15. Alfred Guillaume, *The Traditions of Islam* (Beirut: Khayats, 1966), 135.

16. Ibid., 149. In this same tradition, Bukhari conjectures that when Gabriel appeared to Mary he came in the form of a young man.

17. Attributed to Ka'ab al-Akbar (d. 3/652–653) and cited in McAuliffe, *Qur'anic Christians,* 131–32.

18. The account of Shem being raised from the dead is found in *A Reader on Islam,* ed. Arthur Jeffery (The Hague: Mouton, 1962), 204.

19. Cited in ibid.

20. Attributed to Ma'ruf al-Karkhi, in Ataur-Rahim, *Jesus: A Prophet of Islam,* 223.

21. Ibid.

22. Cragg, *Jesus and the Muslim,* 55.

23. McAuliffe, *Qur'anic Christians,* 131.

24. One accounting of His rescue is that He retreated to Mt. Sinai where a gale caught Him away to heaven. Ibid., 145.

25. The term *jizyah* simply means "tax" (Surah 9:29) and refers to the tax that non-Muslims paid to uphold their status as protected citizens.

26. On the authority of Abdullah bin 'Amr and cited in *The Two Hundred Hadith,* trans. and selected by Abdul Rahim Alfahim (Makkah, Saudi Arabia: Makkah Printing and Information Establishment, 1990), 179.

27. Attributed to Ibn al-Jauzi and transmitted in the *Kitab al-Wafa* according to Ataur-Rahim, *Jesus: A Prophet of Islam,* 228.

28. The Qur'an (in Surah 3:43–45 and 5:109–10) emphasizes the wonders of Jesus while "the tradition tried to establish that the miracles of the Prophet Muhammad were more exalted than the miracles of Jesus." Ignaz Goldziher, *Muslim Studies* (London: Allen and Unwin, 1971), 2:261.

29. McAuliffe, *Qur'anic Christians,* 135.

30. Guillaume, *The Traditions of Islam,* 158. Guillaume cites this tradition without providing information about its initial source.

31. Abdiyah Akbar Abdul-Haqq, *Sharing Your Faith with a Muslim* (Minneapolis: Bethany, 1980), 96.

32. From the *Tanbih al-Ghafilin* by Abu l'Laith al-Samarkandi (died 373 A.H./A.D. 983) in Jeffery, *A Reader on Islam,* 227.

33. This is on the authority of Abu Hurairah and cited in Abdul Rahim Alfahim, *The Two Hundred Hadith,* 177. A variant of this is attributed to Ibn al-Jauzi and transmitted in the *Kitab al-Wafa* according to Ataur-Rahim, *Jesus: A Prophet of Islam,* 228.

34. Article entitled *"Kalam,"* by D. B. MacDonald in *The Shorter Encyclopedia of Islam,* ed. H. A. R. Gibb and J. H. Kramers (Leiden: E. J. Brill, 1991), 210.

35. Al-Ghazali was the most noted Muslim philosopher to Christian readers. By contrast, Ibn Sina (Avicenna) had a slight following among Muslims.

36. For an interesting development of this idea, consult Seyyed Hossein Nasr's *Islamic Life and Thought* (Albany: State University of New York Press, 1981), 60ff.

37. These include philosophy (*al-falsafah*) and what Nasr calls "theosophy" (*al-hikam*). Ibid., 63.

38. Cited in article by Georges C. Anwati, "Kalam," in *The Encyclopedia of Religion,* ed. Mircea Eliade (New York: Macmillan, 1978), 8:231.

39. Called the *Kitab al-fasl fi 'l-milal wa'l-ahwa wa'l-nihal,* which also attacked the Ash'arite opinion regarding the divine attributes. Of this castigation, C. van Arendonk noted, "With regard to the anthropomorphic expressions in the Kur'an [*sic*], however, Ibn Hazm found himself forced to put aside his own method in order to bring these into conformity with a spiritual interpretation." From the article "Ibn Hazm" in the *The Shorter Encyclopedia of Islam,* ed. H. A. R. Gibb and J. H. Kramers (Leiden: E. J. Brill, 1991), 148.

40. Ibid.

41. He mentions, among others, the statement of Jesus: "Some standing here" would not die before the Kingdom of God came (Matthew 10:23; Mark 9:1). Ibn Hazm asked why Christ said that He came not to destroy the law but to fulfill it, and then proceeded to amend certain laws. Ibn Hazm observes that Jesus said, "Why do you call me good?" (Mark 10:18) and then claimed to be the "Good Shepherd" (John 10:31).

42. Cited in J. Windrow Sweetman's *Islam and Christian Theology* (London: Lutterworth Press, 1947), vol. 2, part 1, 249.

43. Ibid., 250.

44. I first heard these arguments while living in a Malay Kampong in Singapore. They seemed especially appealing to Muslims who are not interested in understanding Christianity as much as in refuting its "falsehoods."

45. Cited in Ernest Hahn, *Jesus in Islam: A Christian View* (Hyderabad, India: Henry Martyn Institute of Islamic Studies, 1991), 15; also Jeffery, *A Reader on Islam,* 577.

46. Hahn, *Jesus in Islam,* 19.

47. Hijri years are shorter than Gregorian years.

48. Cited in Cragg, *Jesus and the Muslim,* 47.

49. Cited in F. Peters, *Judaism, Christianity and Islam: The Classical Texts and Their Interpretation* (Princeton: Princeton University Press, 1990), 174.

50. Cited in Jeffery, *A Reader on Islam,* 352.

51. Cited in Andrew Rippin and Jan Knappert, eds., *Textual Sources for the Study of Islam* (Totowa, N.J.: Barnes & Noble, 1986), 86.

52. Article "al-Ghazali" by D. B. Macdonald in *The Shorter Encyclopedia of Islam,* 111.

53. Nasr, *Islamic Life and Thought,* 71.

54. In the article "al-Ghazali" by Bruce Lawrence in *The Abingdon Dictionary of Living Religions,* ed. Keith Crim, Roger A. Bullard, and Larry Shinn (Nashville: Abingdon, 1981), 275.

55. Kenneth Cragg, *The Arab Christian: A History in the Middle East* (London: Mowbray, 1991), 86.

56. Al-Ghazali, *The Alchemy of Happiness,* trans. Claude Field (London: Octagon Press, 1980), 115–16. Al-Ghazali recounts: "Again when people asked Jesus, 'What is the highest work of all?' He answered, 'To love God and to be resigned to do His will.' "

57. Ibid., 20.

58. Nolin states this is from the ruined mosque of the Moghul emperor Akbar. He continues, "Throughout the Muslim world it will be quoted that 'the Son of Man has nowhere to lay His head' in reference to Jesus." From the Abd-al Karim al-Khatib quoted in Kenneth Nolin's article "Al Ustadh al-Haddad: A Review," in *Muslim World* 60, no. 2 (April 1970): 95.

59. Cragg, *Jesus and the Muslim,* 47.

60. Cited in Sweetman, *Islam and Christian Theology,* vol. 2, part 1, 271.

61. Jane I. Smith and Yvonne Yazbeck Haddad, *The Islamic Understanding of Death and Resurrection* (Albany: State University of New York Press, 1981), 68.

62. Sweetman, *Islam and Christian Theology,* vol. 2, part 1, 271.

63. Cited in W. Montgomery Watt, *Muslim-Christian Encounters* (London: Routledge, 1991), 67–68.

64. Although al-Ghazali assumes that part of the text must be corrupted, he feels free to study the Gospel of John because he believes that it contains part of the true *injil.*

65. Cited in Sweetman, *Islam and Christian Theology,* vol. 2, part 1, 282.

66. In an article, "Sirah" written by G. Levi della Vida in *The Shorter Encyclopedia of Islam,* 548.

67. Sweetman, *Islam and Christian Theology,* vol. 2, part 1, 290.

68. Ibid., 297.

69. Cragg, *Jesus and the Muslim,* 46.

70. Ibn Ishaq was born in Medina shortly after the Prophet's death. He devoted much of his attention to the legends of the Prophet Muhammad which, in traditional Arabic fashion, glorified his skill in numerous military campaigns (*maghazi*). These were compiled in a biography (*sirah*) of three volumes. What has been preserved of this are two sections transcribed by Ibn Ishaq's pupil, the Kufi, Ziyad ibn Abd Allah al-Bakka'i. For further information consult the article by C. Brocklemann in the *Shorter Encyclopedia of Islam,* 149.

71. Jesus was able to avoid death because a companion, Sergius, suffered in His place. Sweetman, *Islam and Christian Theology.*

72. G. D. Newby, *The Making of the Last Prophet* (Columbia: University of South Carolina Press, 1989), 208.

73. Cited in Jeffery, *A Reader on Islam,* 567.

74. Cited in ibid., 561.

75. Newby cites the following Hadith: "He (the teacher) was amazed at this son of a widow whom he scarcely began to teach but found that he knows it." Newby, *The Making of the Last Prophet,* 208.

76. Cited in Jeffery, *A Reader on Islam,* 573.

77. Cited in James Robson, *Christ in Islam* (London: John Murray, 1929), 44.

78. Cited in ibid.

79. Cited in ibid., 43.

80. Cited in ibid., 56.

81. Cited in ibid., 55.

82. Cited in ibid., 57.

83. Cited in ibid., 46. According to this source Jesus exclaimed, "Kindness is that which fire cannot destroy."

84. Cited in ibid., 69.

85. Cited in ibid., 74.

86. Cited in ibid., 63.

87. Cited in Jeffery, *A Reader on Islam,* 589.

88. Cited in ibid., 590.

89. Cited in ibid., 579.

90. Cited in ibid., 582.

91. When one of His disciples noted that only Jesus could raise the dead, Jesus quickly pointed to His limitations: "I am not incapable of raising the dead, but, I am incapable of applying a remedy to a fool." Cited in Robson, *Christ in Islam,* 57.

92. Mahmoud M. Ayoub, "Towards an Islamic Christology II: The Death of Jesus, Reality or Delusion (A Study of the Death of Jesus in Tassir Literature)," *Muslim World* 70, no. 2 (April 1980): 107. Ayoub points out that the substitution theory was criticized by the noted Qur'anic scholar Abu 'l-Qasim al-Zamakhsari. Ibn Ishaq said that the King of Israel who sought to kill Jesus was King David.

93. Cited in Robson, *Christ in Islam,* 88.

94. Cited in Jeffery, *A Reader on Islam,* 596–97. A variant of this is attributed to Abu Hurairah and cited in Alfahim, *The Two Hundred Hadith,* 178.

95. Cited in Robson, *Christ in Islam,* 109.

96. Cited in ibid., 50.

97. Cited in Cragg, *Jesus and the Muslim,* 47.

98. Cited in Jeffery, *A Reader on Islam,* 575.

5

God Incarnate

THE MUSLIM REJECTION
OF THE DOCTRINE OF GOD INCARNATE

The Incarnation of God in Christ is the central proclamation of orthodox Christian theology. In this chapter, examination will begin with the Muslim rejection of the Incarnation. A point of agreement that relates to the Incarnation, the Virgin Birth, will be examined for implications in interfaith dialogue. Arising from the Incarnation is the claim of Christ's divinity, which is also discarded by Islam. How can this doctrine be explained clearly to Muslims? In Christ's life the revelation of His divinity centered on two titles, the "Son of God" and the "Son of Man." The latter is infrequently used among Christians but is well suited for the Muslim context. We conclude with the question of how one might discuss with Muslims the Christian idea that God provides salvation through the Incarnation of Christ.

The Muslim rebuttal of the doctrine of God Incarnate accentuates the deep fissure between two distinct concepts of God. The rejection of the Incarnation is seen by Muslims as a defense of God's unity and an attack against polytheism. Muslims maintain that the Incarnation transforms a human being into God. It is blasphemous (*tajdif*) to say that God shares His nature with another.

Christians might consider responding by explaining that many Muslims may not actually hold an accurate view of the Incarnation. The notion that many have about this doctrine coincides with the early heresy of "adoptionism," rejected by both Christianity and Islam (see Surah 18:4). Islam argues that the Incarnation is, in the words of Feuerbach, the "humanization" of the Almighty. They concur with Wittgenstein, who wrote, "Christians are bewitched by a picture of a sinless God crucified by sinful men."[1] Another barrier is the linguistic one. Muslims repeatedly use the word "indwelling" (*hullul*) or "union" (*ittihad*) to characterize the Incarnation. These terms invariably cloud and restrict the Muslim's view of this event.

Islamic soteriology circumscribes the way that Muslims perceive the doctrine of God Incarnate. Muslims ask what is the reason that God must become Incarnate among humanity. It cannot be to liberate: God is already free to rescue whomever He chooses. In light of this, the Incarnation is not essential.

Islam maintains that God is loving but does not need to so completely identify with humanity as to become a person to establish the fact of divine kindness. The Muslim view of God's transcendence means that intimacy with God is not possible because God is distinct in every way from creation. Jewish philosopher Maimonides said, "God is free from passions; God is moved neither by feelings of joy nor feelings of pain."[2] Islam refutes the Incarnation because it is derogatory to God's greatness.

It is not possible to reconcile the Islamic awareness of God's transcendence with the doctrine of the self-revelation of God in Christ. How is it reasonable, Muslims ask, that God could go inside the womb of a woman and experience the uncleanness of conception and childbirth? How is it conceivable that God could dwell within a human form that hungers, excretes, and sleeps? God's greatness make these ideas inappropriate. Muhammad Iqbal concluded,

> God is beyond death and is the essence of life. God does not know what the death of man is. Though we be as naked birds, in the knowledge of death, we are better than God.[3]

Al-Ghazali advances that the Muslim dismissal of the Incarnation of Christ is "not a rejection of divine mercy, but a question of being faithful to the absolute mystery (*ghayb,* literally "hiddenness") of God's oneness."[4] Christians take issue with this logomachy because the Incarnation is the fullest revelation conceivable of the love of God. Christianity does not believe it is possible for Muslims to perceive divine mercy or love apart from the Incarnation of Christ. In Islam, God's mercy is an expression of the divine will and not of the divine nature. Because Christianity believes that the Incarnation is a self-revelation of God, it is dismissed by Muslims as a blasphemous insult to divine glory. The only self-revelation of God is the truth of God's oneness.

THE INCARNATION OF GOD IN CHRIST

Islam rejects the doctrine of the Incarnation because it is seen as demeaning to God's greatness and compromising of God's holiness (defined as divine transcendence). Christianity avows that the Incarnation magnifies God's power and does not undermine God's holiness (defined in moral terms and not just in terms of God's nonrelatedness to humanity). In Christianity, the Incarnation is an extension and complete manifestation of the nature of God since creation. Christians need to explain how the Incarnation does not jeopardize God's unity and is consistent with the New Testament revelation of God's transcendent holiness.

In fact, the Incarnation of God in Christ is the divine answer to the human condition, desirous to enter God's presence but mired in unholiness. This is obviously not the only way to approach this doctrine: The Incarnation is also a revelation of God's nature. Muslims, however, feel they have no need for an additional description of God's essence beyond the Qur'an. Muslims are vividly aware of both the holiness of God and the fact that their sin separates them from God. Holiness, in whatever its form, defines God. It does not describe humanity. The Islamic concept of God makes these two points unambiguous. Muslims agree that only God could breach this difference (and to a limited degree, God has overcome this with the impartation of the Qur'an). There is a tension, however, within Islam of how to portray the nature of God, the nature of humanity, and the nature of revelation between the divine and the human. The Incarnation resolves these three uncertainties with the disclosure of God's nature as Triune. The Incarnation makes the new covenant possible and has been described as "the essential, formative characteristic of Christianity."[5]

Many Christians see the foreshadowing of the doctrine of God incarnate in the Torah's description of God's glory (*shekinah*) and the "theophanies" of this glory descending among humanity. God is willing to overcome the barrier of human unholiness with His presence. Abraham Heschel spoke of these manifestations as "God's self-humiliation (which) are to be understood as God's accommodations to human weaknesses."[6] The willing heart of God toward humanity is apparent in Eden as God walks with Adam in the cool of the day. It is only sin, and not divine intention, that has driven a wedge between God and humankind. The early church fathers developed creeds which formulated that Jesus was "truly God and truly man" (*vere Deus, vere Homo*). The problem of how the divinity of Christ interrelates with the humanity of Jesus remains a major stumbling block between Muslims and Christians.

Some contemporary Christians have stressed that the Incarnation is not an ongoing process. Christ has entered human history in a unique and decisive moment. The Incarnation is a singular act of divine intervention in history in order to reshape history. The specificity of this event empties the Incarnation of any notion that God's visitations among humanity are to be seen as "*avatars*" or periodic appearances among people of different places or cultures. The nonhistorical and eternal God takes on the "flesh" of time.

Philippians 2:7 speaks of the "emptying" (*kenosis*) of the Incarnation. Christ did not renounce divine power but set aside the prerogative of that might to inhabit one body and, in humanity, bring forth "a manifestation of divine glory."[7] This splendor, evocative of the *shekinah* of the Torah, was

God's presence which brought salvation. God has chosen to go "out of Himself in order to gather all things to Himself."[8] God in Christ has left heaven in order to dwell among widows and orphans so that they can be restored to Himself. The Incarnation eliminates the distance which dispossessed humanity has experienced as a result of sin.

Christians take exception to the Muslim idea that it is "unworthy" of God to come among creation. God has chosen by grace to bring conclusive revelation about the divine nature in the person of Jesus. This decision of God magnifies His worthiness. Many Christians would respond to Islam by saying that it would actually be unworthy of God to create and then predestine a portion of creation to a life of suffering followed by eternal torment.

God in Christ provides a revelation of His plan for redemption. The purpose of the Incarnation is to restore fellowship between God and creation in the possibility of profound intimacy. In light of humanity's need for holiness before communion can be realized, God has fashioned in Christ a pathway for individuals to become holy. Before the fall of Adam, God crafted humanity in divine image; the Incarnation is the re-creation of that image in the "second Adam." The initiative begins with God and expresses divine involvement with humanity. Irenaeus explained, "God has become what we are in order that we might share in His perfection."[9]

The Incarnation of Christ is a revelation of divine unity. The doctrine of the Incarnation compelled Christians to develop an understanding of God as differentiated within His unity. Jesus announced, "I go to my Father and to your Father, my God and your God" (John 2:17). Yet Christians worship Jesus as Holy God in human flesh. The conclusion that revelation came through humanity confronted Christians with the fact that they were calling Jesus — unquestionably a human being — one with God.

The Incarnation underscores that the revelation of Christianity is a person and not an idea or set of decrees. For Christianity, the teaching, mission, and nature of Christ are inseparable. The marriage of message and messenger is puzzling and daunting to Muslims, but very much in keeping with the biblical understanding of prophethood. The Bible is consistently biographical and filters the meaning of revelation through the specific experiences of life. Jesus Christ is the embodiment of the eternal mind walking among humanity.

THE VIRGIN BIRTH AND
THE DOCTRINE OF GOD INCARNATE

A principal area of agreement between Islam and Christianity is the miraculous birth of Jesus. This harmony, however, is interpreted differently because of a dissimilar view of God's nature. Care should be taken in communicating to Muslims how the Virgin Birth relates to the Christian belief that Jesus is divine. Islam sees Christ's birth as evidence of His humanity, purity, and prophetic office. Christians do not believe that the Virgin Birth "proves" Christ's divinity, but that it is consistent with the claim that He is the promised Messiah. The Qur'anic narrative of the Virgin Birth underlines the humanity, sinlessness, and special relationship that Jesus had with God (Surah 19:16– 34). The significance in Islam of the Virgin Birth has no relation to the essential nature of God, or the revelation of that nature. Jesus is not born from God but created inside Mary.

The Islamic depiction of the Virgin Birth raises a number of questions. Christ's birth in the Qur'an is merely a statement about God's power. Christianity agrees that God's might is manifest at the birth of Jesus. But it asks the Muslim why God chose this particular demonstration of power. What does this miracle say about the nature of Christ? Why do Muslims stress that Christ's lineage is pure and He is sinless? If Christ alone is blameless, then surely it does not mean His perfection is to serve as an example for Muslims to emulate.

Christ's birth is a miracle that affirms His prophesied Messianic role. Paul declares, "When the time had fully come, God sent forth His Son, born of a woman, born under the law" (Galatians 4:4). Many Christians feel that the words of Isaiah point to Christ:

> Unto us a child is born, unto us a son is given, and the government shall be upon his shoulders. And He will be called, Wonderful Counsellor, Mighty God, Everlasting Father, the Prince of Peace. (Isaiah 9:6)

Unlike other messengers from God, Jesus does not begin in speech but in His involvement with humanity. The Qur'an certifies that Jesus preached from the cradle; in Christianity the infant is silent. The child says or does nothing to merit worship and yet God allows Him to be lauded as holy. The Jesus of the cradle is not revered as a moral teacher, miracle worker, or prophet, but because He is God dwelling in human form.

The Bible expounds that Jesus was divine from the outset of His life. Jesus was untouched by the "original sinfulness"[10] that many suggest the Bible implies is common to humanity. The Virgin Birth of Jesus affirms the *logos* doctrine of God in Christ preincarnate. His birth, by the power of God (Luke 1:35), affirms the Christian revelation of God who is participant. In coming among humanity, Jesus infuses into it the perfection and possibility lost in the fall recorded in Genesis.[11] Jesus is born in purity, among humanity, but in a way distinct from all other individuals. Human birth does not exclude the divine nature of Christ. As Christ is generated, Ignatius tells us, Christ remains ungenerated and eternal.

THE ISLAMIC REJECTION OF CHRIST'S DIVINITY

It is either an absolute truth or an absurd folly to believe that God was in a poor, obscure, Palestinian peasant reconciling the world to Himself.[12] Islam scorns the belief that Christ is divine and centers its rejection around the belief that it is impossible for a human being to share God's nature and be both human and divine.

From the perspective of Islam, the belief that Jesus is God's Son is an affront to the divine majesty. God is greater than such a misconception. The cardinal sin of Islam is to worship another besides God; this is seen as the implication of the doctrine of Christ's divinity. The Qur'an heralds with clarity, "They say: Allah hath begotten a son! Glory be to Him — Nay!" (Surah 2:116); and "It is not befitting for Allah that He should beget a son!" (Surah 19:37). The Qur'an (Surah 9:30) rails against Christians who hold to such heresy:

> The Jews call Uzair a son of God and the Christians call Christ the Son of God. That is a saying of their mouth; (In this) they do but imitate what the unbelievers of old used to say. God's curse be on them: how they are deluded away from the truth.

The Qur'an is unequivocal that no mortal can be associated with God. It clarifies that "The likeness of Jesus with God is the same as the likeness of Adam whom God created out of the earth" (Surah 3:59). In the final day, Islam contends, Jesus will return to the earth and denounce all who have inaccurately venerated Him as the "Son of God." Jesus is quoted in the Qur'an as categorically denying that He is divine (Surah 4:171). Jesus is only a created being and "no more than a messenger" (Surah 5:75–76) in the likeness of Adam (Surah 3:52). Surah 5:19 states that God could "destroy" Christ if it were His will. This verse illustrates that it is beyond Islamic comprehension for God and Christ to be one.

Along with the Fatihah (Surah 1, which is quoted seventeen times a day), the most frequently recited passage in Islam, Surah 112 insists,

> Say: He is God, the One and Only; God the Eternal, Absolute; He begetteth not nor is begotten; and there is none like unto Him.[13]

This term "begotten" is consequential because it is so frequently cited by Muslims. How might Christians respond to this refutation? Christianity does not teach that Jesus was "begotten" (*yulad*) in the physical sense. Rather, Christ is begotten through the Spirit of God. The truth that Jesus is born of God speaks of Christ's intimate union with the Father. In spite of this, John 3:16 is generally interpreted by Muslims as a conspicuous contradiction of Surah 112.

In Islamic confutations of Christ's divinity, Qur'anic references are habitually supplemented by biblical passages. Suspect hermeneutics characterize these forays into the Bible. Much is made of the fact that Jesus says, "The Father is greater than I" (John 14:28), which contravenes the view of God's unity being equal in the Father, Son, and Holy Spirit. It is asked why Jesus shouted, "My God, My God, why have you forsaken me?" which is not seen by Muslims as a recitation of the twenty-second Psalm but an admission that Christ was separate from God. Jesus' announcements, "By myself I can do nothing" (John 5:30), and "Why do you call me good? There is none good but God," are also regarded as "double-think." Muslims cite biblical passages such as references to Ezra, the judges of Israel (Psalm 82:1, 6); and Moses (Exodus 7:1), which call these men "sons of god." The pronouncement of Thomas, "My Lord and My God," should never have been uttered to Jesus.

Muslims are often willing to accept that Jesus, like any other prophet, is invested with divine nature in the reception of revelation. The angels are commanded to "Fall down and prostrate yourselves unto Him" (Surah 15:29) as they are told to do to other prophets. Christians should communicate to Muslims that the divinity of Christ means more than God's divine presence residing within a human being. The Incarnation is not a mythological transformation of the essence of the divine. Muslims should be shown that there is no translocation of a portion of God into the body of Christ.

DIVINITY WITHIN HUMANITY

Christian faith maintains that Christ is both fully human and divine. How can this idea be effectively communicated to Muslims? It is imperative to begin by communicating the Christian understanding of God's nature as participant. Not only the giving of revelation but also incarnational involvement are at the heart of God's nature. The artist of creation takes responsibility for humanity in the act of the Incarnation. God never withdrew from creation in the biblical revelation of His character. The prophetic voice within Israel, the Holy Spirit active in history, and the intricate witness of the natural world speak of God's interactive desire. It was humanity who chose sin and separated itself from the holy God. It was God in divine greatness who provided a way for humanity back to Himself in Christ.

God is the "source" of Jesus. Pauline Christology exalts, "In Him dwelleth all the fullness of the Godhead bodily" (Colossians 2:9). Jesus commands all power over nature (Matthew 8:26–27), demons, disease, and death. He has the ability to know all things (John 2:24–25; 21:17), including the thoughts of individuals (Luke 5:22; Matthew 9:4). Christ is sovereign (Matthew 28:18) and reigns "far above all rule, authority, and power" (Ephesians 1:21).

Christ cannot be understood apart from His complete unity with the Father. There is union between Christ's humanity and divinity: two natures maintained in a single person (*hypostasis*). God in Christ is indivisible, unchangeable, and inimitable. The announcement of Christ, "I and the Father are One," is an authoritative declaration from which all subsequent christological affirmations begin. To say that Christ is one with the Father is not the same as saying that Christ is the Father. Muslims often point to the fact that Jesus prays to the Father. These are not being directed toward Himself but is Christ talking as a son to His father. Christ in "very nature God" (Philippians 2:6) is God the Son in right relationship with God the Father and God the Holy Spirit (2 Corinthians 13:14).

Christ speaks as God in a relatable human voice. Jesus did not appear out of the heavens as a thunderous word, but emerged from Galilee recognized for His regional accent.[14] This accented voice was an opprobrium to those in organized religion (John 1:46) who knew that the Messiah would come from Bethlehem and not Galilee (John 7:42). But God in Christ is recognizable. There can be no reality nearer to humanity than that of fellow creature. Jesus is born, grows, suffers, bleeds, and dies. Nothing can be easier to comprehend. Yet, it remains an unfathomable mystery that humanity can become the vehicle for God's incalculable revelation. The propensity of humanity seems to have been to obliterate the image of divinity, and, in agnostic self-destruction, mar creation and squander the gift of freedom.

It should be clarified to Muslims that the worship of Jesus in Christianity is not the veneration of a human personality or the idealization of a man. This can be done by pointing Muslims to the biblical record of Christ's claims to be divine. The Bible is cogent that Christ does not seek God as we must, but brings God to us. Jesus does not fear judgment but will be the judge of humanity.

The doctrine of the Incarnation is a message of relational salvation. Apart from it, Christianity has nothing to say about the mercy of God. Seeing how low God must bend to enter creation illustrates how far creation has fallen from the original intent of God, which is communion with Himself. In the Incarnation, God completely fulfills the intention of humanity to be crafted in His image. Jesus becomes that image. The divinity of Christ ennobles the characteristics of humanity and restores it to God.

The question that Muslims ask about the Christian doctrine of God and its relation to humanity is whether Jesus was divine because He lived a perfect life, or if He lived a perfect life because He was divine. Was the Incarnation always in doubt, dependent on the daily decisions of Christ, or did Jesus perpetually make proper choices because He was completely God? Had Jesus sinned, would the Incarnation cease to be a reality, because in disobedience God's will would no longer have been perfectly revealed?

Muslim cross-examinations of this nature arise from the inaccurate notion that the Incarnation necessarily implies a mixing of the divine and human natures. Jesus, in His humanity, had the possibility to commit sin. Jesus, as completely divine, grasped the truest nature of sin and thus avoided it. Jesus struggled with temptation but, in submission to God's will, never sinned. Hypothetical speculation is silenced by the purity of Jesus, a truth affirmed in both the Qur'an and the Bible.

In our interactions with Muslims, the impasse of theological intransigence is best dealt with by focusing on the meaning of the Incarnation, not only on its feasibility. The Incarnation is feasible because God, in His infinite strength, has the ability to come into the finite. It is meaningful because God has sent His Son to address the need for individuals to be restored to Himself. The Almighty is nowhere more divine than when being revealed in the humanity of Jesus. Without compromising God's divine nature, Christ changes human essence by allowing humanity to enter the presence of Holy God.

THE TITLES "SON OF GOD" AND "SON OF MAN"

The New Testament employs two primary titles for Christ to communicate that He was God Incarnate. How can these two expressions, "Son of God" and "Son of Man," be discussed with Muslims? Are they interchangeable or is one more applicable than another in speaking with Muslims? Finally, it is important to show Muslims that Christ had a clear understanding of Himself as one who was fully divine.

For early Christians, the title "Son of God" was fraught with Messianic expectation. Its usage underscored the adoption by God (Psalms 2:7) of His chosen servant. Christians used the term "Son of God" as a declaration of Christ's divinity. It reflects the intimate nature between God the Son and God the Father.[15] Perhaps because of commonly held political or eschatological misconceptions, Jesus rarely called Himself the "Son of God." Instead, He dramatized its meaning so unmistakably that He was crucified because this claim was disputed (John 7:25–44; 8:48–59; 18:28–40).

The use of the title "Son of God" poses obvious problems among Muslims. It is not understood because it is considered oxymoronic. Muslims believe that the divinity of Christ does not permit God to remain fully God, nor does it make Christ fully God. Muslims usually comprehend sonship in a physical sense, which obviously does not replicate the Christian understanding of the term.[16] The question "Do you believe that Jesus is the Son of God?" means something different to a Muslim. As a metaphor, it could be clarified that the sonship of Christ means that He is a completely accurate picture of God the Father (Hebrews 1:3) and completely obedient to the Father's will (Matthew 11:27).

The title "Son of God" needs to be thoroughly explained to Muslims as a statement about Christ's divine authority and the fulfillment of Messianic hope. Language used should affirm that Christ is God, revealing Himself in human form (1 Timothy 3:16). Care must be taken to avoid such expressions as Jesus being the "God-Man," which Muslims might perceive to mean that Jesus is partly God and partly human. Most importantly, the unity of God needs to be safeguarded. This is done by emphasizing that the sonship of Christ means that He is completely one with God.[17] Use of the nuance-freighted title "Son of God" is so decidedly beset by complications that Christians would do well to consider giving greater usage to the parallel expression "Son of Man," which seems more applicable in the Muslim context.

JESUS, THE "SON OF MAN"

The title "Son of Man" had historical meaning for the Jewish community at the time of Jesus. It comes from Daniel 7:13–14, in which an end-times personage is entrusted by God with sovereign power. Jesus used the term to explain His mission and identity and is an example of His care to avoid misconceptions. It was meant as much more than a statement about His humanity. Unfortunately, that is what it has come to mean for Muslims.

Although used by Christ, the designation "Son of Man" has not been frequent in the historical development of Christianity. Christians have tended to cast this term aside because it seemed to overemphasize His humanity. Theologically it was avoided because it was seen as unable to "assimilate the fullness of the aspects of Jesus' significance that evolved in the historical development of the traditions."[18] Nonetheless, this title helps show the completeness of God in Christ's condescension and His complete relational identification with humanity (Matthew 26:63–64; 27:11).

How can the appellation "Son of Man" be used to help Muslims understand the Christian doctrine of God? For Islam, the import of Jesus is within the boundaries of His humanity. Islam is in complete agreement with Jesus' injunction to Satan, "You shall worship the Lord your God and Him only shall you serve." Christ intended this term "the Son of Man" not only to define His relationship with humanity but also to point people to the fact that He had been chosen to restore humanity to right relationship with God. The divinity of Christ is what makes that reconciliation possible.

THE "CHRISTOLOGY" OF JESUS

Formative Islamic sources portray the self-understanding of Jesus very differently from the biblical account. This is beneficial to realize because

Muslims frequently cite numerous scriptures in which Christ is said to deny any claim to divinity. In light of this apologetic, it is helpful to present an accurate portrayal of the self-understanding of Christ. Did Jesus hold a "Christology" or was that formed, as Islam postulates, by His followers?

Christ unhesitatingly affirmed His divine origin. Some of the most distinctive pronouncements made by Jesus are the "I AM" declarations of John because they call attention to His claim to be one with God. In His declaration, "Before Abraham was, I AM" (John 8:58), Christ alluded to an eternal, preincarnate nature. In Matthew 18:20 and 28:20, Christ is shown to be omnipresent. For the Jewish listener, these affirmations explicitly mirror the name of God given to Moses (Exodus 3:13–14). These verses substantiate that Jesus believed that He had come from heaven (John 3:13) and was the "Alpha and the Omega" (Revelation 1:8) of divine revelation.

The assurance that He was God was an underlying theme in Christ's declarations about the future. Jesus preached that He would be the one who would serve as judge on the final day (Matthew 25:31–32). He permitted people to worship Him (John 5:23) and did not deny that He was able to forgive sin (Mark 2:5–12). Jesus promised that it was within His power to bestow on individuals who believed in Him the gift of eternal life (John 10:27–28). When Philip asked Jesus, "Lord, show us the Father" (John 14:8–11), Christ announced that those who had seen Him had seen God the Father.

Many references in Christ's teaching are also predicated on His awareness of the divine nature. In the parables, Jesus gave an account of Himself as the vine, and the Father as the gardener (John 15:1). Christ was the "Good Shepherd" and the "Way, the Truth and the Life" (John 14:6). He rarely called Himself the "Messiah" but did not deny this office (Mark 14:61). Intense in Jesus' memory at all times would have been the testimony from heaven, "This is my beloved Son in whom I am well pleased" (Luke 3:22). He repeatedly referred to God as His Father. Christ boldly used the intimate term "Abba" to epitomize His relationship with God. Jesus said that He was One with the Father and commissioned His followers to go to every nation and baptize in His name. Christ announced that He was the "bread of life" who had come down from heaven (John 6:41). Jesus claimed to be the "light of the world" (John 8:12) and the "resurrection and the life" (John 11:25).

These statements are audacious if spoken by a mortal. For Muslims, they can only be explained as textual inaccuracies. The self-conscious understanding of Jesus that is manifest in the New Testament, however, cannot be interpreted as declarations of naive egoism. Christian proclamation to Muslims will explain that Christ's obedience to God the Father is so complete that He is willing even to go to the cross. Christians should show Muslims that Jesus believed Himself to be God, eternal and omnipotent, the Creator of heaven and earth, dwelling in human flesh.

DISCUSSING THE DOCTRINE
OF GOD INCARNATE

When Martin Luther first heard of Copernicus's bold manifesto about the heliocentricity of the universe, he jeered that the Polish astronomer would "turn the world upside down." When Christians invite Muslims to embrace a concept of God based on the Incarnation, they are asking nothing less of their audience. Christianity claims that God can no longer be described as unaffected by human actions. The Incarnation denies that God created the world and then left it alone to stagnate beneath the shadow of His awesome indifference. In Islam, God is above us; in Christianity, God is with us and participant. The Incarnation should be introduced to Muslims not in terms of "what" or "how," but of "who." The "who" of the Incarnation, in content divine, but in form human, is Jesus Christ.

The doctrine of God Incarnate reveals that the sender and the sent are one. The Qur'an promulgates that Jesus is one who is sent (*rasul;* Surah 4:171). This "sending" is not to be understood in either tradition as generational, but as processional. The Qur'an heralds that Jesus is a "Spirit proceeding from God" and a "word from God." So what does Jesus' "sentness" (*rasuliyyah*) mean? There must be an association between the one who sends and the one who is sent. Does not the fact that God sends imply divine involvement? Is God's word of revelation with Jesus, or is it invested within Jesus as is claimed by the doctrine of the Incarnation?

The Islamic approximation of Jesus must be fashioned to accommodate the Muslim concept of God. Christ, as revealed in the Incarnation, is a direct challenge to this conception. It is impossible to fit Jesus as revealed in the Gospels into the straightjacket of Islamic monism. The Incarnation unravels an underlying tension between Islam and Christianity. God may be merciful, but the compassionate kindness of God does not mean that God can share in suffering; nor does it imperil God's transcendence.

Both Muslims and Christians regard God to be transcendent. Christianity, however, advances that God has chosen to make Himself fully knowable. Christians assert that the Incarnation meets the desire imprinted on hearts to see and know God more fully.[19]

Christianity does not claim that God adds something to Himself in Christ, concurring with Islam that divinity is entirely self-sufficient. This paradox, that God in His transcendent strength is capable enough to become human in vulnerable weakness, is central to the doctrine of the Incarnation. As such, it is a revelation of both divinity and humanity. That God could become human shows that the distinction between the divine and human nature is not insurmountable. Humanity and divinity are distinct, but they are not completely alien to one another.

The Incarnation disproves the notion that there is any deficiency in the capacity of God to love. It shows God's love for humanity in spite of its sinful disfigurement. Divine love not only subjugates sin through the Incarnation, but also overcomes the conditions that make evil inevitable. Death is vanquished; eternal life is freely given. Humanity has been "delivered from our offenses and raised again for our justification" (Romans 4:25). Christianity holds that the Almighty has not conquered humanity from without by His sovereign power, but has relationally redeemed it from within by divine love.

Islamic orthodoxy is not prepared to conceive of God in those terms. Muslims, for the most part, do not understand the Incarnation nor, indeed, the historic presentation of Jesus given by Christians. As one Muslim lamented, "No human author has ever succeeded in rendering the Incarnation entirely free of what may only be termed conceptual confusion."[20] The Incarnation, which is graspable by Islam, means only that God breathes His indwelling spirit (*hullul*), or word of inspiration (*wahy*), on the messenger.

Communicating the doctrine of the Incarnation demands it be presented in a way that is pertinent to its audience. The "failure" of its receptivity among Muslims is not in the doctrine but in its explication. The Incarnation is not a notion of divine immanence framed in symbolic language. It has intrinsic meaning that must either be accepted or rejected. Jesus did not only speak the "word of God" (symbols of meaning), but He is "the Word made flesh." The Incarnation lifts revelation out of linguistic limitation into the sphere of experience, the pervasive language of humanity. Although revelation that is relational, and not primarily verbal, is not easily explained, it can be more readily understood at the ontological level. The limitation of personality is nothing compared with the impediment of words to say something about God. The immediacy of the Incarnation circumvents this barrier:

> Any revelatory language must surely be susceptible to translation within a multi-lingual humanity. It needs to be viable and capable of obedience within all the exigencies of human grammars and cultures, in potential correlation to all the vagaries of society and history. . . . Even the most strictly literal language must proceed by metaphor and allusions and these are in the flux of the changing world.[21]

In the absence of the doctrine of God Incarnate, Muslims are without the same degree of emphasis on God's Love which Christians enjoy in light of the tremendous participation that God has within humanity. Islam lacks the perception that God, in His holiness, actively seeks intimate communion with creation. If embraced, the doctrine of the Incarnation could become a key to unlock a host of related issues that have not been answered by Islamic theology. One Muslim author, Shabbir Akhtar, remarked, "If it were true it could be a useful theological resource, lacking in Islam and Judaism for explaining in part the nature and origin of evil."[22]

An explanation of this doctrine means that the messenger will be sensitive to communicate in a way that affirms God's unity. Christians do not raise up another deity; neither do they hold that a human is transformed into God. The Father and Christ are distinct in their persons but indistinct in such a way that the divinity of Christ and the revelation of God's Triune nature are substantiated.

Another decisive concern when discussing the Incarnation is the issue of God's power. Muslims ask, "Was the Incarnation of Christ necessary?" Christians respond that it is an event which took place and the crowning moment of history. The Incarnation forever abrogates the inert immobility of an Absolute Power. This "condescension" is not a failure of God's ability to exercise power over humanity. It is, rather, the path that God chose to display divine power. Islam insists that the Incarnation of God in Christ is not essential in light of God's might. The Bible reveals that the Incarnation is possible because of God's power and necessary because of humanity's separation from God. Kenneth Cragg submits:

> When we present Christ we ask Muslims to believe not less but more in the undefeated sovereignty of God. To believe that God stooped to our need is not to make God less but more, the God of all power and glory. With patience born of faith in this very sovereignty, we must invite all to seek and find Christ in the demonstration that God is God alone, and that all contrary powers are gloriously vanquished and subdued.[23]

The Incarnation is a phenomenon of both history and eternity. The Incarnation was in place in the eternal self-communication of God as Triune. In the Incarnation, Christ has brought something of heaven into the story of creation and returned again to the Father taking into His humanity something of earth to heaven. Neither humanity nor divinity was what it was before the "marriage" of the Incarnation. Christians need to repeatedly remind Muslims that they also agree it is heretical to contend that a human being can become God. The embodiment of God in Christ is not an emergency contingency devised to grapple with the demise of humanity in sin. If the Incarnation is only some stopgap expediency once the atonement of humanity had been achieved, then the Incarnation of Jesus would no longer be in effect.

The Incarnation could also be conveyed to Muslims as the Christian response to the human need for salvation. A fundamental question in all spiritual pursuit is how humanity can know and experience God. Christ discloses God to humanity. In the process, Jesus brings to humanity the process for self-discovery. Once in the presence of God, individuals instinctively cry out, "Lord, depart from me for I am a sinful man" (Luke 5:8). The Incarnation unveils God's holiness in spite of, and in the midst of, every circumstance. Because of the Incarnation, humanity not only knows more about God than Islam says is possible, but is able to actively participate in covenant relationship with God. Jesus displays that the Creator wills to be understood and, to some degree, must be understood for salvation. In Christ, God enters the human condition and conquers the last citadels of human perversity. The God of love takes "self-responsibility" for the evil within creation and bears the brunt of suffering in Christ. Humanity's inability to perceive God is overcome by the desire of the divine to communicate.

Explaining the Incarnation to Muslims is not an issue of metaphysical interest but springs from an irrefutable soteriological imperative. Jesus' death reveals God's involvement in humanity and affirms the "credibility" of divine sovereignty, even over the fact of human rebellion. The mere functionalism of Islamic soteriology avoids God being "tainted" by sin in the process of providing redemption. In fact, in one sense there is no historical narrative or "process" in Islamic soteriology. Christianity says "God is Love." The relational love that brings salvation through the Incarnation is both an act of mercy and a historical revelation of the divine nature. The great paradox of God's grace is that in the Incarnation, God not only acts freely toward creation, but even relinquishes that freedom in order to bring salvation.

It is important to remember that the example of the Incarnation provides its own brightest exposition. In the Incarnation, God communicates with humanity by becoming human. The implications of witness to that truth is that the presentation of the doctrine must also become "incarnational" for those who have yet to receive it. The revelation of God coming as a servant needs to be retold in lives of humility and compassion. From this, worldviews will be transformed and insight will be facilitated. What Thomas said of Christ is what Muslims require of Christians, "Except I see His wounds and the nail prints in His hands, I will not believe" (John 20:25).

A belief in the Incarnation is based, ultimately, in the conviction of faith. The declaration, "Immanuel: God is with us!" is accepted by faith and is beyond the grasp of empiricism. Although the doctrine of God in Christ cannot be made "prove-able," it must be made comprehensible for Muslims. This is possible because Christians claim that the Incarnation is a complete revelation of God's nature expressed in the understandable language of human personality.

NOTES

1. Cited in Shabbir Akhtar, *A Faith for All Seasons* (London: Loewellew, 1990), 180.
2. Maimonides quoted in Jürgen Moltmann, *The Trinity and the Kingdom of God,* trans. Margaret Kohl (London: SCM Press, 1981), 26.

3. Muhammad Iqbal, *The Reconstruction of Religious Thought in Islam* (London: Oxford University Press, 1934), 28.

4. Cited in *Guidelines for Dialogue between Muslims and Christians,* compiled by the Commission for Inter-Faith Dialogue (Cochin, India: KCM Press, 1977), 82.

5. Marcus Dods, *Muhammad, Buddha and Christ* (London: Hodder and Stoughton, 1937), 200.

6. Abraham Heschel is cited in Moltmann, *The Trinity and the Kingdom of God,* 27.

7. O. Weber (*Grundlagen der Dogmatik,* vol. 2:161) is cited in Wolfhart Pannenberg, *Jesus, God and Man,* trans. Lewis L. Wilkins and Duane A. Priebe (London: SCM Press, 1968), 319.

8. Jürgen Moltmann (*Theology,* p. 645) cited in Peter Toon and James D. Spiceland, eds. *One God in Trinity* (London: Samuel Bagster, 1980), 128.

9. In a conversation that I had with an Egyptian Coptic Christian I was told that St. Athanasius clarified the final part of this statement in a way that is much more acceptable to Muslims when he said that humanity is able to fulfill its full destiny and potential.

10. John Calvin states, "We do not represent Christ as perfect or immaculate merely because He was born of a woman without any man, but because He was sanctified by the Spirit, so His generation was pure and Holy, such as it would have been before the fall of Adam" (Calvin's *Institutes,* numbers 11–13; 4), in Jens Christensen, *A Practical Approach to Muslims* (Upper Darby, Pa.: North Africa Mission Publishers, 1977), 456.

11. Nicholas Berdayev in *Freedom and the Spirit* (New York: Scribner's, 1935), 206, claims: "Christ was born of the Virgin in order to hallow afresh the tincture of femininity and to unite it to the masculine principle so that man and woman might become alike 'male-female' as was Christ's birth [*sic*] hallows femininity by reuniting it with masculinity and thus breaking down barriers of sexism created by the fall of man."

12. This idea comes from John Macquarrie, *The Humility of God* (London: SCM Press, 1978), 64.

13. When the Seljuk Turks overran Constantinople and turned Byzantine churches into mosques it is reported that they often engraved into the walls the verse from Surah 112: "God had no Son: He is not begotten and does not beget." This is mentioned by Jürgen Moltmann in *The Crucified God,* trans. R. A. Wilson and John Bowden (London: SCM Press, 1974), 235.

14. "Christ is our contemporary who comes among us, identifying with us, growing among us in obscurity and silence, without pedigree or prestige in society and speaking a strong local dialect." Geoffrey Ainger, *Jesus, Our Contemporary* (London: SCM Press, 1967), 84.

15. The term "Father" to describe God is used over 150 times in the New Testament.

16. One example from the Qur'an that might be helpful in talking with Muslims about Jesus as "the Son of God" might be the phrase *ibn al-sabil* ("son of the road"), which is used in Surah 2:215 (see also Surah 2:177 and 4:36). The term merely conveys likeness.

17. There are seven passages in which Jesus is described as the "Son of God" in the New Testament. They are John 1:1, 18; 20:28; Romans 9:5; Hebrews 1:8; Titus 2:13; and 2 Peter 1:1. Matthew says that Jesus is to be called "Immanuel," which means "God is with us" (Matthew 1:23). The Centurion who saw Jesus die declared, "Surely this man was the (a) Son of (the) God(s)" according to Mark 15:39.

18. Pannenberg, *Jesus, God and Man,* 32.

19. Jesus reported the fulfillment of this aspiration when He announced, "He who has seen me has seen the Father" (John 14:9).

20. Akhtar, *A Faith for All Seasons,* 180. One of the reasons for this confusion is the lack of any Islamic vocabulary acceptable to Arabic Christians to describe the Incarnation. The term used for the Incarnation by Egyptian Coptic Christians is *Tajassud.* In learning this I was recommended by a Coptic believer to look at the text by Athanasius, *The Incarnation of the Word.* He said this was the formula he had used with success in explaining the Incarnation to Muslims. Athanasius tells a parable: A king goes to one place in one town but while he is there the entire town is under his authority. In the same way, God rescues all humanity by entering into one baby.

21. Kenneth Cragg, *The Christ and the Faiths: Theology in Cross-Reference* (London: SPCK, 1986), 55–56.

22. Akhtar, *A Faith for All Seasons,* 180.

23. Cragg, *The Christ and the Faiths,* 264.

6

God's Triune Nature

THE ISLAMIC REJECTION
OF THE DOCTRINE OF THE TRINITY

The Muslim denial of the Trinity is a consistent refrain whenever Muslims and Christians come together to talk about God. The verdict of Islamic orthodoxy is that the doctrine of the Trinity is blasphemous. It is an insult to the single unity of God. Because God cannot have a Son, is not a Spirit, and cannot be called "Father," the Trinity is dismissed as a theological distortion. Muslims often claim astonishment at the naivete of Christians in seeing mathematical, philosophical, and doctrinal cohesion in three discernible gods with separate personalities. The rallying cry of Islam, "God is One!" rings as an apologetic refutation of the Trinity. Christians are branded polytheists (*mushrikun*) because of the belief that Jesus is God. The Qur'an is emphatic:

> O People of the Book! Commit no excesses in your religion: nor say of God aught but the truth. Christ Jesus the son of Mary was (no more than) an apostle of God and His Word, which He bestowed on Mary, and a Spirit proceeding from Him: So believe in God and His apostles. Say not "Trinity": Desist! It will be better for you for God is One God! Glory be to Him: (Far exalted is He) above having a son. (Surah 4:171)

Christianity also largely rejects what Islam does not affirm about God's nature. The Qur'anic view of the Christian triad even suggests that Mary is part of the Trinity (Surah 5:116).[1] Muslims can be asked to explain what Christians mean by "Trinity." There are few Muslims who set forth the doctrine of God in Trinity in a way that is compatible with Christian doctrine.[2] Seyyed Hossein Nasr, a contemporary Muslim criticized for being unorthodox, writes that the Qur'an does not oppose the Christian view of the Trinity, as long as it does not introduce a determination or a relativity to the divine nature. Nasr thinks, "Every question regarding the Trinity can be resolved between Christianity and Islam by a truly metaphysical penetration into the meaning of the fundamental polarization of the One."[3]

Islam frequently labels the doctrine of the Trinity as an attack against the truth of divine unity. Early Muslims, led by the Prophet Muhammad, strove to assure the doctrinal conviction of God's unity as a buffer against polytheism. Thirteen centuries later, this emphasis remains predominant. Islam scorns the Trinity as a division of God into three parts. Muslims deride it as modalism that personifies three of God's attributes. Why, Muslims ask, are not other attributes of the divine nature also existent in personality? Why did not all three become Incarnate if they are not separate from each other?

In spite of these misconceptions, the Qur'an leaves no room for Muslims to accept any version of the Trinity. For Islam, Christians who aver that God is three are in erroneous infidelity against the truth: "They do blaspheme who say, God is one of three in a Trinity: for there is no God except God" (Surah 5:76). The oneness of God is affirmed by Jesus in the Qur'an (Surah 19:91–93). He denounces any connection between Himself and a triad of Gods:

> And behold! God will say: O Jesus the son of Mary! Didst thou say unto men, worship me and my mother as gods in derogation of God? He will say: Glory to Thee! Never could I say what I had no right. Had I said such a thing, Thou wouldst indeed have known it. (Surah 5:119)

Muslim polemicists conclude that the doctrine of the Trinity is a remnant of paganism. It was not spelled out by Christ but developed by St. John and St. Paul. It could not have been inaugurated from God's prophet because it is unreasonable, unnecessary, and confusing. The Trinity, to Islam, is an unnecessary complication of something that God has chosen to express in clarion simplicity. Jesus, the prophet, is a man (Surah 43:59) who could never be the son of the One and indivisible God. Any reproduction, physical or metaphysical, could not apply to God and would compromise His transcendent uniqueness.

THE CENTRALITY OF GOD'S TRIUNE NATURE
IN CHRISTIANITY

The doctrine of God in Triunity emerged as the issues became discernible for the first Christians: Either Christ is God or Christianity is false. Because Jesus was divine and because of the inherited conviction of Judaism that God is One, this foundational doctrine gained acceptance. How then does one explain such a belief? Within Christianity are a number of paradoxes,[4] and

Muslims also find themselves defending problematic enigmas.[5] Such ambiguity seems inevitable when the finite try to explain that which is infinite. Part of the difficulty in discussing the Trinity is that the term itself is a theological and extrabiblical phrase which attempts to say something about the unsearchable personality of God. The term "Trinity" (*Trinitas*) originated as Tertullian's translation of the Greek word *"triad"* (used first by Theophilus in the second century). It has been suggested that the term "Triunity" be employed in its place among Muslims because "Trinity" means "three" and says nothing to affirm God's unity. Nonetheless, since the intended audience of this book are Christians interacting with Muslims, the familiar term will be used interchangeably with the more dialogue-conscious term "Triunity."

The doctrine of the Trinity, formulated by theologians, is drawn from explicit biblical evidence. It is a formulation that acknowledges both the oneness of God and the diversity of divine action. Mathias Zahniser writes that the Trinity is "not a deviation from the biblical assertion of divine unity but a way of understanding it."[6] It fundamentally affects one's view of God. Because of the Trinity, one comes to see God as active and participant in establishing covenant with His creation.

Muslims ask Christians why, if this doctrine is so important, it is not systematically described in the New Testament. The early disciples recited the formula, "Father, Son, and Holy Spirit," and they did so naturally and without explanation. To ask a Christian to detail how the Triune nature of God is possible is equivalent to asking how God is God. The divine cannot be understood in Christianity apart from being God the Father, Son, and Holy Spirit. God is One who reveals Himself in three ways: Creator, Savior, and Spirit. According to orthodoxy, God is the source of this doctrine as He gives Himself in His Son and then sanctifies humankind by the Holy Spirit. The revelation of God is a self-revelation in which God's "Word" is identical to God Himself. As Jungel explicates, "God is the Revealer, the Revealed, and the Revelation."[7]

Muslims regard the many Trinitarian formulations[8] as doctrines of tritheism. God as Father, Son, and Spirit are distinct but not separate. Jesus Christ did not "become" God, He was God. To avoid tritheism, Christianity denies the existence of distinct, self-subsistent sources of being. To avoid monolithic unitarianism, however, Christianity does not accept the concept that there are no distinctions within God. The Trinity exists the moment it is accepted that God was in Christ. God the Father is God; God the Holy Spirit is God; and Jesus is God. This does not equate with polytheism because there is a discernible unity in God's being. The doctrine, then, serves as a statement about the human understanding of God and the experience of a personal God in the ways that He has revealed Himself.

THE BIBLICAL BASIS
FOR THE DOCTRINE OF THE TRINITY

Although the term "Trinity" does not appear in the Bible, the New Testament is infused with a Trinitarian view of God. The primary formula for God's oneness, expressed as a Trinity, is found in Christ's injunction in the Great Commission: To baptize followers in the "Name of the Father, Son, and Holy Spirit" (Matthew 28:19). This spoke of three eternal and distinct persons. God, the eternal One, is not alone but exists in relationship.

The New Testament writers do not elaborate a doctrine of the Trinity because they are more concerned with ethics and soteriology than with apologetic definitions of the divine nature. The Gospels primarily deal with the narrative events of Christ's life without formulating didactic theology, which was a development of the worship, apologetic thought, and experience of early Christians. This provides an example for Christians to also avoid arcane metaphysics in attempts to relate with Muslims the Christian portrait of God's nature. Questions cannot be sidestepped. Neither can they blur the central Christian proclamation that "God was in Christ reconciling the world to Himself."

The doctrine of the Trinity surfaced in continuity with the awareness that Jesus was the Son of God and that the Holy Spirit brought salvation into human hearts. If Jesus Christ is Lord to be revered, then He is one with God. If Christ is God, the Holy Spirit that flows from God and brings revelation is also one with God. The most imperative element in the trinitarian problem is the explanation of the relationship between the Father and the Son. This is a predominant theme of St. John's Gospel. John establishes that there is a unity of spirit between the Father and the Son (John 10:30; 14:16–24).

The oneness of God was periodically reaffirmed throughout the biblical record. Israel began its journey of faith against a backdrop of polytheism, which the prophets incessantly vilified (e.g., Isaiah 42:8; 1 Kings 42:8). Moses warned people never to forget that God was one (Deuteronomy 6:4). In biblical Judaism, God was seen as one with personality who was able to extend Himself beyond the realm of conscious being. God was Word (Isaiah 55:11) and Spirit, active in creation, not through the mediation of angels, but in the power of His own personality. The promised Messiah was described as Immanuel, "God with us," which, for Christians, foreshadows the Incarnation.

The New Testament provides numerous trinitarian references. In the baptismal reports of Jesus (Matthew 3:16–17), in His infancy (Luke 1:35), and in His transfiguration (Matthew 17:5), the Father and the Spirit are present with the Son. Following the example of Matthew 28, other New Testament writers employ a "three-fold pattern" in describing God's nature. The author of Hebrews seems to use the names God, Christ, and Spirit interchangeably

(Hebrews 6:1–6; 10:29–31). This is also evident in St. Peter's letters (1 Peter 1:2; 4:14) and in Jude (Jude 20–21).

Muslims credit the doctrine to St. Paul because it is so predominant in his theology. The apostle often invokes a trinitarian blessing on his congregation (e.g., 2 Corinthians 13:14). He writes to Titus (Titus 3:4–6) and teaches Timothy that God the Father, Son, and Spirit are active in salvation (1 Timothy 2:5; see also Galatians 3:11–14; 4:6; 2 Corinthians 1:21–22). In this latter passage, Paul promulgates the view that God is undivided in substance and without distinction. He also affirms this oneness in his missive to Corinth (1 Corinthians 8:5–6).[9] Throughout Paul's epistles, there is substantive evidence that he is aware of the triadic pattern when describing God's unitary nature (2 Thessalonians 2:13–14). When Paul speaks about God, it is in trinitarian terms:

> For this cause I bow my knees unto the Father, from whom every family in heaven and on earth is named, that He would grant you, according to the riches of His glory, that you may be strengthened with power through His Spirit in the inward man; that Christ may dwell in your hearts through faith. (Ephesians 3:14–16)

The Muslim contention that the doctrine of the Trinity is limited to the writings of Paul cannot be substantiated. It is a revelation of God's nature which is not explicitly outlined but which underpins all other Christian theology. It does not contradict God's oneness, but correlates that oneness with the Christian revelation of God as Father, Son, and Spirit.

THE MISSION OF CHRIST AND
THE DOCTRINE OF THE TRINITY

Christians espouse that, in His deity, Jesus is omnipresent, loving, holy, and worthy of worship. Without an understanding of Jesus as one in divine Trinity, the mission of Jesus (beyond being anything more than a moral exemplar) to restore humanity to right relationship with God is beyond comprehension. Christianity without Christ's divinity is a form of Judaism. It is in the revelation of the cross of Christ that a "social," or relational, perception of God as Trinity is best seen. God is God in personality. Humanity must relate, not to an abstract ideal, but to God as He is. Personality is hallowed in divinity. Humanity is understood as being in God's image because both humankind and divinity share personality and complexity. It is the mission of Christ in the Trinity to express the truth of the personality of God, as well as to reconcile creation to God.

For Christians, the cross of Christ cannot be bifurcated from the God of Heaven. "God is Love," but in being "Love" God is not a metaphysical conception. The nature of God as Love is expressed in the trinitarian relationship of God the Father, Son, and Spirit. Islam casts aside the soteriological mission of God in Christ as an affront to the nature of God's oneness. In Christianity, the cross shows a tremendous unity between Father, Son, and Spirit in their mutual willingness to be identified with each other and with humanity even to the extent of affliction and death. God the Father and God the Holy Spirit "suffers" with God the Son in the darkness of Calvary. The Triune God becomes experienced as "Love" in the reality of the cross.

Neither the Muslim nor the Christian doctrine of God can exist without reference to God in relationship with others. Jesus is revealed as a "Word" from the Father from whom He proceeds and returns. Christ's purpose on earth is to reveal God and establish a covenant between divinity and humanity. In the cross, God the Father reconciles divine love with holiness. In the resurrection, God is revealed as (Christ) triumphant over death and eternally alive. Pentecost portrays God, the Holy Spirit, speaking to and transforming individuals in power, giving birth to the church. For Christians, God cannot be expressed apart from trinitarian terms. The Trinity of God reveals the mission and will of God, as well as the nature of God.

DISCUSSING THE NATURE OF THE HOLY SPIRIT

Related to the broader issue of discussing Christian faith with Muslims is the challenge of explaining the Christian understanding of the Holy Spirit. This is integral in exposition because Islam teaches that God cannot be defined as a "Spirit." God has many "holy spirits"; in Islamic cosmology these are angels.

The Nicene Creed reads that the "Spirit is worshiped together with the Father and the Son." St. Paul tells the early church community, "The Lord is a Spirit and where the Spirit of the Lord is there is freedom" (2 Corinthians 3:18). This is the life-giving, divine Spirit of God, which "proceeds" from the Father and the Son. Jesus announced to the Samaritan woman, "God is spirit and they that worship God should worship in spirit and in truth" (John 4:24).

Humanity's capacity to respond in any way to God is a gift given through the Spirit. God, the Holy Spirit, is the speech of God within the heart, which enables human faith to respond to the provision of transforming salvation. When St. Peter told Jesus that He was the Christ, Jesus replied that this was a work of the Holy Spirit (Matthew 16:17). The God who came for humanity in the person of Christ indwells humanity by the power of the Spirit. God, the Holy Spirit, moves revelation beyond the historical and objective into the realm of the personal, communal, and covenantal. The Christian view of faith, sanctification, and communion between God and creation is made possible by Jesus but made accessible by the agency of the Holy Spirit. Apart from the Spirit of covenant, an individual cannot discern the nature of spiritual reality. God's guiding Spirit is the divine indwelling light and fire of God's nature.

In the Bible the Holy Spirit is so closely linked with God that the Spirit is seen as being one with God. The Spirit is the divine breath (*ruah*) creating life and effecting change. The Spirit of God is described as one who is invested with personality. The Spirit grieves (Isaiah 63:10), guides individuals (Psalm 143:10), and instructs them (Nehemiah 9:20). God's presence came as an intermittent gift in times of need (such as when the Spirit "rushed" onto the prophets: Judges 14:6; 1 Samuel 11:6; see also Numbers 11:17–29). The Spirit is referred to in relation to God's presence throughout creation (Psalm 139:7). Christians relate the Messiah of prophecy with the Spirit of God (Isaiah 11:2; 42:11; 61:1). God promises that one day the Spirit will be poured out on all humanity (Joel 2:28–30).

The New Testament provides a vivid picture of the work of the Holy Spirit among the first Christians. The vibrant early church believed that the prophecy of Joel was fulfilled on the day of Pentecost (Acts 2:1–13; Romans 8:9). The Spirit of God is mentioned over sixty times in the book of Acts,[10] portraying the dynamic force of God being poured out on humanity — filling and dwelling within individuals. Jesus asked the disciples to wait in Jerusalem for power from heaven. Christ promised that the "Comforter" would soon come as God's presence among them to live within them (John 14:15–29). The Spirit is a "spirit of truth" (John 14:17) who gives insight. The Holy Spirit enters the church and gives gifts to individuals (1 Corinthians 12:1–12), and God's presence at work brings fruit of character into believers' lives (Galatians 5:22–23). Paul declares that each person's body is to become a temple of the Spirit (1 Corinthians 6:19). The Spirit helps "us in our weaknesses" (Romans 8:26) and brings humanity into eternal life (Galatians 6:8).

The picture of the Holy Spirit in Islam is far from conclusive. In some instances it is a spirit sent from God, while in other situations it is implied that the Spirit of God is another name for the work of God. It is also mentioned that Jesus is a "Spirit" from God although this description is never embellished to explain the relationship. What Christians call the Holy Spirit is viewed by Muslims as the angel Gabriel (Surah 19:17), or other angelic beings who aid God in the forwarding of the divine will among humanity. The general conception among Muslims is that the Spirit is a created, empowered entity who is not coeternal with God, and who does not share in the divine nature.

The Islamic comprehension of revelation also affects the perception of the Holy Spirit. When Muslims speak of revelation, they are referring to a past and completed act of God. The Christian understanding of the Holy Spirit reveals that God is active in the ongoing covenantal mission of revealing Himself to humanity, in the same way that revelation first came to the disciples. This progressive work of the Spirit continues the process of redemption in specific human circumstances and makes the truth of God relevant to individuals and to communities of faith. Each generation, through the agency of the divine Spirit, must be shown the unique "purposes of God" (Acts 13:36). Through the Holy Spirit, God's work of imparting revelation about His nature, character, and will is an ongoing process across the uniqueness of each generation.

Christians contend that, although the Son has come into history in human form, the Spirit continues to reveal God's nature among humanity. The Spirit works, in the words of John V. Taylor, as the "Go-between God," who goes between humanity and divinity to foster communion. God's Spirit brings freedom to creation bound beneath the influence of oppression and the weight of history. The Spirit proceeds from the Father and the Son and aids them in accomplishing this ongoing work of deliverance. The Spirit enables believers to become vessels for God Himself and carry forward the work of the divine kingdom of righteousness and justice. At the outset of His ministry, Jesus quoted Isaiah:

> The Spirit of the Sovereign Lord is upon me because He has anointed me to preach good news to the poor. He has sent me to proclaim freedom for the prisoners and recovery of sight to the blind, to release the oppressed, to proclaim the year of the Lord's favor. (Luke 4:18–19)

In Christian pneumatology, the person of the Holy Spirit manifests God's desire to bring deliverance and healing. The Spirit, active in creation, works to set at liberty that which has "groaned and travailed together" since the advent of sin (Romans 8:21–22). This desire of the Holy Spirit is indicative of God's active role in the process of redemption and should be given prominent place in the explanation of Christian soteriology among Muslims. The absence of any agency approximating the Holy Spirit in the Islamic concept of God (apart from, perhaps, the Qur'an) underlines a pronounced difference in the way that God's nature is understood. Without the activity of the Holy Spirit, the fruit and gifts dynamic in personal Christian lives (and that which should be most vital in the experience of faith) are beyond attainment.

DISCUSSING THE DOCTRINE OF THE TRINITY

Anthropologist Eugene Nida once surveyed a number of evangelical Christian leaders asking them to explain their understanding of the Trinity. From these responses, he concluded that "ninety percent of all Evangelicals surveyed worship three Gods!"[11] Nida's analysis was that these misrepresentations were born of carelessness in explanation and had nothing to do with respondents' doubting the veracity of the Trinity. This illustration exposes one of the most notable roadblocks in discussing the doctrine of the Trinity with Muslims: the inability of many Christians to present this doctrine with cogency. As a result, Muslims have thought that Jesus was a third god in contention with two other gods or part of a three-god counsel.

The Triune nature of God is the *mysterium logicum* of Christian theology, but an awareness of mystery is no substitute for reasoned explication. Christians should be able to explain the relevance of this doctrine for their lives. There is no argument that can be forwarded to establish the truth of the doctrine of a Triune God. It is an article of faith. It is also a belief rooted in the claims of the New Testament. The Trinity must be presented without the spinning of speculative riddles and be vitally related to the nature of God seeking relationship. Complicated explanations should not be devised and need not be defended. This is especially true if anything said about God's nature obscures the evident oneness of God.

It is self-contradictory to explain the doctrine of God's Triune nature apart from a thorough understanding of the Christian concept of a God who seeks to be known by His creation. Yet, Muslim apologetic literature often begins by demanding an explanation of the Trinity without any consideration of the other doctrines of Christian faith. The Trinity needs to be presented as a belief which upholds God's oneness and affirms that this oneness is complex. Christians do not exalt the "threeness" of God but claim that His oneness is expressed as Father, Son, and Spirit.

Discussions on the mysteries of faith are not productive if they advance misconceptions. Christians must explain their views to Muslims progressively while repeatedly affirming God's unicity as well as the "logic" of the Trinity inherent in the claim of Christ's divinity. It could be explained that the Holy Spirit enacts the will of God in individuals' hearts and, ultimately can only be satisfactorily grasped once a person has been "apprehended" through faith. The New Testament proclamation becomes revelation once it is accepted for what it is, and not in some distorted form.

Muslims are able to grant that it is as difficult to explain how God exists in three ways at once as it is to delineate how God's divine essence relates to His qualities separate from His attributes. Christians should present the doctrine in the context of affirming the oneness of God and the certitude that the divinity of Christ is not limited by His humanity (2 Corinthians 5:19).

Melanchthon taught that the adoration of the secrets of God was a better quest than efforts to investigate them.[12] It is a truth to be defended from heresy and not a doctrine to be advanced divorced from the promise of God's deliverance of humanity. The "mystery of godliness" (1 Timothy 3:16) and the depths of wisdom about God's nature (Romans 14:33–34) flow from God, not from a humanity unable even to ascertain its own condition. It may not be possible to explicate the Triune nature of God in all of its dimensionality. It is much less difficult, and far more important, for Christians to emphasize to Muslims that they do not worship three gods. The unity of God should be framed in a light distinct from mathematical singleness. Many formulas devised to express the doctrine of God's Triune nature have foundered on the precipitous shoals of metaphor. Analogies can only help in a limited way and are often misleading.[13]

Christianity teaches that it is only possible to grasp the unity of God's person when that oneness is expressed as a Trinity. Muslims should note that Christians do not observe God as an abstract concept, but as a living personality in active relation with the world. The doctrine of the Trinity exists to defend the unity of God in the context of His manifold involvement with creation. It is a doctrine that frees the concept of God from a strict mathematical monism that "limits" God and makes Him, by definition, incapable of love and (in transcendence) beyond the possibility of explaining revelation.

The Qur'an urges, "Call upon God, or call upon Rahman: by whatever name ye call upon Him, for to Him belong the Most Beautiful Names" (Surah 17:110). The unity of God within Islam can be exhibited in countless ways. In His oneness, God is "complex" and not simplistic. This is similar to the underlying logic of the Christian doctrine of God. Divine unity is greater than feeble human understandings of oneness without distinction.

Jesus, as He is described in the Bible, cannot be presented distinct from God's essence; Christianity claims that He is a divine self-revelation. The union of Christ with the Father is an agreement unshrouded in Christ's unstinting obedience to the Father's will and the Father's ready identification with the Son. Christians believe that God has revealed Himself as loving Father, approachable through the Son, and accessible through the life-giving power of the Holy Spirit. The Spirit of God unites Father and Son in a "joyful communion of love."[14] The Father is eternally alive in His Spirit and perfectly made known in Jesus Christ.

NOTES

1. This idea is alluded to in Yusuf Ali's notes: "Here the Christian attitude is condemned which raises Jesus to an equality with God; in some cases venerates Mary almost to idolatry; attributes a physical son to God and invents the doctrine of the Trinity, opposed to all reason." Yusuf Ali, note to verse 4:171, note 675, page 233. This idea may have sprung from an obscure Christian group known as the Collyridians.

2. Tahanawi, a compiler of religious terms in India, wrote in the *Kashshat Istilahat al-Funan* (Calcutta, 1862): "According to the Christians, the 'persons,' *aqanim* are three of Allah's attributes and these three are knowledge, being and life. The significance of

being is 'Father,' that of life is the Holy Spirit and that of knowledge is the Word (*kalima*) and the Christians say the person of the Word becomes Jesus" (from H. Spencer, *Islam and the Gospel of God* [Delhi: SPCK Press, 1956], 11).

3. Donald Wismer, ed., *The Islamic Jesus: An Annotated Bibliography of Sources in English and French* (New York: Garland, 1977), quoting Seyyed Hossein Nasr in *Les Musulmans: Consultation islamo-chrétienne,* ed. Muhammad Arkoun (Paris: Beauchesne, 1972), 139. I have heard Christians offer that the Trinity can be established from the Qur'an. This is a fruitless endeavor because this doctrine emerges out of the distinctly Christian revelation of God's nature. Attempts to demonstrate that the Qur'anic notion of Jesus being a "Word from God" is a declaration about God's personality is also beyond Islamic orthodoxy. The argument that the invocatory sentence of the Qur'an is trinitarian (because God is referred to as Allah, Rahman, and Rahim) is untenable for the same reason. Emphasis on references in the Qur'an where God is described in royal plurality (e.g., Surah 19:17; 21:91) represents a cross-faith hermeneutic that stands alien to the traditional Islamic interpretation of the Qur'an.

4. The term "paradox" (*para* = beyond, *doxa* = opinion) need not be defined as that which is essentially self-contradictory. God may be beyond our comprehension but that is because we are limited.

5. The "externality" of the Qur'an, the relationship between God's attributes and His essence, and the relation between revelation and transcendence are a few that this study has examined.

6. Mathias Zahniser in a paper read at the Wilmore United Methodist Church entitled, "The Christian View of God's Unity" (Wilmore, Ky.: unpublished paper, January 1993).

7. Eberhard Jungel, *The Doctrine of the Trinity,* trans. Horton Harris (Edinburgh: Scottish Academic Press, 1976), 16.

8. The Cappadocian Fathers in the fourth century taught a "social" unity that moves precipitously close to tritheism. Modalism taught that God is revealed in successive manifestations. Arianism, or "sub-ordinationism," taught there was a hierarchy within the Trinity. All of these were refuted as heresies by church authorities.

9. In a difficult passage, St. Paul explains, "When He has done this (put everything under His feet), then the Son Himself will be made subject to Him who put everything under Him, so that God may be all in all" (1 Corinthians 15:28). It has been suggested that this does not connote that the Son is inferior to the Father but that Christ will return the administrative function given to Him to the Father. This commentary on 1 Corinthians 15:28 was written by Walter Wessel in the *New International Study Bible* (1985): 1756.

10. "Eighteen of these sixty-two times the Holy Spirit is described in terms of a person who speaks, forbids, appoints, sends, bears and witnesses." Arthur Wainwright, *The Trinity in the New Testament* (London: SPCK, 1962), 201.

11. Related by Don McCurry in a lecture "Christianity and Islam" on November 4, 1993, at the Immanuel Kerk in Ermelo, Holland.

12. Melanchthon ("Loci Communes, 1521" in *Melanchthon's Werke II,* ed. R. Stupperich [Gutersloh, Germany, 1952], 7) is cited in Jürgen Moltmann, *The Trinity and the Kingdom of God,* trans. Margaret Kohl (London: SCM Press, 1981), 1.

13. An effective analogy advances God's nature as "a Dance of Love" with God as "Love," the "Lover," and the "Beloved." C. S. Lewis, *Beyond Personality: The Christian Idea of God* (London: Centenary Press, 1944), 26.

14. McCurry, "Christianity and Islam."

7

God in Covenant

For Christians, the God revealed in Christ is a God of covenant. The covenant plan of God finds its fulfillment in Christ as mediator between God and humanity (Acts 4:12; see also Acts 10:43; 1 Timothy 2:5). Discussing this view with Muslims raises a number of issues that should be addressed. How do Christian views of salvation contrast with Islamic perspectives? What do these differences say about a differing concept of God? How does the view of human sinfulness relate to the concept of God in both religions? Earlier, it has been noted that Muslims refer to Jesus as the Messiah. What does this mean? How should the revelation of the Messiah, as one sent to be a mediator, be explained to Muslims?

Salvation in Christianity comes from the life and death of Christ. Islam, however, has a divergent portrait of Christ in its formative source materials. Christians believe that God was in Christ in the cross and that divine power is manifest in the empty tomb. Christians should ask Muslims what role theodicy, ethics (described in the New Testament as the "kingdom of God"), and eschatology play in this process. Finally, how might the message of salvation through faith be expressed when interacting with Muslims?

ISLAMIC CONCEPTS OF SALVATION

Muslims primarily view salvation in terms of God's provision for the devout to avoid destruction on the day of judgment. Muslims seek deliverance from the inferno which all must face: "There is no one of you but shall approach it. That is a fixed ordinance of the Lord" (Surah 19:71). This verse has been interpreted by some to mean that individuals will first experience hell before being rescued into Paradise. If the goal of salvation is deliverance, how is this achieved? The Qur'an reveals that God is merciful toward frail humanity and has not made it strenuous for them to attain His favor. God's kindness undergirds the Muslim view of soteriology.

Humanity's acquiescence before God is an underlying aspect of the Muslim quest for salvation. The Qur'an notes that the "mark of a believer" is a forehead flecked with the dust of frequent prostrations. People are loyal slaves before the Almighty. Happiness and, ultimately, salvation are won through submission (*islam*) to God.

Forgiveness from past mistakes is another goal in the Islamic pursuit of salvation. The Qur'an repeatedly encourages Muslims to "seek forgiveness from God." One's heart is not to side with evil (Surah 4:110–12) but to ask God for remission of sins and a "new heart." In seeking forgiveness, one is preparing for future judgment and is also gaining protection (salvation) in this life of evil. Repentance characterizes every believer, including the Prophet Muhammad (Surah 11:114). If one is repentant, God, in His mercy, will be forgiving.

God has called humanity to perform righteous deeds and, in so doing, gain merit for salvation. Life is a battle to be righteous in opposition to the spirits of seduction and death (such as Harut, Marut, and Azrael). The "hypocrites and polytheists who imagine an evil opinion of God" will fall to the bottomless pit, while believers will enjoy the gardens of bliss "beneath which rivers flow" (Surah 49:5–6). Paradise is a place of eternal freedom, health, wealth, and joy. God is the beneficent framer of this utopia, but He is not resident there. God does not commune with humanity in the same sense that Christianity describes God involved in covenantal fellowship. Any sense of "intimacy" that one might have toward God is better viewed as a right relationship to God based on submission to His holy will.

God's revelation provides the guidelines for salvation. These requirements are summarized in the five pillars (*arkan*, literally "supports" or "basic elements") of faith, which are the foundational guidelines of Islamic orthopraxis. These pillars are the means of salvation,[1] serving as signposts toward Paradise (Surah 11:14; 99:6–8). As one "strives in the way of God" (*jihad*), the hope is that one will become "cleansed" (Surah 9:103) in God's sight.

The most conspicuous of these pillars for salvation is the "bearing witness to" (as opposed to simply believing) the creed of Islam (*shahadah*). I was reassured by one Muslim that all of one's deeds are put on a heavenly scale. One's good deeds are weighed against the evil performed, but if the *shahadah* has been recited once, God will pardon all transgressions. The ready recital of the creed makes one a Muslim and places one within the community of faith. Its repetition helps Muslims gain a vision of reality which recognizes that God is everywhere and active in everything. In Christianity, it is Christ who is the Savior through faith; in Islam it is God who graciously redeems individuals as they appropriate the *shahadah,* the supreme expression of truth.

The emphasis on the recital of the creed seems to underline the notion that the gaining of salvation in Islam is primarily a process of acquiring knowledge. God has asked humanity to accept nothing that is beyond the realm of logic. The purity of heart one is to cultivate is the rational pursuit of an individual before God. Humanity is not capable of knowing God, but God has made humanity capable of knowing themselves and has given reason to bring humankind to truth.[2]

Salvation (*tasdiq*) is the recognition, appropriation, and outward implementation of truth. Education brings regeneration and protection from evil. Revelation is the process whereby God educates humanity to become righteous. This knowledge must first be gained and then appropriated in order to be effective (Surah 10:39). As one passage relates, "That is your belief (*zann*)[3] which you believe (*zannantum*)[4] about your Lord and it has ruined you" (Surah 41:23). Belief is inadequate in itself. One's faith can be false and based on intellectual judgments not rooted in revelation. A person may postulate that something is true, but one must relate every belief to that which is truth (*haqq*). Faith (*iman*) is mentioned seventy times in the Qur'an; in more than fifty of these, it refers to people's wrong opinion of God's decrees and that their religion is misguided.

Each person is "thrown" to the mercy of God's will (*iradah*). Ultimately, it is not a matter of whether or not a person repents but the course of God's will. Only God can cancel sin. Punishment is not the unavoidable consequence of sin. This is because God is not obligated to either penalize or forgive the sinful. There is no injustice in this (Surah 49:17). God has no dictate that forces Him to bring anyone into Paradise and no need for any sacrifice to "satisfy" His holiness. God passes over the guilt of some without apology for His choice. Salvation is the work of God alone, and each person must humbly take refuge in none but Him.

Christianity concurs that salvation is a divine work beyond the ability of an individual to obtain. A basic disparity between Islam and Christianity is how this is accomplished. Islam informs that God decrees some to be saved and leads them into salvation, while not extending that prerogative to others. This has led to a fatalistic attitude toward the hope of salvation where an individual can secure no assurance of redemption. God will reveal on the final day the verdict for each life. Humanity is not free to determine its own future any more than it is able to go against God's perfect will.

Muslims have asked me if the Christian doctrine of salvation by faith implies that a person can sin without restraint and then gain God's forgiveness. It is asked if the free gift of salvation provides an exception from the demands of righteousness.[5] In Islam, the incentive of obedience is trepidation regarding the consequences of disobedience. Free from this constraint, why would individuals not seek their own interests if they conflicted with the demands of righteousness? Christianity affirms this suspicion in light of humanity's fallen nature. The solution of Christianity, however, is not the reformation of the heart through terror but the granting of a new nature motivated to be righteous by the power of God's Spirit.

Islamic soteriology is borne from the Muslim concept of God. The "gospel" of Islam is that, while individuals (such as Adam) make mistakes, God is willing to teach them how to repent and provide instruction for them to return to the straight path. Humanity must yield in obedience to the truth that God has given; the question of salvation will then resolve itself. The way of salvation is the course of obligation (*fard*) in following the requirements of God.

Muslims summarize their hope of salvation as the affirmation of the truth of a conviction ("I bear witness . . . "). Christians trust in the nature and work of Christ on their behalf. Islamic faith is internalized, then exteriorized in righteous deeds. Both Islam and Christianity call adherents to surrender to the will of God. Both assert that faith is more than a series of propositions to accept and that faith must be lived. The two concepts, similar in many regards, are ultimately contradistinctive because of a dissimilar understanding of God's nature. Christianity holds that the divinity of Christ presupposes His ability to save. The Incarnation of God in Christ makes known the divine predisposition to bring salvation. Because of the mission of Christ within the Trinity, Christianity is a thoroughly soteriological creed.

In contrast, the theme of atonement (*kaffarah,* literally to "hide" or to "cover") is far less predominant in Islam. It is not entirely lacking because the Qur'an does provide a singular mention of Abraham's offering his son (Surah 37:107). There is only one allusion to the idea of "ransom" in the Qur'an and that is to refute its feasibility: "Every soul that hath sinned, if it possessed all that is on the earth, would feign give it in ransom" (Surah 10:54; see also 3:91). In orthodox Islam, there is no reference to sacrifice by blood; there is no atonement for the sins of another. Some claim that individuals have no free moral agency and are not mired in a fallen nature. Some, however, argue that although one's deeds can be determined by divine foreknowledge, human beings still maintain a sense of free choice. For Muslims, there is no requirement for another to deliver. The revelation of God is sufficient and able to be obeyed. Most telling, the Qur'an speaks of "salvation" in the sense of going free or escaping (*najat*) only once, and this is a reference to the willingness of Moses to intercede for Israel in Egypt:

> And O my [Moses speaking] people! How (strange) it is for me to call you to salvation while you call me to the Fire! Ye do call upon me to blaspheme against God, and to join with Him partners of whom I have no knowledge; and I call you to the Exalted in power, who forgives again and again! (Surah 40:41–42)

The Islamic concept of God reveals that the divine is loving and holy. Humanity is capable of achieving salvation without the life and death of Jesus. Muslims believe that the requirements of a holy God are able to be met. Salvation is earned through God's grace and submission, righteous deeds, repentance, and the fulfillment of the pillars of faith. Salvation means deliverance from hell (Surah 50:30) and, to a lesser degree, protection from the evils of this life.

Salvation is never "guaranteed" for the Muslim because there can be no assurance about the direction of God's will, including the likelihood of one's final salvation. Individuals are capable of fulfilling God's laws, but the end result of that action is not certain. Christianity teaches that individuals cannot accomplish the law of God but can come to a degree of confident certainty about their relationship with God through Jesus Christ. A satisfaction in obedience but a dissatisfaction in hope characterizes the Islamic effort to accomplish what God has required.

A CONTRASTING UNDERSTANDING OF SIN

In Islam, humans do not inevitably sin because of an inherited nature but are guilty of sin when they become disobedient to God. This affects how individuals perceive their need for God, a fact that Christians have not always wrestled with in their encounter with Muslims. Sin and suffering are the outworking of God's sovereign power and in light of His unfathomable (but perfect) will.

What is considered to be sin for the Muslim? Sin is that which is against a known law of Islam. Deeds that are performed in ignorance of the divine law are not considered "sinful." There are actions which some Muslims consider sinful but others do not.[6] With the exception of association (*shirk*),[7] and unbelief, all offenses are of equally minor importance in terms of their relation to God's gift of salvation. Theoretically, to pray with unwashed hands is as reprehensible as telling a lie because both are instances of disobedience. In practice, however, there are gradations in the severity of transgressions. The most heinous are those committed against the larger community. One Hadith observes that the "taking of interest has seventy parts of guilt, the least of which is as if a man commits incest with his mother."[8]

Numerous terms in Muslim theology are used to describe sin. Probably the two most common are *ithm* and *dhanb,* which connote doing that which is forbidden or morally wrong.[9] One term, *khati'ah,* is used five times in the Qur'an and "seems to have the idea of failure to attain God's standards,"[10] but the meaning is ambiguous. Humanity commits vile deeds or "crimes" (*fawahish*). One of the most severe sins is unbelief (*kufr*).[11] Individuals are mired in depravity (*fujur*), corruption (*fasad*), viciousness (*fisq*), misfortune (*su'*), and evil (*sharr*).

The sin of Adam is mentioned on three occasions in the Qur'an (Surah 2:35–39; 7:19–25; 20:117–23) in accounts that bear many similarities to the Bible (Genesis 3:1–24). The Qur'an puts most of the blame for the fall with Satan, while Genesis describes Adam and Eve as deliberately choosing a path of disobedience. The story in the Qur'an ends with Adam's returning to the garden, which implies that what had originally been lost was once again reinstated by God's kindness.

Individuals do many evil deeds, but there is no formulation within Islam that these are the result of an inherently sinful nature.[12] Humanity did not suffer because of Adam's sin. The pattern in which God has made humanity (*fitrat Allah*) is present today in the birth of each child without corruption. The Qur'an maintains that people are naturally "good" (Surah 30:30). Sin is not a "genetic" perversion of human nature but the result of the will of God in each person's life — a sort of *karma* for individual disobedience. Islam describes sinfulness as consisting of isolated acts of rebellion. In light of this, Muslims could be asked if they believe that humans are predestined by the divine will to commit acts of wickedness.

In Islam, God does not judge sin harshly. "If God were to take humanity to task for their wrongdoing, He would not leave them a living creature" (Surah 16:61). God is lenient because He knows that humans are inherently weak (Surah 4:28); God will "make the burden light" (Surah 4:28). If one prays for forgiveness, then probably God will forgive. The unrepentant face no such respite and will invariably perish in the seven layers of fiery damnation.

The view of sin in Augustinian Christian ontology is that it is an evil resident in human hearts (Jeremiah 17:9). God created humanity in His image and without sin. Disobedience entered into the human experience with the trespass of Adam. St. Paul moralized that "none is righteous" (Romans 3:10), and the prophet wrote: "All we like sheep have gone astray" (Isaiah 53:6). St. John asserted that all unholiness was an affront to God (1 John 3:4). The most serious consequence of wickedness is that it separates individuals from God (Habakkuk 1:13; Isaiah 59:2). God is a loving Father who seeks communion with His prodigal children in spite of their sinful past (Luke 15:11–31). Before an individual can be restored, sin must be dealt with and forgiven by the Father. This idea is without parallel in Islam, where sin does not "affect" God or one's relation to God.

God, in holiness, cannot tolerate anything in His presence that is unrighteous. This is why biblical revelation explains that death is the fruit of sin (Deuteronomy 24:16; James 1:15). Sin not only hinders prayer (Psalm 66:18), as it does in Islam, but it also binds people to become slaves to its power (Proverbs 5:22; John 8:34). Sin cannot be removed by human effort or acts of righteousness. God's holiness requires that all injustice be eradicated. Disobedience is shown to be an infringement against God's glory because it flouts the fact of His power: Sin is putting one's self before God. Because individuals are incapable themselves of dealing with the problem of sin adequately, God has come in Christ to bring deliverance from the moral and spiritual consequences of sin, which are evil and suffering. For this reason St. Paul says, "The wages of sin is death, but the gift of God is eternal life through Jesus Christ our Lord" (Romans 6:23).

Christians and Muslims both claim to be entirely dependent on God's mercy for salvation. In Islam, sin is viewed in strictly legal and social terms; in Christianity, it is an offense against God. Both religions agree that the morass of disobedience is the common denominator in every life, and even to every prophet[13] except one. Both the New Testament and the Qur'an acknowledge that Jesus was pure (*zakiyy*) and without sin (Surah 19:19; 1 Peter 2:22; 2 Corinthians 5:21; 1 John 3:5). Christians should ask Muslims if there is any significance within Islam to this "faultlessness" (to use Pickthall's translation of *zakiyy*) of Jesus. Christ's purity is able to purify humanity from sin (1 John 1:7).

JESUS, "THE MESSIAH" AND MEDIATOR IN COVENANT

The Messianic idea is held by both Muslims and Christians, but it is understood in very distinct terms. The Messiah (*al-masih*) is a title that might be employed to help Muslims understand the role of Christ as the mediator of the covenant which God desires to establish with each individual and with each community. When presenting this title, the Christian should realize that, although ascribed to Jesus on eleven occasions in the Qur'an, the term is never explained.

According to Christianity, the people of ancient Israel expected God to send the Messiah into their midst to represent God among them.[14] The prophets foresaw a divine person who would come to earth in human form (Psalm 110:1; Isaiah 7:14). God's promised deliverer was to be known as the "Messiah" ("Anointed One," Daniel 9:25). He would be more than a prophet; He would be a divine king whose rule would be eternal (Micah 5:2). Isaiah foretold that the Messiah would be God among humanity (Isaiah 9:6–7), the "Servant of the Lord" who would have the ability to bear the infirmities of humanity (Isaiah 52:13–53:12).

For Christians, the Messiah's role is central to the revelation of God as participant in covenant with humanity. Beginning in Genesis (Genesis 3:15) it is established that blood needed to be shed to cover the nakedness of humankind in sin. The biblical idea of sacrifice assuring covenant is clearly wedded to the mission of Christ in the mind of the early church (2 Corinthians 5:21).

Early Christians pointed to the "Lamb of God" (John 1:29) who served as God's Passover provision from the angel of death. In Christianity, it is God's grace expressed in Christ which secures right standing with God (Romans 5:8–11; Hebrews 10:12). At Bethlehem, the angels announced that the child was "Christ the Lord!" the anointed of God (Luke 2:11). Andrew told his brother, "We have found the Messiah!" (John 1:41). Martha professed, "Yes, Lord, I do believe that you are the Messiah, the Son of God, who has to come into the world" (John 11:27).

Islam does not subscribe to the notion of God's entering into covenant relation with humanity beyond the promise of experiencing blessing in exchange for obedience (see Surah 5:7, 12, 13). Any suggestion of a doctrine of covenant in the Qur'an (such as Surah 2:118; 6:152) has nothing to do with communion between the Almighty and humanity. There is no possibility for human beings and God to communicate apart from the revelation that God has already given. According to Muslims, a view which proffers that God is personal and self-sacrificing is not worthy of His greatness.

The Christian view of a God who seeks covenant teaches that humanity has an individual and collective need (Psalms 49:7) for a mediator. God "cuts" a covenant with humanity in the perfect sacrifice of Jesus (Romans 5:18–19; Hebrews 8:6). God has allowed Christ who "knew no sin" to take sin upon Himself in order to restore humanity to communion with Himself (2 Corinthians 5:21). Jesus, in His unique position of intimacy with God (Surah 3:45 describes Him as *khalilu-Ilah,* the "friend of God"; this title is also given to Ibrahim), and in His flesh, is able to represent God to man and man to God. The New Testament declares that Christ came to "die for our sins, once for all, the righteous for the unrighteous to bring humanity to God" (1 Peter 3:18). Jesus expresses God's love in His willingness to become the acceptable sacrifice (1 John 4:10) that God required. As He suffers for others (John 10:15), Christ reveals God's intense desire to establish covenant relationship with humanity.

It is instructive to note that, in spite of the arguments of orthodox Islam that no mediation is needed, saints and prophets have emerged as points of veneration and aids in intercession across the Muslim world. This may be because Muslims also sense their need for one who can stand between their imperfection and the Almighty. I have also touched on how prophets such as Muhammad have gained christological stature as Islamic history progressed. This tendency confirms Tillich's idea that the primary function of soteriology is the formulating of Christology.

For Christians, salvation is not only a conceptual doctrine but also a person. Jesus alone needs no mediator between Himself and the Father. He alone is able to provide a relational pathway for others. The purity of Christ satisfies the Father in purity. Because He is divine, Jesus can annihilate all distance between humanity and God. At His crucifixion, Matthew records that the veil of the temple was ripped in two (Matthew 27:51), signifying that Christ's work made it possible for humanity to enter God's presence (see also Hebrews 9:1–14). Everything in Christian soteriology depends on God's seeking out humanity, offering reconciliation, and then making that propitiation possible.

The incarnate Christ embodies the revelation of God as active and participant among humanity. The Islamic concept of God makes it unthinkable that Jesus could be a mediator between God and humankind. Islam predicates that the only mediator available is the "mediation" of the Qur'an between humanity and truth (and not between humanity and God). According to Christianity, Christ's mission was to fulfill the role of mediator, "just as it was written about Him" (Mark 14:21). Jesus on the Emmaus road unveiled that the covenant plan, which began with "Moses and the prophets" (Luke 24:25–27), showed that God's holiness required a holy mediator. St. Paul declares,

> God our Savior wants all people to be saved. For there is one God and one mediator between God and people, the man Jesus who gave Himself as a ransom for all people. (1 Timothy 2:4–5)

ISLAM AND THE CROSS OF JESUS

In reading references to the cross of Christ in formative Islamic sources, one feels that these sources would prefer to provide a rendering of Jesus that avoids a cross. Ambiguity marks its citation, because the cross mars an otherwise orderly picture of one who is a noble prophet.

The first issue that Muslims must address is whether or not Jesus actually died on the cross. Certain verses in the Qur'an seem to support the conviction that He was crucified (Surah 3:55; 19:33). Surah 4:157 appears to cite that Jesus did not die on the cross but was rescued by a substitute. This passage dominates contemporary Muslim interpretation with its statement, "They did not kill Him, nor did they crucify Him but they thought that they did."

From this, Muslims postulate that Jesus was not crucified but was "gathered to God." Muslims emphasize that the prophecies of the Bible are further proof that it only "appeared" to be Christ (*shubiha lahum*); it is written that the Messiah's face was marred beyond recognition (Isaiah 52:14; 53:3–4). Muslims register that during the trial, the accused "opened not His mouth" but finally shouted from the cross, "They know not what they do!"[15]

This supposition does not seem to correlate with the Qur'anic affirmation that the Bible is authentic. It is arduous to conceive how such a predominant theme, prophesied and repeated in the Bible, could have been corrupted. Other Muslims have doubted this assertion on the grounds of its logic. Kamel Hussein, in *City of Wrong,* opined,

The idea of the substitute for Christ is a very crude way of explaining the Qur'anic text. They [Islamic theologians] had to explain a lot to the masses. No cultured Muslim believes in this nowadays. The text is taken to mean that the Jews thought they had killed Christ, but God raised Him unto Himself in a way we can leave unexplained among the several mysteries which we have taken for granted on faith alone.[16]

The basic idea of the Islamic substitution theory is that God confounded the adversaries of Jesus and delivered His chosen one from death. It may be seen as commendable to propagate this idea because it delivers the prophet from distress.[17] In the process, however, it misconstrues the mission of Jesus, which had nothing to do with self-preservation. Islam sees the rescue from the cross as divine vindication. Jesus is so obedient that He is even willing to die, but God is able to deliver Him from His enemies. Because Muslims see no need for a sacrifice for sin, Jesus did not need to die and was delivered into heaven. What is the source of this view? Muslims may have been influenced in this discussion by docetic Christianity,[18] which alleged that it was actually a visage of some human on the cross but not Christ who died. In any event, there is obvious confusion of identities within the Islamic picture of the cross. For Christianity, a Jesus divorced from the cross is a "Jesus" who no longer resembles Himself.[19]

Muslims view the cross as a symbol of defeat and not a proclamation of divine love. They seek to exalt God and not to denigrate Him to such ignominy as suffering and death. The cross is a place of disgrace, not majesty. It is an offense to God and to the prophet of Islam. The rejection of the cross is a logical consequence of Islamic theology, which claims that there is no need for a mediator to deal with sin. Islam understands that if the cross is significant for salvation, then all other revelation would be superseded. One cannot remain a Muslim and believe that Christ's death has redemptive value to save individuals from sin (Surah 5:164). In rejecting the cross, Islam refutes the pivotal theme of Christian soteriology (1 Corinthians 15:3). St. Paul wrote, "Christ was clearly portrayed as crucified" (Galatians 3:1). This is not true of the Islamic portrayal of the cross, a rendering often clouded in a morass of abstruseness.

THE CROSS OF CHRIST
IN THE CHRISTIAN DOCTRINE OF GOD

For Christians, the cross reinterprets God. To Muslims it can be explained as the fullest revelation of God's nature as passionate love and the central fact of biblical soteriology. The cross can be introduced to Muslims as the perfect example of Christ's obedience to the will of the Father. It is a revelation of the horrific nature of sin but also a place of victory where the sovereign God unfurls His power and conquers sin. Finally, the moral authority of the cross over evil and the forces of darkness challenges Christians to live sacrificially as they proclaim that "God is Love!"

In church history, the significance of the cross has been the focus of centuries of theological discussion. Tertullian and Origen held that it was inescapable because a ransom for sin needed to be paid to Satan (who held humanity captive since the fall). Ignatius and Augustine reworked this concept by saying, in a way that echoes Islamic perception,[20] that Satan was confounded and God's plan of salvation was accomplished in Christ's death. Anselm of Canterbury taught that the satisfaction of God's law was the message of the crucifixion. Luther referred to it as "humanity's happy exchange" in which humanity surrendered alienation from God and received forgiveness. In later, dialectical theology, the cross was held to be a revelation of love: "God's eternal Yes! to humanity."[21]

How does the twisted figure of Jesus on the cross reinterpret the way God is to be understood? The cross revolutionizes the image of God from one who is a distant enemy to be dreaded (because of His power) into one who has himself participated in removing every obstacle to fellowship. In the cross, the relational love of God is freely given and undeserved (1 Peter 5:10). Christ died each person's death (Romans 6:23) and went into the darkness of hell to bring life.[22] The cross becomes the supreme proof of God's loyalty to humanity (John 19:30; 2 Corinthians 5:18). The probity of God is displayed in His willingness to provide Christ as sacrifice although He could have exercised His power to avoid it (Matthew 26:53). Even humanity's "insignificance" (Psalm 8:3–4) is no barrier for the greatness of God. The infinite worth of the life of Jesus given for humanity imparts infinite value to humanity.

The cross, a hideous torture reserved for criminals in the Roman empire, is the most unlikely place for God to reveal His full love to creation. Christianity believes that God has chosen, within uttermost humiliation, to bring revelation about the extent of His love (Romans 3:24–26). The cross contains both the justice and love of God. The love demonstrated on the cross robs the powers of evil of their force and is consistent with God's holiness. One poet has written, "It was not Judas for money, nor Pilate for fear . . . but the Father for love"[23] that sent Christ to die.

God in Christ crucified vividly elucidates the distinction between the Muslim and Christian concepts of God. God as "Father," God "becoming man," and individuals becoming "children of God" are all ideas unacceptable to Islam. Surely, Muslims say, God could have chosen another way instead of the cross. Perhaps, but for Christians the cross lies at the center of God's covenantal plan. Rahner remarked that death "expresses God."[24] Here, the Almighty takes a crown of thorns and stands among humanity in weakness.

Christ restores humanity to God and, in Hegel's words, "eternally reconciles Himself with Himself."[25]

The cross can be discussed with Muslims in terms of Jesus' obedience to the divine will. A Christian might use the language of Surah 5:111 (Pickthall) as I once did in Uzbekistan to explain that we now "believe in God and bear witness that we have surrendered unto God" as revealed in Jesus. Muslims can more easily comprehend coming to God through the cross in this way because in both religions the Messiah surrenders Himself to God's control without reservation. In both traditions, this allegiance is rewarded with vindication by God and deliverance into heaven. As other prophets have been slain (Surah 2:61, 91; 4:155; 5:70), Jesus anticipated the same fate as a result of His obedience. In Gethsemane, Jesus reaffirms this absolute conformity to God's will. This surrender leads to Christ's final exaltation (Philippians 2:9–10).

Christ's shout from the cross, "It is finished!" (*tetelstai!;* John 19:28), announces the completion of all that He had anticipated throughout His life and ministry. Jesus fulfills all scriptures,[26] and makes God's relational covenant attainable. Speaking of Himself, Christ revealed, "Unless a grain of wheat fall into the ground and die it abides alone" (John 12:24). For Christians, were Jesus to be divorced from the cross, He would no longer be an expression of absolute submission to God or be congruent with the thrust of His own message of deliverance.

The cross also explains the nature of evil and the cruel perversity of humanity in nailing Christ to its frame. The cross reveals the seriousness of this depravity and the extent to which God goes in resolving its force. The cross cannot be grasped apart from an understanding of the nature of sin. Because God is just, sin must be dealt with. God cannot contradict His own character and merely decree sin to be eradicated. To eliminate sin dismissively would not be an expression of God's power; it would be an indication of His inability to deal with it thoroughly. Acting in this way would be arbitrary and would minimize the gravity of sin. Sin defames both the moral order and the relational divine law. As an affront to both Creator and creation, sin must be challenged on both levels.

The cross can be described to Muslims as a place of victory over the powers of evil. It is an event that underscores the sovereignty of God, is deliberately chosen, and is not the result of uncontrollable circumstances. Jesus said its obligation was why He had come into the world (Matthew 20:28; John 12:27). It is not a place where a prophet battles his opponents but a place where God conquers evil. The cross becomes a throne of triumph for Jesus (Romans 6:4; 1 Corinthians 15:56–57; 2 Timothy 1:10; Hebrews 2:14–15). It shows that no satanic scheme can prevail against God. Christ was not crucified to "satisfy" Satan but to lead to his defeat.

For Christians, the cross is an event that has covenantal ramifications for each person and carries with it an existential obligation implicit in its proclamation. René Girard stressed that the moral authority of the cross moves people to lives of sacrificial worship and service. St. Peter spoke about Christ "whom you crucified" (Acts 4:10); the responsibility of His death, as well as its acceptance, is charged against each person. Christians espouse that Jesus died for each person (John 10:11; Romans 5:8; Ephesians 5:2). His death forever changes how individuals approach God and conclusively resolves the need for sacrifices to be offered (Hebrews 10:11–25). Christ's sacrifice is to be appropriated personally in the celebration of the Eucharist and in faith (1 Thessalonians 5:10; Titus 2:14). The personal receiving of the death of Jesus returns an individual to right relation in covenant before God (1 Peter 3:18).

The tragedy of the cross provides a relational model for Christians among Muslims. The love of God that it reveals encourages believers to live out the moral implications of God as Father with self-emptying love for others. Jesus summoned His followers to imitate His own submission (*islam*) and participate in taking up the cross daily. This bearing of the cross will mean faithful witness in covenant with people in spite of rejection. The message of the cross inspires believers to respond to critics with the affirmative patient love implicit in the prayer, "Father, forgive them, for they know not what they do." Christ's death was once, for all, but the church is called in witness to a Eucharistic retelling and "reliving" of its truth to every person and culture. The "stigmata" of Jesus becomes the ongoing mark of His disciples. St. Paul remonstrates that all Christians must "crucify" their selfish (Romans 6:6) and sinful nature (Galatians 5:24) because God has "crucified the world to us" (Galatians 6:14). An accurate portrayal of the biblical concept of God will be characterized by the pervasive centrality of the message of the cross.[27]

In a normative sense, the cross disproves the conceivability of syncretism between Christianity and Islam. It is a constant reminder of what is clearly definable about the covenantal Christian doctrine of God. To the rational sensibilities of Islam, the cross is a profane affront[28] and an accursed horror (Galatians 3:13) inappropriate for God. Christians believe that the cross rescues humanity, menaced by the curse of sin and without the resources within itself for salvation. Christianity teaches that

God was pleased to have all of His fullness dwell in Him, and through Him to reconcile to Himself all things, whether things on earth or things in heaven, by making peace through His blood, shed on the cross. (Colossians 1:19)

DISCUSSING THE IMPORTANCE
OF CHRIST'S RESURRECTION

The resurrection of Jesus can be related to Muslims as a lustrous expression of God's life-giving power. St. Peter declared, "God raised Him from the dead, freeing Him from the agony of death, because it was impossible for death to keep its hold on him" (Acts 2:24). Jesus dies to save humanity and He is alive in resurrection power to sustain humanity. Salvation comes to those who apprehend the power of this resurrection by faith (Romans 10:9). Without the resurrection, Christianity is a false, futile illusion and Christians "are, of all people, most to be pitied" (1 Corinthians 15:16–18).

Christian hope is set in motion with the resurrection of Christ. When the apostle John was an aged sage, he retold of a youthful race with Peter to the tomb (John 20:3) after Mary had announced that it was empty. This message energized the early church to declare, "The Jesus that we speak of has been raised by God" (Acts 2:32). The resurrection lodged within the hearts of these Christians a certitude that Jesus was one with God. His resurrection is described as the basis for comprehending Christ's divinity (John 20:28; Romans 1:4–5). The truth of the resurrection confirms a view of God who is victorious over all circumstances. In Christianity, the ascension is the deliverance of Jesus to the presence of the Father (Colossians 3:1; Ephesians 1:20–21), but it is at a different time (after death) and for a different purpose than is stated by most Muslims. Jesus in Islam is raised to avoid the murderous intent of His adversaries. Christian theology deduces that, in spite of any human plans, if Jesus is divine then His life will not end in death but in His return to the Father. In resurrection power, Jesus conquers death and the power of evil. In Islamic terminology, the resurrection is a complete vindication of God's blessing: Jesus was buried and His enemies did all that they could do to keep Him confined. His power, however, was stronger than their efforts.

It is important to relate the relationship between the crucifixion and Jesus' ascension into heaven. Christ heralded, "I am He that liveth and was dead, and behold I am alive for ever more!" (Revelation 1:8). The resurrection is an outcome that is rejected by Islam because (by and large) the cross has first been disavowed. The consensus is that Jesus, like Enoch, was translated into heaven. In light of the Islamic interpretation of death (the taking of a soul from a body), Christ must now be ascended both body and soul into Paradise. The ascension of Christ in Islamic sources is stripped of any soteriological significance.

Both Christians and Muslims assert that Jesus is now alive in heaven waiting to return to the earth. Muslims can be encouraged to consider several questions: If Jesus was only a prophet, why has God kept Him alone alive for two thousand years? Has His body not known the effect of time? If the only purpose of His being raised was to rescue Him from His enemies, could He not have returned after His opponents had perished?

Christians might relate to Muslims that the resurrection of Christ springs from His divine nature. Jesus' life after death comes from His life before birth. Jesus is now in heaven, forever clothed in human flesh, but alive by the power of the Spirit (Romans 8:11) never to die again (Romans 6:9). The reign of Christ in heaven reveals that believers have a future hope and should strive to live in His resurrection authority (Philippians 3:11). The resurrection transcends human nature and transforms human mortality. Jesus told His followers, "Because I live, you shall live also" (John 14:19).

Jesus has been exalted as the "prince" of life (Acts 5:31). The mystery of Christ's death for Muslims is explained in the power of His resurrection. The bold nature of this belief compels Christians to speak to all peoples (Matthew 28:10). After its occurrence, Peter preached with the newly found eloquence of conviction because its truth had profoundly transformed his life.

The resurrection speaks of God's desire for covenant with humanity. Jesus not only ascends into heaven, as He is said to do in Islam, but in the resurrection returns again to His disciples. Even when Jesus no longer is "required" (because of mediation) to come among humanity, He returns. The risen Lord relishes surprising the faithful with the truth of His power: "I am not a ghost," Jesus declares, "look at my hands and my feet" (Luke 24:38–39). Muslims may have locked their hearts against its message, but the event of the resurrection shows that God is able to break through barriers and stand in authority among those who doubt (John 20:19, 26). Our proclamation is to "Come and see" (Matthew 28:6) the place where Jesus has overcome death. This will be done through a retelling of the biblical account related in Muslim terminology and through the vivid example of lives transformed by the reality of the risen Christ.

DISCUSSING CHRISTIAN ESCHATOLOGY

Christians will find a receptive chord among Muslims in the declaration of Christ's return because they also believe that Jesus will return to the earth. Christian revelation, however, is premised on the divinity of Jesus and reveals that He is all-powerful in His return.

Both Islam and Christianity explain that Jesus will return to judge humankind and subdue the anti-Christ (*al-dajjal,* literally "the swindler" or "imposter"). This point of concordance is based on one verse in the Qur'an (Surah 43:61) and over seventy Hadith. Christ's return is a major theme in the Bible and is referred to over three hundred times (notably Matthew 24–25; 2 Peter 3; and 1 Thessalonians 4:13–5:11).

There is, however, an expansive contrast between the Muslim and Christian perceptions of the role of Jesus at the end of time. Islam predicts that Jesus will come again to finish the ministry that He began before Muhammad. Christ will castigate Christians and affirm the truth of Islam by leading a "struggle" (*jihad*) against infidels and polytheists. Jesus will be the last prophet because He was raised from the earth without being crucified. In the end times, He is finally able to marry, reign as king, and then die a natural death.[29] In this Islamic rendering of His return, Jesus is completely human and is depicted as a vengeful warrior.

How can Christians explain to Muslims the Christian understanding of God's nature through this expectation of Christ's return? At no time does Islam claim that the second coming of Jesus has any soteriological ramifications. Jesus comes as a judge to represent God, rectify wrong, and determine, as God's emissary, whether individuals will go to hell or Paradise. One supposes that His sentencing will encompass the other prophets (although this is not explicitly stated). The Christian can ask why this key responsibility was handed over to Jesus if He is merely one of the prophets. The Bible claims that Jesus is the magistrate on the final day because He is the Son of God (John 12:45). Eschatology is helpful in the Christian discussion of God's nature because it is a theme which is relevant to the Islamic goal of salvation as deliverance from judgment and consistent with the role that Christ plays in His return. Christians could ask Muslims to consider how one's view of God relates to eschatological hope.

Christians could also encourage Muslims to reconcile the belief in the return of Christ with the insistence that He is human. The idea that a person (and not an angel) with a corporeal body could dwell uncorrupted in Paradise for two thousand years and then return to the earth is an extraordinary claim that Islam makes of Jesus. Christians maintain that this is possible because Jesus is one with the Holy Spirit of God, the Father (*ruh-ullah*, Surah 4:171), and is "from above" (John 8:23) instead of from the dust that formed others.

Christian faith explains that God is driving history toward the fulfillment of His purposes for creation. In His life, Jesus inaugurated the eschatology of God that will be fully realized in His return. In the "last days"[30] Jesus has declared His kingdom among humanity (Luke 17:20–21). Each individual needs to respond to Jesus as the Lord of this era to determine their participation in Christ's future kingdom (Matthew 10:32). Christ is the "last Adam" (1 Corinthians 15:45); humanity finds restored relationship with God through sharing in Christ's life, death, and resurrection. Because of Jesus, the eschatological hope of Christians has become, not only deliverance from hell, but the fulfillment of humanity's destiny to "become like" Jesus in intimate relation with God (Romans 8:29; Philippians 3:21; 1 John 3:2). In the "fullness of time" the hope of Christian faith is that in His "second coming" (Hebrews

9:28), Christ will establish a reign of social justice, cultural harmony, and relational unity.

Biblical eschatology has a role to play in engaging Muslims to consider the Christian doctrine of God and the implications of the orthodox Islamic view of Jesus. The differing portraits of Paradise, with God absent in the Islamic rendering and predominant in Christian accounts, say much about the future hope offered in the two faith traditions. The return of Jesus to secure that hope speaks of Christ's divinity and of the need for each individual to prepare for His return. St. Peter asked the question, "since everything will be destroyed in this way, how shall we then live?" (2 Peter 3:11). It is also a valued component of Christian interaction with Muslims because it played a central role in the preaching of the early church. What must be repeatedly emphasized to Muslims is the revelation, dramatically evident in biblical eschatology, that God is One who comes among humanity in love as an active participant.

DISCUSSING THE PROBLEM OF SUFFERING

Again I looked and saw all the oppression that was taking place under the sun: I saw the tears of the oppressed, and they have no comforter; power was on the side of their oppressors and they have no comforter. And I declared that the dead . . . are happier than the living. . . . But better than both is he who has not yet been, who has not seen the evil that is done under the sun. (Ecclesiastes 4:1–3)

The concentration camp in Buchenwald during one Sunday afternoon in World War II was the setting for a most bizarre tribunal. Elie Wiesel tells of a group of intellectuals assembled in their prison kitchen for the purpose of placing God "on trial." The "charge" was that God had neglected humanity and was blind to human suffering. Witnesses came forward for both the prosecution and the defense. A group of imprisoned rabbis served as the judiciary. With a unanimous verdict, God was found guilty of being unjust and uncompassionate.[31] The rabbi judges then led the trial participants in a time of prayer.

How do Muslim and Christian perspectives about God relate to their understanding of human suffering? How is theodicy, the relationship between divine justice and the existence of evil, addressed in the Qur'an and in the Bible? Is this a starting point in talking with Muslims about the Christian doctrine of God's covenantal nature as participant and compassionate? Islam's response to suffering is based on a view of God who is separate beyond humanity. Christianity describes God's nature in the personality of Christ as actively entering into suffering and redeeming it with significance through the divine presence.

The love and power of God meet in the cross of Christ to answer skeptics who say that suffering proves that either God is not all-powerful or that He is not all-loving. The love that God had for humanity was not inhibited by the realities of suffering, death, and torment. Indeed, the cross, on which Jesus offered Himself, is the very picture of hell itself in its torture, abandonment, and pain. Jesus, who knew no sin (2 Corinthians 5:21), entered into the anguish of humanity and experienced the full dynamic of what it means to be human.

The cross is a place of torturous inhumanity. Islam avers that the cross was a place too vile for God and too impotent to hold any promise for salvation. Christians believe that the cross shows that there is no cost too great for God to pay to ransom His creation. In the cross, "God stretched out His hands to embrace the ends of the earth."[32] Christ crucified responds to the claim that it is unjust of God to be all-powerful and yet remain detached from suffering.

Islam has no answer to the problem of suffering as it relates to God's nature because of its revelation that God is wrapped in unknowable transcendence. As a result, sin is not understood and the relationship between sin and suffering is never delineated. Christians can describe how Genesis shows that the plight of humanity is the fruit of disobedience to God. Creation was initially made "good" (Genesis 1:31). The result of the intrusion of sin into humanity is death, fear, physical and emotional distress (Genesis 3:15–19), hopelessness, lust, bondage, and harassment from supernatural powers of darkness. Suffering is the harvest of sin (Galatians 6:8). God is active in restoring humanity to a place of "protection" (although clearly not immunity) and eternal blessing.

The Islamic view of God places the responsibility of suffering with God and, thus, provides no answer to its mitigation. In Islam, God is the first and the last cause of all situations, including suffering. If one undergoes hurt, it is because this is the will of God. Islamic determinism often leads to a degree of passivity and devaluation of life, which is difficult for many Christians to accept. To the Muslim, opposition to suffering cannot lead to success and circumstances cannot be altered. These conclusions lead to little expectation of progress (Surah 6:126; 7:155; 76:31). What remains in orthodox Islam is an antimony: one's destiny is sealed by God, but one is called to go on fighting the battle for morality. This leads Muslims to fiercely deny they are "fatalistic" while, at the same time, acknowledging that God in His sovereignty shares no power to act (or decision) with any other. Nasr writes:

> Were Islam to be fatalistic it would not be able to conquer half the known world in seventy years. It is actually absurd to call one of the most virile, patriarchal, and energetic civilisations which the world has

known, fatalistic.... What is, however, emphasized in Islam is that freedom in an absolute sense belongs to God alone. Nevertheless, we share
in this freedom and therefore bear the responsibility of having to choose.
Were this responsibility not to be incumbent upon us there would be no
real meaning to religious faith.[33]

Agnosticism often concentrates its attention against an impersonal concept
of a Deity who offers no response to the problem of suffering. The Islamic
view of God says that it is beyond the majesty of God to participate in
suffering.[34] Islamic theology coincides with Greek philosophy that suffering
cannot be considered an appropriate attribute for deity. If God is capable of
anguish, the logic proceeds, God cannot also be absolute. God must be the
self-sufficient unmoved-mover. The world is God's creation; He can in no
way be subservient to it. God cannot suffer if, at the same time, He is the one
who creates (and has mastery over) suffering. The Islamic concept of God
speaks of salvation completely divorced from the issue of suffering in this
life. Muslims believe that suffering comes as a test from God, and the only
redress for suffering comes in God's will and in Paradise. Christ on the cross,
by contrast, embodies suffering in His life. God in Christ takes suffering into
Himself and sanctifies it. The promise of the new covenant is born from the
broken bread of Christ's body and the poured-out wine of His blood.

Christianity maintains that God is capable of anything, including suffering.
God is not chargeable on a moral level for allowing evil. It is the consequence
of human decisions to misuse God's gift of free moral agency. Furthermore,
God in Christ is not apathetic or distant. Islam holds that salvation is a gift
from God, who is able to give mercy because He is above the plane of
humanity. God cannot embrace suffering any more than He could be human
and, at the same time, still be divine. Christianity agrees that suffering is a
characteristic of humanity but it is an attribute that must be redeemed, not
ignored. Christian doctrine concludes that if God is incapable of suffering,
then He is also incapable of love.

In the tragedy of the cross, God is love, and God exists in love. The God
who bleeds in Jesus gives His life-giving blood to those He loves in stark
contrast to metaphysical Islamic theism. God's infinity is able to relationally
embrace the finiteness of humanity: God is even able to have spikes driven
through the hands of that finiteness. The impassable view of God, portrayed
in Islam, criticizes the cross as unbecoming of God. For this reason, Islam
cannot say that "God is Love."

Jesus crucified is a victim. His crucifixion was not a "quiet" death but was
marked by great anguish (Mark 14:33) and "loud cries" (Hebrews 5:7). In
death and life, Jesus fully participates in the travail of pain. Christianity shows
the Almighty active and participant within humanity. Muslims are repulsed

at the suffering of the cross and rescue their prophet from its grasp. The New Testament provides a different perspective: Christ is shown to taste the full extent of human anguish in order to provide salvation for humanity: "Christ learned obedience through the things that He suffered" (Hebrews 5:8).[35] Jesus, in His submission to suffering, becomes the ideal mediator between God and humankind. Christ is the Christian resolution to the problem of suffering. Jesus faced the extremities of human suffering, even the feeling of being forsaken by God. To the early church, this fulfilled the hope of the promised Messiah who would be profoundly "touched by the feeling of our infirmities" (Isaiah 53:4; Matthew 8:17; Hebrews 4:15). They believed that Isaiah foretold a "Suffering Servant" who would be immersed in a life of wretchedness. Christ lived a life of denial (Luke 9:23–25) and of daily "dying" before His death. In this process, and in the face of temptation, Christ's purity was never compromised.

The Incarnation and the crucifixion of Jesus "tangle" God and humankind inexorably together in the passion and compassion of life. The cross bridges the chasm between the anguish of humanity and the relational ability of God to deal with suffering. John Stott observes:

> I could never myself believe in God, if it were not for the cross. In the real world of pain, how could one worship a God who was immune to it? . . . I have turned instead (of Buddha) to that lonely twisted, tortured figure on the cross, nails through hands and feet, back lacerated, limbs wretched, brow bleeding from thorn pricks, mouth dry and intolerably thirsty, plunged in God-forsaken darkness. That is the God for me! He laid aside His immunity to pain. He entered our world of flesh and blood, tears and death. He suffered for us. Our sufferings become more manageable in light of His. There is still a question mark against human suffering, but over it we boldly stamp another mark, the cross, which symbolizes divine suffering.[36]

The problem of suffering has its end point in biblical eschatology. In the "New Heaven and Earth," suffering will finally be abolished as the curse of sin is cancelled (Isaiah 65:17–25). Until the day that "there will be no more tears" (Revelation 21:4), God does not take away suffering but infuses it with relational meaning by His presence (Romans 8:17). God in Christ answers a child crying in unmerited suffering in Afghanistan, Kurdistan, Palestine, or Belfast, with His own cries from the cross. The cross says to humanity that God is not silent but active and participant.

It is not difficult to observe evil in the world and exclaim, "If I were God. . . ." Jürgen Moltmann's theology was forged by the experience of surviving a concentration camp in Nazi Germany. For Moltmann, God was to be exculpated because of His unrestricted identification with humanity in the midst of such suffering:

> like the Cross of Christ, even Auschwitz is in God Himself. Even Auschwitz is taken up into the grief of the Father, the surrender of the Son and the power of the Spirit. . . . God in Auschwitz and Auschwitz in the Crucified God — that is the basis for a real hope which both embraces and overcomes the world, and the ground for a love which is stronger than death and can sustain death. It is the ground for living with the terror of history and the end of history, and nevertheless remaining in love and meeting what comes in openness for God's future. It is the ground for living and bearing guilt and sorrow for the future of man in God.[37]

Creation "groans" (Romans 8:19) since the entry of sin into the world, but every anguish is conclusively echoed by the groans of God in Christ on the cross. Without this "entanglement" of God in humanity and in the suffering that defines that experience, the screams of Auschwitz and Buchenwald would go without answer, as they do in Islam. The intentionality of Jesus who "must die" (Mark 8:31) puts God's response to suffering in an entirely different light. Christians can communicate to Muslims that the anguish of the crucifixion not only "explains" the problem of suffering but also resolves it in the eternal embrace of a covenant-making God whose essence is love.

DISCUSSING ETHICAL "SALVATION" AND THE KINGDOM OF GOD

Some Muslims remonstrate that Christianity is otherworldly and irrelevant to many of the daily concerns of life. Muslims ask why Christianity has no *shari'ah* law, or why Christians do not follow the Torah law of Moses.

Jesus, in the inauguration of His ministry, announced His mission in terms which stated that the rule of God was to be over everything an individual or a community did. Karl Barth said that "Jesus lifted humanity from the ground of our own (individual) being beyond our being"[38] into community with others. Christ was a person who lived His life for others. Even though He was branded as an "outsider,"[39] He was immersed in the social and moral issues of His time. At His birth, political leaders saw Him as a threat to the status quo. Christ challenged them throughout His life as an itinerant teacher, and this confrontation precipitated His death. Jesus did not preach a life of faith calling for domestic piety and interiorized religion. He lived among the peasants instead of seeking refuge in the isolated religious holy places of His day. Christ preached in marketplaces and in fields a message brimming with revolutionary implications for the ethics of the businessmen, farmers, and fishermen who heard His message: the kingdom of God. Unfortunately, the message of the kingdom of God is rarely stressed by contemporary Christians. This is especially inauspicious in the context of interaction with Muslims because the message of the kingdom would find a ready audience among those who see their faith expressed primarily in communal, social terms.

While hanging on the cross, Jesus did not only speak to God about humanity; He also spoke to humanity about their lives in the light of His death. The kingdom of God is a domain whose ramifications touch every area of life. When applied to individuals, this kingdom attacks paternalistic or ethnocentric pride and smashes self-aggrandizement. Christ determined to build the church (Matthew 16:18) as a far-reaching kingdom governed by the just laws of God.

Every ethical premise within Christianity begins in the revelation of God's nature. Whatever humanity can say about itself must first be stated in terms of humanity's concept of God.[40] The standard of goodness is the personality of God (Mark 10:18). The will of God is that which is "good and perfect and acceptable" (Romans 2:18). The underlying ethical demand in Christianity is to imitate God the Father (Leviticus 11:44) as revealed by Jesus (Ephesians 5:1).

The moral teachings of the Bible are expressed as commands that relationally flow from God's nature. The covenant that God established has far-reaching implications for social justice and inaugurates a new nation: the covenant community. This corporate solidarity "brings people near" (Ephesians 2:12) to God and to each other. Christ's announcement of the kingdom forged a new code of action and attitude (as opposed to new "laws"), which would work to change character and inspire godly action based on proper motives.

The Beatitudes of Jesus (Matthew 5:1–12) are often seen as the starting point for an understanding of the kingdom of God. The Beatitudes build into followers a dissatisfaction with fallen nature and summon them to a new standard. Muslims whom I have spoken to about the Sermon on the Mount have often dismissed its ideals as unachievable. The Islamic ethic, they respond, is forged around collective self-interest and is more pragmatic, if not quite so grandiloquent. Jesus' mandate to "turn the other cheek" (Matthew 5:39), for example, is without parallel in Islamic ethical justice.[41] Islamic law does not criticize a person who chooses to forgive in this way, but stresses that the offended has complete right to receive justice for what has been suffered. Christians readily agree that the guidelines of the Sermon on the Mount are contrary to human natural standards. The solution to this problem is that God has sent the Holy Spirit, who makes available supernatural moral power, to do what otherwise might seem impossible (Matthew 5:48).

The Christian revelation of God as love makes a previously unattainable standard of ethical behavior possible. This revelation is at the heart of God's effort to initiate covenant with humanity. For Jesus, love is the summation of the biblical ethical law (Mark 12:28). Christ extends its significance to include every person, not only to those within the covenant community. *Agape* love is based on the relational character of God and operates free from any prerequisite such as "loveableness." Inclusive love is the vital core of Christian ethics because it flows from God's nature.

In both Islam and Christianity, salvation is related to ethical obedience. This is relevant and comprehensible to Muslims but rarely developed by Christians. Those who have entered the kingdom that Jesus announced are marked with a desire to obey God's way. When "God's kingdom comes," then "His will is done," in individuals and in the community. Jesus provides those within the kingdom the power to bring the intention of obedience into fruition. Christian obedience ties the weight of the cross against the back of self-centered egotism. The ethics of the kingdom establish themselves first in the heart and then in the wider spheres of life.

In a real sense, people are the center of Islamic ethics because God is unknowably transcendent. The motivation to be obedient to God's moral imperatives could be described as self-survival before God's power to inflict suffering and throw one into hell. Submission to God's will is self-protection from the same fate that awaits evildoers. The idea of the kingdom of God within Islam (the community [*ummah*] based on social laws [*shari'ah*]) is designed to build on this earth a foretaste of Paradise as it relates to politics, war, taxes, and other practical dimensions of life. Islam disdains what it sees as a lack of specificity within Christian ethical guidelines.[42] This may be because it has not been communicated that biblical ethics should not establish structures for political domination but covenantal structures for social service.

The justice issues of the kingdom of God are fundamentally ethical and not power-based political concerns. Christ said that His kingdom was "not of this world" (John 18:36) and, as such, relates to all the world and to every cultural milieu. Jesus did not summon followers to direct their attention to addressing political and governmental structural vicissitudes. The corrupt "powers" of society were not to be refashioned but completely reinvigorated. The inscribing of justice on hearts (Jeremiah 31:3) meant that external cultural forms could become new wineskins for the enactment of God's kingdom. Christians are called to be "salt and light," working for justice and peace. They are not called to forcefully impose their political claims but to establish "covenants" within local communities. Islam sees this model of a powerless minority beyond political structures as an abdication of the possibility that Christians might have to bring effective and comprehensive social change. Naturally, many Christians throughout history have attempted to merge God's

Kingdom with Caesar's kingdom. The results of this institutional marriage, however, are usually disastrous.

Christians cannot deny the protestation of Muslims that much of Christendom has strayed from the strength of Christ's social and ethical imperatives.[43] Nietzsche disparaged, "Basically, there was only one Christian, and he died on the cross."[44] Jesus on the earth today would not relate to many of the materialists, hedonists, militarists, or racists who call themselves Christians. This pattern of inconsistency has not gone unobserved by Muslims. Seyyed Qutb said that Christianity was ethically impotent and irrelevant because it is

> an individualist, isolationist, negative faith. It has no power to make life grow under its influence in any permanent or positive way.... Christianity is unable, except by intrigue, to compete with the social and economic systems which are ever developing because it has no essential philosophy of actual, practical life.[45]

The contention of Muslims that Christianity is otherworldly and offers no vision for ethical salvation is countered by the theme of God's relational kingdom. The most successful rebuttal is not the development of new "Christianized" economic and political forms, but a spirit of servanthood characteristic of the Sermon on the Mount. Jesus, in both Christianity and Islam, is known as a servant (Surah 19:30; 43:59) who "disdaineth not to serve and worship Allah" (Surah 4:172). Christ took up the washbasin of service and humility (John 13:3; Philippians 2:6) and led with the authority of compassion in action. The fact that God responds to human suffering establishes an ethic for Christians based on compassion in response to suffering. This ethic has worked to abolish slavery, build hospitals, guard human rights, fight war and sectarianism with nonviolence, cure disease, and ease suffering in countless situations since the first announcement of God's coming Kingdom from that small hillside in Galilee.[46]

DISCUSSING CHRISTIAN VIEWS
ON THE NATURE OF SALVATION THROUGH FAITH

Faith is the doorway into understanding the Christian doctrine of God. Christianity is a religion "proven" by faith. To help Muslims understand this, faith must be defined. According to Christian tradition, it is faith which allows an individual to experience communion with God. Through faith, the God who has entered humanity in the Incarnation is received as deliverer. Through faith, God's Spirit invades individuals' hearts and establishes within them a communion table for fellowship.

Explaining to Muslims that eternal life comes through relationship with Christ provides a legion of hurdles that must be vaulted. That Christ is the "only way to the Father" (John 14:6) is anathema to Muslims. How, Muslims wonder, could the eternal truth of God be bound up in the haphazard facts of history as suggested by the Incarnation? It is not difficult for Muslims to accept the command of the Bible to "obey the sovereign God" (Deuteronomy 6:6). What is difficult is to see why obedience is valid only when it springs from the affection of the heart (Deuteronomy 10:12), which is genuine faith.

The Christian emphasis of salvation's being a gift of faith challenges the idea in Islam that the righteous deeds of individuals "repay a debt" owed to God for His kindness (Surah 35:29–30). The law must be put into effect against those who are rebellious (Surah 5:45). The cross is defamed by Muslims because it undermines the demands of the law by introducing the idea that forgiveness can be received by faith.

The New Testament writers claimed that one's salvation is assured by relational faith in Christ. Christians find assurance in Jesus who has paid the full measure of obedience required by God. Islam cannot accept that faith is able to provide assurance of salvation because salvation is completely in God's hands. The guarantee that Islam relies upon is that God is willing to forgive and be generous toward the righteous.

Unlike Christianity, faith in Islam is not as closely linked to belief as it is to the endeavor of moral righteousness. The Islamic term for faith, *iman,* is not synonymous with belief. One's beliefs might be incorrect. Belief, in the sense of confession, does not appear in the Qur'an and is widely seen to be only one component of God's will. To believe in the creed is one of the pillars of Islamic faith, but it stands in relationship with the other pillars. In Christianity, relational faith is a saving response. Islam regards the Christian idea of faith as a correlative of belief and thus anthropocentric. The accusation is made that the Christian view of salvation requires humans to "judge" God rather than to be judged by God.

Salvation in Christianity comes through relational faith in the person of Jesus. Throughout church history, Christians have concluded that God can be discerned in only a very limited way outside of biblical revelation (Romans 2:7–11), but God cannot be known in any way that contradicts or denies biblical revelation. Those who reject the gift of God in Christ are without "excuse" (Romans 2:1) and are in disobedience to divine revelation. Repentance and faith are described as an openness to God and a willingness to receive God's gift of transforming grace. Humanity's present condition is transformed by faith in that reality. Christ not only removes sin (as God forgives sin in Islam), but also heals the relational fissure that fostered the sinful nature. Transformation occurs through faith in the Lordship of Jesus.

On the cross, Jesus has already expressed the surrendered obedience that Islam believes God requires of individuals, but which Christianity maintains they are not able to achieve. The obedience of Christ illustrates for Muslims why Jesus had to die on the cross. On the cross, Christ is not appeasing an angry God, but is expressing a God who is love. Faith in the atoning work of Christ, the only one able to span the chasm between God and man, is the reception of God's gift. The actuality of sin and the demand for obedience reveal to humanity the need for God to intervene on their behalf. God is not obligated to do this because He is all-powerful. God, in His mercy, has chosen to deal with sin and provide salvation. In this way, humanity can once again enter into covenant relationship with God.

Christians must work to reinterpret a covenantal understanding of salvation through faith in a way that is applicable and relevant to Muslim understandings of God's will. This analysis has looked at the ways ethics, theodicy, and eschatology can be points of contact in this process. Discussion has been given to the question of how to use terms, such as faith, to describe the decision to accept the gift of salvation and to illustrate how the concept of obedience can be utilized in talking with Muslims. A contextualized discussion with Muslims will also emphasize Christ's teaching of the kingdom of God more than the contemporary tendency to stress Christ as one's "personal" or individual Savior. The theme of God's relational will (John 4:34; 5:30) can help Muslims more accurately interpret the biblical revelation of salvation. Christians should point to Christ's role as triumphant victor over death and suffering and the promise of His return as judge.

Christians asked to talk with Muslims about faith should explore with their Muslim friends the thread of covenantal redemption that runs throughout the Bible (Genesis 3:15; Exodus 12; Isaiah 53:5–12; John 1:29). But Christ's transforming power must first be evident in the genuineness of our lives before it can be received as conceptual truth. Muslims will need to hear more than words to be able to see an incarnation of the Word of God in our experience. The most penetrating presentation of Christianity will be seen when its truth has been made "flesh" and bountifully alive in us. We must live, as did St. Paul, a life made meaningful in forgiveness and fellowship with God:

> I have been crucified with Christ, nevertheless I live, yet not I but Christ lives in me. And the life which I now lead in the flesh I live in the faith of the Son of God who loved me and gave Himself for me. (Galatians 2:20)

NOTES

1. Frithjof Schuon, *Understanding Islam,* trans. D. M. Matheson (London: Allen and Unwin, 1963), 38–39. The five pillars of Islam are (1) the recital (*tashahhud*) of the Creed, (2) the pilgrimage (*haj*), (3) daily faithful prayer (*salat*), (4) almsgiving (*zakat*), and (5) fasting (*sawm*) during the month of Ramadan. One tradition which I have been

told by Muslims is that salvation is freely given to children who die prematurely or wives who receive the approval of their husbands.

2. Muslims have related to me that Muhammad once said, "He who knows himself knows his Lord," referring to the importance of accurate self-understanding.

3. The Arabic term *zann* implies erroneous knowledge or an incorrect opinion.

4. "Surmise" is a better translation here than the word "believe." The meaning of this passage is that "knowledge" can often be little more than speculation which cannot be substantiated.

5. See Romans 6:2, 6.

6. An example of this is how money is dealt with. For some, money is the "root of all evil," and those who are not faithful stewards and kind to the poor will suffer. One Hadith states: "Allah's apostle said, whoever is made wealthy by Allah and does not pay the *zakat* on his wealth, then on the day of Resurrection, his wealth will be made like a bald-headed poisonous snake with two black spots over the eyes. The snake will encircle his neck and bite his cheeks and say, I am your wealth, I am your treasure" (Bukhari, 2:276–77).

7. A level of hell (called *laza*, literally "flame") blazes expressly for Christians who claim Jesus was the Son of God. This term occurs only once in the Qur'an. Apostasy from the faith, the killing of a believer, and adultery are the three legal reasons by which one can be executed. Only *shirk* is an "unforgivable" sin. The primary references in the Qur'an to hell are Surah 23:110–18; 53–56; 69; 74. In Surah 88, the Qur'an provides a vivid description of Hell: "On that day many faces will be downcast, toiling, weary, scorched with burning fire, drinking from boiling spit; no food for them save bitter thorn fruit which doth not nourish nor release from hunger" (Surah 88:2–7, Pickthall).

8. Attributed by Zwemer to the *Mishkat al-Masabih* and Osborne's *Islam under the Khalifs of Baghdad,* 63. In Samuel Zwemer, *The Moslem Doctrine of God* (London: Oliphant, Anderson and Ferrier, 1905), 52.

9. According to Martin Goldsmith in *Islam and Christian Witness* (London: Hodder and Stoughton, 1982), 48.

10. Ibid. The term is described in *The Shorter Encyclopedia of Islam,* ed. H. A. R. Gibb and J. H. Kramers (Leiden: E. J. Brill, 1991), and the article *"khati'ah"* by A. J. Wensinck, in *The Muslim Creed* (Cambridge: Cambridge University Press, 1932), 249, as being able to mean an error in logic or an unintentional action, which is based on its usage in Surah 4:92.

11. Relating to the term *kafir,* which originally meant a lack of gratitude but has come to refer to one who is an infidel. *Shorter Encyclopedia of Islam,* article *"Kafir,"* W. J. Bjorkman, 205.

12. This is affirmed by Seyyed Hossein Nasr, *Ideals and Realities of Islam* (New York: Praeger Books, 1967), 24. Nasr states, "In Islam, however, there is no original sin. There is no single act which has warped and distorted human will. Rather, man by being man is imperfect, only God's being is perfection as such."

13. Each prophet was shown by Qur'anic revelation to be disobedient in at least some way: Adam (Surah 7:22–23), Abraham (Surah 26:82), Jonah (Surah 37:142), and the Prophet Muhammad (Surah 47:19). God chides the Prophet Muhammad for turning away a beggar and for certain false perceptions. God then called upon the Prophet Muhammad to seek forgiveness.

Orthodox Islam teaches that the prophets are *ma'sum* or unblemished, because once God forgives their sins they continue to stand as His messengers. They must be "obedient" in order to receive revelation. This reflects the distinction made between "disobedience" and "sinfulness." The prophets make mistakes but are not "sinful." Hence, I have used the word "disobedient" in this passage.

A further note should be mentioned about Surah 19:19 in which Jesus is described as "pure" (*zakiyy*). This term can also simply be translated to mean "smart," and thus does not have to refer to sinlessness. Interestingly, there is no mention of Jesus' ever being disobedient; that is not the case with the other prophets. Al-Ghazali translates the term *zakiyy* to be "holy," while Pickthall chooses the word "faultless."

14. See also Isaiah 42:1–9; Psalms 69:4, 7–9, 20–21; 16:10–11.

15. Kenneth Cragg, *Jesus and the Muslim* (London: Allen and Unwin, 1985), 55.

16. Muhammad Kamel Hussein, *City of Wrong,* trans. Kenneth Cragg (Amsterdam: Djambatan, 1959), 222.

17. According to Cragg, *Jesus and the Muslim,* 57, al-Ghazali claims that in the garden of Gethsemane, Jesus prayed for deliverance from death: "O God, I have reached a point where I am unable to repel what I abhor or to accomplish what I hope. Things have passed into the hands of others. I have become a prey in my task. There is no poor man in a poorer state than I. O God, do not let my evil adversaries gloat over me or my friends think evil of me. Do not allow my piety to be my calamity nor let this world be my maximum distress. Do not give me into the hand of those who would have no mercy on me, O thou ever living one, O thou eternally abiding."

18. Geoffrey Parrinder, *Jesus in the Qur'an* (New York: Barnes and Noble, 1965), 109–10, quotes J. B. Lightfoot in *The Apostolic Fathers,* 156–57, in a discussion about early Christian heretics who taught that Jesus was not crucified: "There early arose in some Christian circles a reluctance to believe that Jesus, as a divine being and Son of God, could really die. Ignatius, writing about A.D. 115, said that some believed that Jesus 'suffered in semblance.' The apocryphal Gospel of Peter in the second century said that on the cross Jesus was silent, since he 'felt no pain,' and at the end 'the Lord cried out, saying, "My power, my power, you have left." And when he spoke he was taken up . . . ' The apocryphal Acts of John, about the middle of the second century, said that Jesus appeared to John in a cave during the crucifixion and said, 'John, unto the multitudes below in Jerusalem I am being crucified and pierced with lances and reeds, and gall and vinegar is given to me to drink. But unto thee I speak.' And later it said, 'Nothing, therefore of the things which they will say of me have I suffered.' "

19. An excellent treatment of this issue is to be found in Colin Chapman's book, *You Go and Do the Same* (London: Church Missionary Society, 1983), 81–85.

20. I am reminded of the Qur'anic phrase, "God is the best of schemers." Satan did not realize what he was doing, according to this theory, and so he was used by God.

21. Attributed to Bultmann in Wolfhart Pannenberg, *Jesus, God and Man,* trans. Lewis L. Wilkins and Duane A. Priebe (London: SCM Press, 1968), 280.

22. The Bible does not explicitly claim that Christ was tormented by Satan in hell. The references to Christ in Hades in early Christianity imply that He preached to those who had previously died but had no opportunity to apprehend salvation through faith in His atonement.

23. Octavius Wilson, quoted in John Stott, *The Cross of Christ* (Leicester: Inter-Varsity Press, 1989), 61. Of this author, Stott says he found this poem in a book by Wilson called *No Condemnation in Christ Jesus,* published in 1857.

24. Quoted in Jürgen Moltmann, *The Crucified God,* trans. R. A. Wilson and John Bowden (London: SCM Press, 1974), 202.

25. John Martin Creed, *The Divinity of Jesus Christ* (Cambridge: Cambridge University Press, 1938), 50. Creed cites Hegel in *Die Absolute Religion* (166) as the source of this idea.

26. Throughout church history many Christians have found in the Hebrew Bible what they believe are prophecies that foretell the coming of Jesus Christ. These include that Christ will be mocked and crucified (Psalm 22:16–18; Mark 15:16–20); sold for thirty pieces of silver (Zachariah 11:12; Matthew 26:14); wounded and beaten (Isaiah 53:7; Luke 22:63–65); remain silent throughout the ordeal (Isaiah 53:7; 1 Peter 2:23–24); be spat upon (Isaiah 50:6; Mark 15:15); refuse vinegar offered to Him to drink (Psalm 69:21; John 19:28); have soldiers divide His clothing among themselves (Psalm 22:18; John 19:23); that His bones would not be broken (Psalm 34:20; John 19:32–33); and be pierced by a sword (Zachariah 12:10; John 19:34).

27. St. Paul, in the book of Galatians explains that the cross is to be both preached (Galatians 3:1–3) and experienced (Galatians 2:19–21).

28. Goethe (in *Die Geheimnisse: Ein Fragment*) was amazed that the cross could become an inspiration for art: "There the cross stands, thickly wreathed in roses, but who put the roses on the cross? The wreath grows bigger so that on every side the harsh cross is surrounded by gentleness." Quoted in Moltmann, *The Crucified God,* 35.

29. These are based on Hadith cited in chapter 4.

30. St. Peter said Christ was made manifest at the "end of times" (1 Peter 1:20). This idea that humanity is in the final epoch is repeated in Hebrews 1:2, in 1 Corinthians 10:11, and by John in 1 John 2:18. It is also in Peter's preaching at Pentecost (Acts 2:17).

31. Cited in Phil Parshall, *The Cross and the Crescent: Reflections on Christian-Muslim Spirituality* (Wheaton, Ill.: Tyndale House, 1989), 93.

32. Quoted from St. Cyril of Jerusalem in Moltmann, *The Crucified God,* 34. It is interesting to note that the plaque placed over the head of Jesus was written in Greek, Hebrew, and Latin, the languages of trade, religion, and politics.

33. Seyyed Hossein Nasr, *Islamic Life and Thought* (Albany: State University of New York Press, 1981), 4.

34. Buddhism defines liberation as deliverance from suffering. This follows the initial affirmation, the first step to enlightenment, the recognition that life itself is (defined by) suffering.

35. The Hebrew Bible implies that God uses suffering to bring individuals to repentance. See Amos 3:6; Isaiah 45:7; Psalms 39:9; and in the New Testament, Acts 2:23 and Matthew 26:39.

36. John R. Stott, "God in the Gallows" in *Christianity Today* (January 27, 1987): 30. The Spanish writer Miguel de Unamuno stated that either God lets people suffer or He suffers Himself.

37. For Moltmann, our declaration of faith becomes: "God suffers with us, God suffers for us, God suffers from us."

38. Quoted in Geoffrey W. Bromiley, *Introduction to the Theology of Karl Barth* (Edinburgh: T. & T. Clark, 1979), 19.

39. Geoffrey Ainger, *Jesus, Our Contemporary* (London: SCM Press, 1967), 26, writes: "He comes to us, as He came to Caiaphas that night, from outside of our cozy resting places. He belongs to us, as He did to the church of His day and yet He is the outsider. Whenever churchmen speak of the problem of the outsider they are speaking of Jesus Christ. Whenever any human community forms a protective barrier against others, however natural and inevitable that barrier may be, Jesus comes to it from the other side."

40. This is even true in atheism or agnostic existentialism where God is said to be irrelevant to human interrelationships.

41. Another example seen as too difficult for mortals is Jesus' command to forgive "seventy times seven" (Matthew 18:21–22).

42. Generally, the New Testament speaks in general terms leaving individuals to draw their own applications. This factor has greatly facilitated the ease of Christianity's being accepted by a wide range of cultures. There are some areas in which specific guidelines are established in the New Testament. These include sexual sins (1 Corinthians 6:9; 2 Corinthians 12:21), sins of the "tongue" (Ephesians 4:29; Colossians 3:8; James 3), rules for household conduct, and the right relation between believers and secular authorities (Romans 13; Titus 3:1; 2 Peter 2:13–15).

43. The record of the Islamic community, which does make the claim of corporate salvation, is equally woeful on this account.

44. Nietzsche (*Werke VII,* 265) is cited in Moltmann, *The Crucified God,* 35.

45. Attributed to Sayyid Qutb, *Social Justice in Islam* (Washington, 1953), 278–79, and quoted in Kenneth Cragg, *The Call of the Minaret* (London: Oxford University Press, 1956), 247.

46. It has been said in response that the Christian moral ethic has not been "tried and found wanting but has been found difficult and left untried." This statement has been attributed to Georgia Harkness. I first heard this from a missionary to Asia, Greg Webb. Geoffrey Ainger says the church must respond to this challenge to be more militant in our ethical proclamation of the Gospel: "The call to respond to what God is doing in the world today is a call to insecurity. It is a call to spontaneity in ministry which can only adequately be described in terms of the work of the Holy Spirit and of a servant community which has begun to live the life of faith." Ainger, *Jesus, Our Contemporary,* 108.

8

An Attempt at Drawing Up a Balance Sheet

The basic distinction between Islam and Christianity is a difference in the conception of God's relational nature. Often correspondence between adherents of the two faiths is mired in contestation that, even if resolved, leaves unaddressed the fundamental question: "Who is God?" Christians are frequently preoccupied with soteriological concerns without first addressing underlying assumptions of how the nature of God informs Muslim soteriology. Christians should focus on that which is most substantive, bypassing contentious questions such as discrepancies within revered scriptural texts. Discussions on the Trinity, the divinity of Christ, and the Incarnation will be futile unless they flow from an inquiry into how God's nature is to be apprehended.

How Muslims see Jesus is predicated on how they view God. Unfortunately, many renderings of Christ to Muslims do not begin with this premise. Both Muslim and Christian sources of revelation focus on God's nature; this provides an ideal starting point for interaction. In Christianity, "God is Love" and, thus, participant. In Islam, "God is One" and, thus, beyond finite human comprehension. Christianity calls individuals to enter into covenant relationship with God. Islam calls individuals to worshipfully assume their proper place of worship and submission to God's will and revelation. Both religions conclude that the other tradition's view of God is decidedly anthropocentric.

Because of this, Christians discussing their faith with Muslims need to focus on how best to explicate this contrast and not become entangled in less cogent issues. This will mean three things: First, Christians should carefully study the Muslim understanding of God so that their explanations will be relevant and graspable. Second, the Christian doctrine that God is Incarnate in Christ must provide the methodology for how we communicate the message of Christian faith. Third, Christians are called to proceed in dialogue with

Muslims in the expectation that this effort can be meaningful and mutually beneficial in spite of numerous theological difficulties.

Christianity judges that the Muslim portrayal of God is circumscribed because it rejects the Incarnational revelation of God as active and participant among humanity. This denial results in ethical and ontological questions becoming distorted in their orientation. A prime example is the view of sin within Islam and the refutation that humankind is fashioned in God's image. Islam focuses adherents on the penalty of sin and not on how it affects one's personal relation to God. Sin is defined in horizontal, as opposed to vertical, terms. Because humans are born free from the taint of sin, there is no requirement that they undergo a radical change of heart. Sin is defined as the failure to attain God's standard and that which must be avoided in order to circumvent divine judgment.

Muslim views of eschatology and soteriology are elements of faith that are often unrecognizable to most Christians. This is because of the Muslim premise that God is primarily a unitary transcendent power rather than an active participant among humanity. The starting point for Christians is the cross, while the launching pad of Islam is the emigration of Muhammad to Medina (the *hijrah*) and the establishment of the Islamic community in political authority. Suffering and ethical constructs are addressed from different starting points; discussion on such agendas, which does not first deal with the contrasting views of God, is likely to be ineffectual.

Islam "believes" in Christ but its view of Him is derived from its view of God. The Qur'an is the glass through which Muslims look at Jesus and their starting point for conclusions about His person. As a result, Jesus is regarded as a prophet for the people of Israel, who confirms the Torah, predicts Muhammad, works miracles, and will return to abjure heretical Christian misconceptions about His divinity. Jesus need not be a mediator because one can live directly before God's will and His revelation. Mediation is not required of God. Christ obviously cannot be worshiped as divine because He is born into humanity as a vulnerable child. Jesus is not sent by God as an expression of divine love to sinners (Romans 5:8) because God does not love those rebels who are unrighteous. Divinity cannot reside in Jesus on the cross because God is far removed from human suffering and limitation.

Christian doctrine is rooted in the conviction that God desires to be intimately and relationally known by His creation. Relationship is possible because God has created people with the capacity for fellowship. The Incarnation shows that God understands humanity in the fullest sense because He participates within it.

In both traditions, the Creator is transcendent. Both religions agree that this Creator exists apart from, and is not subject to, the material universe. What is divergent is the conclusion drawn by Islam that, because God is outside of time and space, He cannot enter those elements to the degree required by the Incarnation. The transcendence of God in Islam demands that God give revelation through these ascended beings and not deal directly with humanity. God's transcendence demands this intermediation. The Bible affirms the self-sufficiency of God in saying that "The Father has life in Himself," but also affirms that He has "granted the Son to have life in Himself" (John 5:26).

Islamic theology is grounded in the conviction that God is primarily to be understood as being all-powerful. The appropriate response of the individual before the Creator is to lie prostrate in submission to the power of His divine authority. God decrees that humanity, fashioned from mud, should bow before Him in servitude (Surah 51:56). God appropriately commands obedience because He is supreme, and will receive obedience because His plan is incontrovertible. God's sovereignty means that He is imperturbable and not affected by human wickedness. To say that God is grieved by evil is an insult to divine majesty, which is beyond being affected by human inconsistency. The greatness of God is His leniency toward sin and the fact that He makes it simple for individuals to escape the penalty of hell.

God's greatness means that He cannot be known and that individuals cannot have a "personal relationship" with Him. One is called to adhere to the divine law that He has established and which serves as a barrier between divine greatness and human imperfection. Christian soteriology also begins with a concept of divine law but it is presented as that which is given as a result of God's love. Individuals can only fulfill this law through Christ, who enables men and women to participate in the moral excellence of holiness.

Both Islam and Christianity believe that God is immutable (Surah 6:34; Psalms 102:25–27; James 1:17) but are at variance on how this immutability is expressed. Christians do not agree with Muslims that the Incarnation is a contradiction to God's unchanging nature. Christianity affirms that God the Father was always in Christ and eternally in coequal trinitarian relationship with the personality of Christ and the Holy Spirit.

Muslims and Christians both profess that God is immanent and that this immanence does not mean that He is pervasive in physical or material substantiality. Christianity avows that God is "over all and through all and in all" (Ephesians 4:6). What is immanent about God in Islam is His will (and the revelation of His will), which cannot be altered, and His power, which cannot be questioned. Christianity sees God's will in terms of His desire to establish covenant with His children as a Father seeks ongoing communion with His family (1 Timothy 1:15; Luke 19:10). Revelation, then, is also ongoing and continual. God, in Christianity, is powerful, but His power is expressed in the personality of Christ who redemptively suffers in order to bring an alienated humanity back into intimate *koinonia* relationship.

The revelation of the Qur'an does not declare that "God is Love." God's power is without limit while His "love" has clear boundaries. God is described as compassionate, but His mercy is unmistakably directed to those on whom His favor rests and is not without "limit." In Islam, it cannot be said that God "weeps" or is grieved over those who are apart from His pleasure. Because God cannot be described as a "personality" within Islam, His immanence cannot be construed as relationally participatory in any mutual sense. God cannot be "intimately" known in the same way that Christianity claims is possible through the reception of Christ into an individual's life. Muslims believe that God's nature cannot be known and, further, that it is not soteriologically necessary to comprehend anything about God's nature beyond His unity and His greatness. The Christian doctrine of God as participant in covenant invites individuals to worship One with whom they mutually and intimately relate.

The biblical theme of covenant is represented as a mutual relationship whereby an individual is called to both know and love God. The biblical emphasis on God's compassionate nature as a father who forgives (Psalm 103:8–13) is also the primary revelation that Christ brought about God in the inauguration of the new covenant. Worship in Christianity cannot be defined as the submissive and nonmutual relationship that a slave maintains toward His master. Christ has proclaimed that

> I no longer call you servants, because a servant does not know his master's business. Instead I have called you friends, for everything I learned from my Father, I have made known to you. (John 15:15)

Christian worship is directed to "our Father" (Matthew 6:9–12) who is both personal and loving (Ephesians 3:15; see also 2 Corinthians 6:18). God chastens individuals as a "father chastises his children" (Hebrews 12:6) and is active in human life. The success or failure of one's existence is not confined to whether or not one is delivered from hell but in terms of one's intimacy with God as His "sons and daughters" (2 Corinthians 6:18). God feels human affliction (Isaiah 63:9) and wrestles with individuals in order to direct them to Himself. God is described as Love and He who has lavished love on humanity (1 John 3:1). God has "showed His love among us" (1 John 4:8–10) in Christ crucified and as a relational participant among His creation.

Second, the Christian conception of God Incarnate is one of mutual engagement. God in Christ meets people where they are and not where God is. God exerts effort toward His beloved. The Incarnation speaks of God's desire to send Himself among humanity in a way that can be comprehended. It speaks of the desire of God both to communicate with the world and to enter into covenant relationship with humanity. It reveals God's attitude toward people and, as such, also charts the Christian's course of mutuality and love in relation to Muslims. The Incarnation is a divine descent that is an unmistakable expression of God's active participation amidst human depravity and ignorance. The Christian is called to similarly "participate" within Islam and seek to understand (even "embrace") the Muslim worldview. This will mean being immersed in the message, language, and issues within Islam.

Communicating the doctrine of God incarnationally will affect the way in which Christian witness is expressed among Muslims. It will mean that there will be "no quarrelling" (2 Timothy 2:24–26) in the Christian's interaction, but rather a spirit of mutuality and gentleness consistent with the spirit of Christ. It will mean that our "conversation will be full of grace" (Colossians 4:6) and not bound up in anti-Islamic reproach. It will mean that our declaration to Muslims will be presented with supernatural authority as it was in the life of Christ. The Christian witness will be marked by a willingness to pray for the sick and oppressed and by a corresponding willingness to work toward their health and deliverance. Agape love expressed by Christians will foster mutuality: unbounded respect for Muslims and a sense of full appreciation and listening, sympathetic participation in the lives of Muslims.

Our example of how to interact with Muslims is the elenctic and patient dialogical approach of Christ. When Jesus was just twelve years old He engaged in dialogue with the religious leaders of His day. This event (Luke 2:45–46) finds Jesus sitting among His audience, listening, asking questions, understanding their responses, and providing responses of His own to the questions that were asked of Him. It is a vivid picture of mutuality and respect being fostered. Christ identified with others and saw His interactions as a process of bringing healing and reconciliation. More than simply adding to the biblical revelation of God's nature, Christ came to embody and translate the truth about God into the world of the everyday and the common. God in Christ used (and transformed) everyday elements such as a hill of execution and an empty tomb to reveal truth. In conversations, Christ never imposed His will but mutually interacted in a way that affirmed the integrity of those with whom He spoke. This is consistent with God's nature. God seeks mutual relationship, not unquestioning acquiescence. The patient posture of Jesus disclosed to His audience that they were loved. At the conclusion of His life, it was said that Jesus wept, not only for His friends, but also for those who had resisted His grace-filled message of inner peace, and inclusion and invitation to God's great banquet feast of eternal life (Luke 19:41). I have discussed how the homiletic patterns of St. Paul were "incarnational" in his approach to those who did not yet believe that Jesus was one with God. Paul's preaching was founded on a tremendous empathy (e.g., 1 Corinthians 9:19–23) with his audience. The apostle was willing to sacrifice his own salvation, if that were possible, in order to attain the deliverance of his countrymen. St. Paul employed no single method but adapted his presentation to each audience. In his preaching he was respectful and often sought to raise questions in the minds of his listeners, then strove to explain his message in the most direct and compelling way that he could find. The missiological approach of St. Paul was rooted in personal experience, centered on Christ, characterized by encouraging his audience to study the scriptures, focused on areas of receptivity, expressed in relational language that was flexible, and contiguous with what his audience had already received.

Mutual dialogue should not be held as a technique employed to subversively "conquer" Muslims. Christian interaction with Muslims should never become a self-centered monologue masquerading as interaction, or a form of polemic devised to advance propagandic proselytism. Rather, dialogue should proceed in such a way that negative barriers are mitigated while entrenched ideas are challenged. Interfaith dialogue should not be restrictive but should include the inclusive and mutual analysis of theological ideas, ritual forms, and relational dynamics.

Vulnerability is a constant factor throughout the process of genuine, mutual interaction as individuals, together, search for God. Christians enter into discussions with Muslims willing to change and expecting to learn. In this approach there is no allowance for possessive attitudes toward truth, which lead to rigid conformity and, ultimately, to spiritual sterility. The Christian motivation for engaging in this process is the passionate love of God who incessantly sought us and heartily encouraged us to enthusiastically share the good news of Jesus that has transformed our own lives. Since God took the initiative with humanity, Christians are able to take the initiative to enter into relationship with Muslims.

Interaction with Muslims does not require agreement but rather a mutual willingness to understand. In dialogue with Muslims, differences need not be suppressed and syncretism need not result. Indeed, differences should be openly discussed and even "celebrated." Christians take this posture because of the conviction that God's truth is relational, self-authenticating, and able to "protect" itself.

Kosuke Koyama, a Japanese missionary to Thailand in the years before he began his long and fruitful teaching career in North America, wrote that the Thai villagers to whom he related saw everything about him and his message of Jesus as alien and, thus, threatening. He responded by crafting among these farming peasants what he called "waterbuffalo theology." The waterbuffalo was the most important element in most people's lives outside of themselves. What Koyama hoped to do was to "float" the gospel message free from the messenger and cause it to rest with incarnational relevance among his audience. He based this intent on the conviction that Christ is present in the world through the work of the Spirit. The task of the Christian was not to "bring" Christ to the Thai people, but to "find" and celebrate Him already resident among them in their rice fields and in their best hopes. When Koyama pursued this sympathetic course, he was much more successful in gaining a receptive response to his bold proclamation about the authority of Christian revelation. This combination of rooted message and fluid, transparent method resulted in the founding of a thoroughly indigenous church, rooted in beliefs that were understandable and relevant to the local Thai population.

This will mean in the Muslim context that Christ becomes increasingly relevant to Muslim cosmology. As Christians increasingly focus on this Muslim context, the gospel will become increasingly "Islamic." It will adapt and transform itself and become more apparently good news to Muslims. Communication will be more sensitive and more understandable. The hope of increased Christian presence among Muslims is that, through the guidance and ongoing revelation of the Holy Spirit, the burden will become "easier" and the yoke will become "lighter." The gospel message itself will remain as zestful as ever, but it will be increasingly "seasoned" with local spices and presented in familiar lilting accents. This was how Jesus met people in His life: in their villages and outside their shops and on their dusty and familiar streets. He went to them. Christ met individuals on their own level and was willing to work to diminish external barriers to interaction. As a result, Christianity has not developed a *"sunnah"* or pattern, as has Islam, on how to wash one's hands and a host of other incidentals. The focus must consistently be on the Christ of God and not on secondary issues. Christ focused on people and saw their identity in terms of His hopeful and empowering understanding of their potential for covenantal relationship with God. His gospel is a message to be presented with compassion, never in condescension.

After thirteen hundred years this posture is markedly infrequent and rarely advocated. Instead, Muslims are sketched as adversaries and "demons" to be avoided. Today's predominant streams of missiological "dialogue" with Islam could be described in two possible ways: "Islamicizing" Christianity through a preoccupation with contextualization independent of theology, or "Christianizing" Islam, which readily accepts most Islamic theological positions and underscores frail traces of common ground. Historically, the most predominant type of interaction is neither of these approaches. Defensive assertion and aggressive diatribe against Islam without any dialogical component have been much more common. A vision for incarnational interaction with Muslims rejects all three of these avenues in encountering the Muslim view of God. Instead, a dynamic, vibrant engagement of the Christian witness with Islamic theology and the Muslim worldview is advanced. This demands a thorough understanding of Islam and a deliberate striving for an adherent's perspective and deep appreciation. This means that the statements that Christians make about the Islamic view of God will be consistent with what a large majority of Muslims actually believe. For this reason, the intensive interaction of Christians among Muslims will be characterized by nonarrogant questions and a desire to learn about Islam.

This position is an essential foundational cornerstone in the "waterbuffalo theology" that will emerge among Muslims. Christians will avoid stereotypical representations of Allah and the "songless void" of Mohammedanism. "Waterbuffalo theology" in an Islamic context will entail the cultivation of an emotional and sympathetic appreciation for the rituals and symbols of Muslim lives. It will be a joyful, proactive proclamation about the abundant bounteousness of God's love and not a whining, negative, and hostile attack against fourteen hundred years of Islamic history, theology, and culture. As part of this dynamic, in fact, the Christian will work to foster a celebratory appreciation of the rich literature and artistic and spiritual genius of those who call themselves Muslims. Interfaith discussions will be thoroughly "baptized" in the Muslim world without feeling obligated to recite the creed of Islam.

The Muslim's primary felt need must be identified and then addressed in the proclamation of the Christian doctrine of God. Clues to discovering how Muslims view God are found in examining what Muslims feel an individual must do in order to please Him. Further, how Muslims perceive God is evident in the emphasis of Islamic theology that "God is One." This need not be questioned. Christianity needs to be explained in such a way that God's unassailable unity is confirmed.

Christian interactions need also to be sensitive to Islamic cosmological views. Muslims tend to value interdependence more than autonomy. Strength is found in the security and interrelatedness of other believers. Efforts should focus more on a family or societal approach than on methods that emphasize one's individual response to Christianity.

This book has mentioned other worldview issues to which the Muslim's search to please God relates. These include the need for community, honor, blessing, spiritual vitality, and freedom from guilt. In spite of the claims of Islamic orthodoxy, the conclusion of my interaction with Muslims is that Muslims, like all other people in the world, are seeking some level of intimacy and personal relationship with their eternal Father and Creator. Islamic mysticism is proof of this. A longing for God is vividly apparent in the life of the Prophet Muhammad and is lavishly expressed in the zealous and frequent rituals of Islamic devotion. Interestingly, I have yet to meet a Muslim who claimed to value an assurance of Paradise comparable to the way that many Christians confidently talk about their eternal destiny, rooted in their understanding of the Bible (e.g., 1 John 5:13).

The end result of an incarnational witness among Muslims is a competent, relevant proclamation of the Christ of God. This will be judged by the loving character of the messenger as much as by the impactful content of the message. If it is true, as Christianity claims, that lavish and self-sacrificial love characterizes God's revelation in Jesus Christ, then this same kind of love will invariably be expressed in countless ways to Muslims. What will be attractive to Muslims about Christianity is the beneficial fruit that this love is shown to produce, not the inedible and unpleasant briers and brambles (cf. Luke 6:44) of theological assertion and argumentation.

Finally, we should remember that although meaningful interfaith and intercultural understanding is demanding, it is also achievable. One reason that Christians sense that effective interfaith communication of the doctrine of God is not procurable is rooted in a condescending attitude inherent in a large degree of Christian interaction with Muslims. This is reflected in the unwillingness of Christians to use the Qur'an in spite of the fact that it is the primary and treasured ancient source for grasping an appreciation for Islamic spirituality and theology. I have tried to present a number of ways of how the Qur'an can help Muslims better understand the Christian doctrine of God. It is a source for numerous starting points in Muslim-Christian interaction (e.g., Surah 3:45–49; 10:64). The fascinating and extensive Qur'anic portrait of Jesus should also be studied, not to be proven inaccurate, but because its subject, Jesus Christ, is the central focus of the Christian revelation of God's relational nature.

It is apparent that few people in the world could be considered more "God-conscious" than those in the Muslim community. The "problem" is not that Muslims worship a different God but that God is understood differently in Islam than He is in Christianity. This difference provides a fascinating opportunity for both faiths to learn and understand more about the nature of God. Muslims direct their quest for God toward the Creator of the universe and the self-sufficient, eternal God. Some Christians may consider the Muslim search for God to be incomplete, but it should not be seen to be misdirected. Christians should appreciate that faith in God in any expression and a desire to live a moral and positive, responsible life of holiness relates to the potential offered in the Christian doctrine of God to know Him in intimate, covenantal relationship. In my encounter with Muslims who have become Christians, I have never heard it expressed that their spiritual quest for truth, which began in Islam, was discontinuous with their decision to believe that Christ was one with God. Many who have been taught as children about God in the Qur'an have come to see that their understanding of God has been "completed" in Christ and not independent from the foundation that they had received in Islam.

Some Christians feel that there are two streams of hopelessness that must be forded. One stems from a response to Islamic theological intransigence, and the other from its cultural extensiveness. Theological barriers include: arguments that the Bible has been altered, Christ cannot be divine and need not have died to atone for sins, God is not Triune, and the Bible prophesies the coming of the Prophet Muhammad. This negativism, caricaturized as pragmatism by many Christians, is usually sustained with a more dogmatical, and less relational and missiological, perspective of pregnant expectation. Those who hold to negative, dismissive perspectives about Muslims need to be reminded that the Incarnation emerged from the backdrop of a pluralistic society that embraced other religious views beyond orthodox Judaism. Further, Christian theology may begin to "explain" Christianity but it does not define or encapsulate it. Christians are not called to a hostile, crusading jihad to defend their theological traditions and positions, but to follow Jesus Christ as He walks the dusty streets of the Muslim world. Christian theology can be malleable in its expression without compromising its content. It has been my observation that many of the patriarchal evangelical "architects" of Christian interaction with Muslims often doubt that exposition of the doctrine of God is possible because of a seemingly impregnable bulwark of ethnic and sociological hurdles that they describe as garrisoning individual Muslims against Christian ideas. It is no wonder that they have not inspired many young people to participate in interfaith witness and dialogue. The argument critics and pessimists advance is that any insight gained on a doctrinal level will fall short because of the palpable extensiveness of Muslim society. From this perspective, what is telling is not Islamic theology but the all-inclusive nature of the Muslim way of life. Adherents of both opinions must be challenged to consider how implicit in these postures is a denial of the relevance of the Incarnation of Christ to Muslims. The second stance is more dangerous than the first because it denies the tenability of meaningful interfaith discussions with Muslims about the nature of God. Adherence to this disparagement is marked by a dearth of eagerness to interact with Islamic political, sociological mores and aesthetic sensibilities to the exclusion of theological discussion. This explains why there is almost no interfaith theological discussion today between Christians and Muslims. Interfaith discussion is much more likely to be "problem"-centered (e.g., dealing with terrorism, environmentalism, war) than it is to be theological, contextual, and historical.

The Christian message of the Christ of God among Muslims should be sustained by the conviction that its communication is realizable. This belief is held in spite of institutionalized theological or cultural problems because of the New Testament assertion that God the Holy Spirit is active in the world today. Christ said, "when the Spirit comes He will guide you into all truth" (John 16:13), and this hope is applicable for Christians among Muslims.

And just as was true in the early church's response to Paul's conversion, many Christians express the suspicion that conversion is even possible (Acts 9:10–19; Galatians 1:21–24). Christians should return to a confident biblical perspective, which contends that God has prepared both the proclamation and the reception of the message (Romans 1:18–2:16).

It is the historic belief of the Christian church that interfaith discussions with Muslims about the loving Christ of God has the capability of progressively transforming lives, breaking down barriers of isolation and alienation, and healing broken hearts. The experienced reality of the Holy Spirit encourages Christians to strive for imaginative and original representations of biblical revelation as a response to important and careful Muslim questions about the logic of Christian doctrine. A component of this interaction is the historical conviction that Muslims, in order to understand the purpose of their own faith (to please God), should be encouraged to first come to grasp the Christian revelation of Jesus, who is able to fulfill that intention.

Do Christians actually believe that the coming of Jesus provides the center point in the history of humanity? If so, how will that idea be expressed in interfaith discussions? Do Christians truly believe that Christ can fulfill the aspirations of Muslims to become those who are truly submitted to the truth about God? If so, Muslims will need to hear extensive evidence to that effect. Christ in Islam is a mysterious and noble figure who is miraculously born, lived performing amazing deeds, then was supernaturally transported to God's presence until He will powerfully return to judge humanity. Muslims know that Christ is the center of Christian faith and they know that Christ is a divine act of God. What they do not know from the Qur'an, their experience, or, for the most part, from their interaction with Christians is how He reveals, or helps express, the relational nature of God. Were it not for Jesus, the biblical, Talmudic, and Qur'anic revelation about God's power and oneness would be almost identical. Christ becomes the axial difference between the Muslim and Christian answer to the question: "Who is God?"

A differing view of God is the primary theological issue that should be addressed in the Muslim-Christian encounter. Christianity states that God is the one who reveals, whose oneness is expressed as three personalities within the Triune relationship of Father, Son, and Spirit. Christianity claims that God "suffers" and loves in incarnational participation in order to restore humanity to right relation with God through His initiation of an eternal covenant. For Christians, the incarnational love of Christ exemplifies how this interfaith communication should proceed by involvement, mutuality, and willing, personally sacrificial engagement among Muslims. The prospect of discussing with Muslims Christian theological ideas may seem daunting, but it is possible. This confidence is not rooted in naive optimism, although it is an expectation that has been missing in most of the past annals of Christian history. It is a conviction that is founded on the faith that the revelation of God in Christ is relevant and able to work forcefully when presented in fresh contextual pertinence in the power of the Holy Spirit.

The New Testament describes Christians as those who have received the revelation that God is a Father who can be known in relational covenant. This is not the message of Islam, but it is a message for Muslims. "Father" is not one of the ninety-nine "beautiful names" of God in Islam. What should our response be to this omission? Perhaps like the apostles, many Christians have "fished all night for a catch" in the shoals of cultural contextualization and theological harmonization but have caught nothing. Perhaps, like those disciples, Christians have engaged in a fruitless "dialogue" or have fought shrill debates with Muslims. These often result in nothing but the meager harvest of mutuality or self-satisfaction. The invitation to come to Christ may or may not result in people who call themselves Muslims beginning to call themselves Christians. But Christians are called to obey Christ's command, and once again put the nets of incarnational presence into the waters of the Muslim world. In so doing, Christians may find themselves reconsidering long-held negative presuppositions toward Muslims.

This exploratory, dynamic process will call upon the Christian to rethink and restate what is "kerygmatic" about Christianity. It is the love of God expressed in Christ, the Christian doctrine of a God of covenants, whom Christians must proclaim. It is in the power of the Spirit that this message is to be communicated through the impact of relevant words and transformed lives. Most Muslims have rejected Christ because they have yet to see Him. Most Muslims have not understood Christ's relational mission and have rejected Christians and Christianity. Christians, with incarnational clarity, should invite people (and themselves in the process) to "consider Jesus." We have no other gospel.

Perhaps the most hopeful single note that I have experienced in my interaction with Muslims is the consistent interest I have seen in the person of Jesus Christ. In interfaith interaction the legend of St. Christopher is instructive. It is said that, as a young man, he wanted to serve the "strongest of Lords." After much searching, St. Christopher came to the conclusion that the infant child, Jesus, born in obscurity and poverty in an animal manger, was actually the divine ruler of all the world. Certainly, God coming in Christ does not come as Muslims expect, and in so doing defies their expectations of what God should be like.

The message of Christianity is not that "our God" is true and "your God" is not, but the revelation that God is Love and actively seeking humanity to be participant as revealed in a new covenant (Jeremiah 31:31–34) between God and humanity. Jesus leads Christians in the *hajj* toward Mecca to "seek our brethren" (Genesis 37:16) within the house of Islam. Our prayer in this journey echoes the first intercession ever recorded in the Bible, the cry of Abraham, our mutual father in faith, who pleaded, "O that Ishmael might live before you!" (Genesis 17:18). May the Muslims who interact with those of us who are seeking to follow Jesus benefit by meeting us, gaining a clearer understanding of the Father, heart of our great and loving Creator God. There is no other God but God.

Appendix 1

The Relationship in Islam between Muhammad and Jesus

The Prophet Muhammad is the final recipient of revelation. Any understanding of Jesus which Muslims develop cannot unfold independent of the role that God has already given to the Prophet Muhammad. This issue is dismissed by many Christians, or overlooked by those who narrowly focus only on Christ as presented in the Qur'an.

Both Jesus and Muhammad are prophets. Jesus as described in Islam has been given revelation from God (Surah 19:30). The Prophet Muhammad has received the final revelation, however, and all other messengers are of a less ascendent position. Jesus served as an inspiration to Muhammad because he felt that his objectives were similar to those of Christ. Both prophets were accused of sorcery, insanity, and demon-possession.[1] Muslims see parallels which lead to the deduction, in the words of Muhammad Khalid, that "Jesus and Muhammad are on the road together" (*a'na ala-l tariq Muhammad wa-l-masih*).[2]

How should Christians respond to the Prophet Muhammad? This question has unnecessarily bedeviled Christian interaction with Muslims. The Great Commission does not include a mandate to defame the Prophet Muhammad. As an enemy of idolatry, it is not difficult to respect his tireless and dedicated battle against polytheism. He is as much a prophet as any biblical iconoclast. Criticisms about his polygamy must also be charged against Abraham or Moses. Neither can the Prophet Muhammad be seen as an usurper of Christianity, because the issue is not religious domination but the truth about revelation from God. As an "Arabian Luther," the Prophet Muhammad was a towering figure in his day. What can be known with some degree of certainty about his morality was that he was sympathetic toward the weak and zealous to uphold God's honor.[3]

Muslims and Christians invariably maintain contrasting views about the Prophet Muhammad's role. For Muslims, understanding Christianity is contingent on grasping the relationship between Muhammad and Jesus. I once talked with a Muslim in Malaysia who despaired, "We are willing to accept that Jesus was a prophet. Why cannot you adopt the same view of Muhammad?" Those Christians who do agree that Muhammad was a prophet usually make this affirmation in a tentative way, which is also inadequate to Muslims. This is because the Qur'an announces that the authority of the revelation given through the Prophet Muhammad extends over those given to Jewish and Christian sources. Both Islam and Christianity agree that the Prophet Muhammad was only mortal. The point of the Islamic view of God, however, is that there are no "christs" or "saviors" besides God. As Shabbir Akhtar points out, "The greatness of God means that if Islam did have a 'christ,' it is Allah; not Muhammad, not the Qur'an, not even Islam."[4]

Muslims are often determined to explain how the Christian *injil* foretells the advent of the Prophet Muhammad. He is greater than Jesus because he is the fulfillment of all the prophetic ministries that precede him. The conviction that Jesus foretold the Prophet Muhammad is established on the basis of Surah 61:6:

And remember Jesus, the son of Mary, said: "O Children of Israel! I am the apostle of God (sent) to you, confirming the Law (which came) before me, and giving glad tidings of an Apostle to come after me, whose name shall be called Ahmad." But when he came to them with clear signs, they said, "This is evident sorcery!"

Jesus, in Islam, fulfills the function that John the Baptist carries out in Christianity. John 14:26 is the primary New Testament passage that Muslims say refers to the Prophet Muhammad. In this verse, Jesus is not prophesying the coming of the Spirit on the day of Pentecost, but the "praised one," which refers to Muhammad. This is built on the notion that the term in the Bible (*prklts*)[5] is not to be read as "the comforter" (*parakletos*) but as the "praised one" (*periklutas*). When translated into Arabic, this becomes "Ahmad" from which the name "Muhammad" is derived. Christians might point out to those quick to draw these conclusions that Jesus also predicted that the one coming would be sent by the Father in the name of Jesus (John 14:26), would be unseen (John 14:17), would live forever with the followers of Christ (John 14:17), and would come to them shortly as the disciples waited in Jerusalem (Acts 1:4).

Muslims assert that the Prophet Muhammad fulfills the work of Jesus because his ministry succeeds where Jesus has faltered. Jesus made tremendous spiritual progress but failed in the material realm because of His own gentleness and because of the fierce opposition from the powers of entrenched religious legalism. This insufficiency, combined with the subsequent corruption of the *injil,* made the end result of Christ's earthly ministry ineffectual.

Further, Jesus never emerged into manifest political success during His tenure on the earth. The Prophet Muhammad, in contrast to Jesus, was an acknowledged member of the dominant tribe in Arabia and resident in the predominant city of that country. Muhammad was much better suited than the dispossessed, poor Galilean to bring political changes that could lead to the preservation of the revealed truths from God.

Jesus still holds an honored place in Islam[6] but has been eclipsed by the brighter light of the Prophet Muhammad. Islamic Hadith, devotional literature and mystical literature (and to some degree theological sources) have promoted a likeness of Muhammad that is increasingly "Christ-like." To Islam, the portrait of Christ in the New Testament is ultimately irrelevant because of the superiority of Muhammad and the trustworthy Qur'anic account of Jesus. It is not Jesus, but the Prophet Muhammad, Muslims premise, who is the central figure in the historic search of humanity to perceive something of God.

NOTES

1. The Qur'an tells us that some considered the Prophet Muhammad to be a demon-possessed, mentally disturbed poet: Surah 10:2; 15:6; 17:50; 25:9; 37:35; 38:3; 41:5; 44:13; 52:29–30; 68:2; 69:41–42.

2. Cited in Kenneth Cragg, *Jesus and the Muslim* (London: Allen and Unwin, 1985), 52.

3. I was told by a Malay that, according to a tradition, a man asked the Prophet Muhammad how he could best commemorate the recent burial of his mother and Muhammad replied, "Dig a well and give water to the thirsty."

4. Shabbir Akhtar, *A Faith for All Seasons* (London: Loewellew, 1990), 187.

5. According to Muslims with whom I have spoken, the Greek script would only list the consonants in the earliest copies, so the word *prklts* could be open to either interpretation. This is not correct. In the earliest copies it is clearly to be shown as *parakletos*. A complete study of this issue can be found in the book *In the Family of Abraham,* ed. Ann Cooper (Tunbridge Wells: Gospel Communications, 1989), 42–49.

6. According to Martin Luther, Islam taught that the Prophet Muhammad sits at the right hand of God while Jesus sits on the left. In Donald Wismer, ed., *The Islamic Jesus: An Annotated Bibliography of Sources in English and French* (New York: Garland, 1977), 7.

Appendix 2

The Portrait of Jesus
in Early Islamic Mysticism

> The hermitage of Jesus is the Sufi's table spread;
> Take heed, O sick one, never forsake this doorway.
> —Rumi, *Mathnawi,* III. 298

INTRODUCTION

Formative Islam embraces a wide spectrum of spirituality traditions and expressions. One of these, mystical Islam, is centered on the task of the individual's seeking right relationship with God. Many of the "signature marks" of mysticism are resident in other aspects of Islam. Mystical Islamic vocabulary, for example, is clearly rooted in the Qur'an. The goal of "desiring the face of God" (Surah 2:272) did not evolve from external sources, but is said to reveal a different way of struggle (*jihad*) toward obedience. More than anything else, mystics within Islam are what Leonardo da Vinci called "disciples of experience."[1]

It is challenging to identify when the mystical dimension of Islam began. In some respects, the Prophet Muhammad was the first "mystic" of Islam. There is, however, a clearly traceable development within Islam from dogmatic orthodoxy to a desire to gain spiritual experience. The first notable mystic in Islam was probably Husayn ibn Mansur al-Hallaj (244–309 A.H./A.D. 858–922), a Persian who wrote in Arabic. He was tortured and crucified by the Abbasids for his heretical esoteric preaching. By the tenth century, others followed al-Hallaq and compiled handbooks for Sufi devotees.

These early mystics showed a profound reverence for Christ as the greatest *faqir* (one who possesses spiritual knowledge and insight). Ibn al-Arabi quotes extensively from the Bible and emphasizes prayer and fasting as the most important tools in developing spiritual perception. Al-Jilani, before Ibn al-Arabi, preached the need for a spiritual director to lead a person in humility, charity, and self-surrender to God. The fruit of this depth of obedience is the indwelling (*hulul*) of the spirit of God transcendent within humanity. Al-Jilani exalts,

> In all the eye discovered, only God I saw, like a candle I was melting in His fire amidst the flames outflashing, only God I saw. Myself within my own eyes I saw most clearly but when I looked with God's eyes... I passed away with nothingness, I vanished and lo, I was still living by only seeing God.[2]

Christ described in Sufi Islam emerges as quite distinct from His portrayal in the Bible, and even from the Jesus recounted in the Qur'an. He is characterized in ways that clearly facilitate Sufi's need for an example in a way in which the wealthy, warring Prophet Muhammad cannot satisfy. What emerges is a "Jesus we can scarcely recognize. He is neither the historical man of Nazareth, nor the divine being that Christian theology declared Him to be."[3]

Jesus appears as a "seal of sanctity" who typifies a special kind of "christic" wisdom. Jesus is able to guide people to experience God in the same way that He has come to know God. Christ is the epitome of one who has suffered and illustrates the mystical belief that suffering is able to transform evil. A Sufi should pursue Christ to the cross in order to cultivate intimacy with God: "Whoever turns his countenance to God, must press his back against the cross. His soul cannot mount heaven alone.... It is four nails that deliver the candle of the soul."[4] In its early years, Sufism was highly diffused in both theological and geographical terms. Because of this I have chosen to select representative authors and key descriptions that are repeated in order to draw a clearer impression of how this movement dealt with Christ.

THE PORTRAYAL OF JESUS
IN THE WRITINGS OF IBN AL-ARABI

Abu Bakr Muhammad Ibn al-Arabi (560–638 A.H./A.D. 1165–1240) was called an "animator of the faith" because of his influence. Ibn al-Arabi's most noted tome is the *Wisdom of the Prophets* (*Fusus al-Hikam*) which, in twenty-seven chapters, focuses on the idea that the human nature of the prophets was infused with divine wisdom. What these prophets have attained, others can also achieve.

Ibn al-Arabi begins his investigation by looking at the "wisdom of prophecy," which was placed within Jesus. This is what enabled Christ to perform miracles. What Jesus did was the result of God's breath (*nafas*) which flowed freely through Christ because of His heightened sense of obedience. Christ's powers are accessible to any vessel who is submitted to God. The reason for strength within Jesus was what Ibn al-Arabi labeled "the localization of God"[5] and divine power. When Jesus was able to raise the dead, "It was Him and yet not Him, just as anyone who reflects on this action is amazed at a human person who revives the dead."[6]

Jesus was able to do more miracles than others because He was more intimate with the divine. Jesus understood the "superior" world of faith, and it was easier for Him to operate in it than in the "inferior" realm of common life. God purified the body of Jesus and elevated His spirit by giving Him special gnostic insight. Christ is a symbol to Ibn al-Arabi of how an individual can, by close relation with the Creator, live in a higher dimension of possibility.

When Ibn al-Arabi surveys the instruction of Jesus, he notes the themes of almsgiving and humility. He records that Jesus forgave His enemies and yielded to others. Jesus' life strikes Ibn al-Arabi as being feminine. This may explain why he considers Christ particularly sympathetic to women. These factors spring, Ibn al-Arabi concludes, from the fact Christ was born from His mother without a father.[7]

Ibn al-Arabi describes Jesus as one who had received special revelation from God. His words are to be a "sign to others" (Surah 23:4). It is distressing to Ibn al-Arabi that the teaching of Jesus has been so corrupted and misinterpreted by Christians.[8]

Jesus is summarized in Ibn al-Arabi as being "the seal of all the saints,"[9] who has gone before. Christ was a man without equal in terms of His familiarity with God. Ibn al-Arabi elevates Christ to a level equal with Muhammad as a prophet and taught that His life was an outworking of the truths that were later revealed in the Qur'an.

THE PORTRAYAL OF JESUS
IN THE WRITINGS OF JALAL AL-DIN RUMI

Jalal al-din Rumi was born in Balkh (present-day Afghanistan) in A.H. 604 (A.D. 1207; died 672/1273). He was a prosaic theologian who, late in life, had a dramatic mystical experience. He claimed to have had a direct vision of God. After this, he wrote an anthology dedicated to the honor of his mentor (the itinerant Sufi Shams-al-din Muhammad Tabrizi, died 645/1247), the forty-thousand-verse *Diwan Shams al-Tabrizi*.[10]

The God that emerges in his poetry is the God of orthodoxy who is separated from humanity by "70,000 veils of light and 100,000 stages of the spirit." Rumi, however, describes this God in vivid, romantic imagery which seems to contradict the idea there is a great distance between God and individuals. He depicts God as the "hidden treasure," the "painter," the "heart ravisher," and the "Solomon of substance."[11] He says that God is a merciful and loving "friend," active in seeking relationship with humanity.

One confirmation that intimacy is attainable between individuals and God, according to Rumi, is found in the example of Jesus. Christ is not to be worshiped, but serves as a beacon to help others attain this level of love. God has taken Jesus into the fourth heaven:

> When Jesus found the ladder of God's light, he hastened to the top of the fourth dome.... Since Jesus has gone to the fourth heaven what need had he for a church! I am now tired of this house, for like Jesus, I have a house up in the fourth heaven. From now on, let me sit with Jesus on top of the fourth heaven.[12]

Jesus can serve the pilgrim as a guide and an indicator of how far one still has to travel. According to Rumi, the surest way to reach this heaven is to "become Jesus' companion! Otherwise," Rumi advises, "do not aim for the azure spheres."[13] Jesus is a mirror by which one can see into the heart and understand one's self. When Jesus is reflected in the "inner mirror" of one's soul, then one is coming closer to God: "If you see an ugly face (within), that is you, and if you see Jesus and Mary, that is you."[14] One metaphor, frequently repeated in Rumi's script, is the idea that intimacy with God is analogous to being drunk. Jesus lived in this state of ecstasy before God. Rumi warned, "Hark, O Heart! Be not deceived by every intoxicant! Jesus is drunk with God, but his ass is drunk with barley."[15] The source of this inebriation is that Jesus is radically given over to God without reservation. The heart of Jesus is infused with the image of God within.

According to Rumi, life is defined through the experiencing of denial. Jesus exemplifies this truth. Christ lived a life of self-debasement and had a "poverty of spirit"[16] which led to His prayers' being answered and to His peace of mind. When persons are filled with the cares of this world, they are not free to explore the world beyond sight. Christ is proof that triumph over physical circumstances comes through spiritual maturity. He lives as a homeless indigent whose only affluence is His knowledge of God.

Jesus does not gain His acumen because He is an ascetic, but He is an ascetic because He is erudite. Wisdom is *a priori* and beyond the realm of intellect and a gift from God. Jesus in His cradle announced to those who listened, "Without having become a youth, I am a *shaykh* and an old man."[17] Revelation is to be received and not to be learned through the mind. Consciousness, in Rumi's philosophy, inhibits insight. This intimacy with God cannot be quantified: "Within the breast, Allah painted a form, fatherless like Jesus, (but) were Ibn Senna to try and understand it he would be an ass on the ice."[18]

The time to gain this level of communion with God is before death. Illumination must come within "while your Jesus is still on the earth; for when He goes to heaven then you will be lost."[19] Because Jesus has suffered pain, and because of His intimate rapport with God, He can be trusted to guide the soul to safety. The path of love, not the trail of knowledge, is the way forward into oneness with God.

Although Rumi has an obvious fascination with the life of Jesus, he feels there is no contradiction between this and Islam because Jesus is a Muslim prophet. The "breath of Jesus" became a formula that Rumi used to describe the attainment of enlightenment. The breath of Jesus "was not like very ordinary breath," because it brought with it an "infusion of the universal soul."[20] The breath of Jesus brings new birth and imparts the spirit of God as it was revealed in the drunken revelry of Pentecost.

Rumi has undisguised abhorrence for Christians and their corruption of the stories of the prophets. Rumi is particularly grieved that Jesus is the object of worship as He is illustrated in icons. Rumi believed that St. Paul ingratiated himself into the ranks of the early church at the behest of a "Jewish monarch" in order to undermine its ranks by encouraging Jesus to be venerated as a god.[21] Everything that Rumi observes about Christ, it would seem, is derived independent from the influence of Christian sources.

THE PORTRAYAL OF JESUS
AS ONE WHO ACHIEVED UNION WITH GOD

Sufism begins with the goal of a direct experience of God. Because of God's "impersonality" within orthodoxy, Sufism became synonymous with this quest. Sufism sought to shift the focus from the realm of action to the state of one's heart. One's motives become as critical as one's external obedience to the law. This is one of the reasons Christ is so highly regarded within mystical Islam. Another reason is that Sufi writers have long scoured the lives of the saints (*pirs*) and sought to emulate their examples. This propensity has its first expression in the extensive devotional material about the life of Muhammad. Sufism, over time, built on this tradition, and gave increasing reverence to Jesus as one considered close to God.

Mystical Islam[22] is dedicated to what al-Ghazali called "a thirst after comprehension for things as they really are." Beyond intellect, the seeker is called to meditation and other efforts that lead to various ecstatic experiences. This combined with the orthodox doctrine of God's transcendent impersonality led to the conclusion that to achieve union with God, one must overcome human limitations. Without a view of God's coming among humanity in everyday life (the Incarnation), Islamic mysticism sought to ascend to God and experience "enlightenment."

In this quest, Sufism taught that individual personality needed to be "abandoned"[23] in order to participate in God's transcendent nature. God's immanence made this experience achievable. Another proof of the potential for union with God was the experience of others. Christ was the ultimate example of one who was a "friend" (*wali*, literally saint, or holy man) with God. Because Christ was still alive in Paradise and because He was human, He was an ideal "guide" in this quest. Jesus was the culmination of prophetic cycles: the last prophet before the Qur'an and the first prophet, in His return, after the Prophet Muhammad.

In Christ's obedience, Sufism saw one who was a perfect being who could teach others how to attain perfection. Tirmidhi states that Jesus' sinlessness is both a challenge and a judgment. Jesus is a perfect master who led a perfect life on this earth. In Paradise, Christ has become angelic and "superhuman." In His ascension, Jesus entered Paradise through the "gate of power" (*qadr*) and not through the "gate of death." In His birth, Jesus entered life through the "gate of majesty" (*'izzah*) and not the "gate of lust."[24]

THE PORTRAYAL OF JESUS
AS A TEACHER OF MYSTICISM

The Qur'an declared that the revelations of Christ came directly from God. According to Islamic mysticism, Jesus' message was that "Jesus wisdom" (*hikmah 'isa wiyyah*) consisted of elements that focused on the love of God. As a teacher, Jesus moved people from materialism and lust into a concern for spiritual reality. A central thrust in His message was that wisdom could not come without the renunciation of the world. One Sufi said that Jesus taught, "The world and the hereafter are like two women which a man is trying to please at the same time. When one is pleased, the other is annoyed."[25]

The portrait of Jesus in Sufism is of one who has dedicated Himself to poverty (*faqr*), eating only what could be found hanging from the trees.[26] Jesus went about dressed in a cloak of wool filled with holes: "every rip and tear of which represented all the pangs of suffering which had stung His heart."[27] Because Jesus has suffered and is familiar with poverty, He is able to empathize with common people. Christ represents the aspirations, not of power, but of weakness. This is why He is chosen to serve as judge on the final day. His privation and meekness in that day will silence the complaints of those who have also known injustice.

Jesus' renunciation of luxury facilitates His ability to become one who has drawn near to God (*al-muqqarabin*). Those who leave the lust of this world and seek what lies beyond by following the example of Jesus will gain eternal wealth. Those who fast and follow His model in deprivation will be filled with God's presence. As one Sufi warned, "Gold and women are nothing but instigators of sorrow; leave them behind like Jesus, son of Mary."[28]

Another predominant idea of Jesus is His thematic accent on love. Attar wrote, "When God showered His grace on the breath of Jesus, the world was filled with passion."[29] Sufism agrees with orthodoxy, however, that what Jesus showed was love for God and was not a revelation of the love of God. The love that Jesus displayed to God would be better translated "passion" rather than the intimacy (*agape*) described in the Bible. The love poetry written by the Sufis seems distinctly erotic — a reflection of the idea that the dynamics of sexuality are akin to the transcendent experiences of ecstasy to which one should aspire.

Sufism teaches that the love Jesus shared with God is latent within all individuals. In Sufi literature, God is frequently rehearsed as the "Beloved" (*al-habib*). The heart of the worshiper is increasingly caught away from mundane ritual and religious observance. The zeal that Jesus displayed toward God enabled Him to reach the fourth heaven and come close to perfection (*ila 'l-kamali 'l-haqiqi*)[30] and near to complete union with God.

CAN SUFISM BE SEEN AS A BRIDGE BETWEEN MUSLIMS AND CHRISTIANS?

The appreciation that Sufism bears for Jesus provides the frailest of bridges between Islam and Christianity. Attempts to correlate Christian theology with Islamic mystical experience risk becoming blurred in a subjective haze of relativity. Clearly, Sufism venerates a portrayal of Jesus more than other dimensions of Islamic experience. This reverence, however, remains rooted in a concept of God that is monistic. This means the distinctiveness given to Jesus in Christianity as divine, if it exists at all, could be described as pantheistic. Jesus is never perceived as a "savior" but is confined to being honored as an ascetic capable of emulation, but not deserving of worship.

Sufism has established other "christ" figures besides Jesus within its development. The most obtrusive of these, Mansur al-Hallaj, was also crucified for preaching the truth. The uniqueness of Jesus is that He alone was fatherless and conceived by the respiration of the Holy Spirit. Many others resemble Jesus in their intensity and godliness.

Christians, in dialogue with Muslims, have seen in the Sufi cognizance of Christ's union with God a point of reference to explain the Incarnation. Jesus, as the "Spirit of God" (*ruh'Allah*), was a perfect spirit. He is described by Sufism as a "theophany" (*mazhar*) of the all-comprehensive name of God. Because Jesus was the truest devotee of God (*'Abd Allah al-haqiqi*), He was able to perform miracles. Sufism teaches that divine life was breathed into Jesus, an idea rejected by orthodoxy. This idea of God's breath in individuals (such as the Prophet Muhammad and Jesus) is not a revelation of God, but a fulfillment of human potentiality. Sufism held that this divine indwelling (*hulul*) did not imply that Jesus was divine.

The Sufi understanding of "divine indwelling" (*hulul*) does not parallel the Christian teaching of the Incarnation. It is, instead, a precept of neo-Platonism, which advocates that anyone can be filled with the divine nature. To Ibn al-Arabi, Christ is "god" to the same degree that everyone else can become "god."[31] The same breath of life that filled Jesus is the "breath of Jesus which hourly brings forth another dawn and causes a sleeping world to raise its head from the earth."[32] Although some Christians have reasoned that the Sufi doctrine of God's divine indwelling meets a felt need that Islamic orthodoxy cannot fulfill, it also makes Jesus a man who receives God's power. Even within Sufism, the concept of God rooted in Qur'anic revelation makes it inconceivable for God's transcendence to be bridged by His immanence. The unity of God cannot be distinguished in separate personality, although it can be diffused (according to Sufism) into all personality (pantheism).

On one level this doctrine of *hulul* makes it easier for Sufism to accept the idea that a person can become a "child of God." The emphasis, however, is on achieving a special status with God. One does not gain intimacy with God because of the work of Jesus but, in Sufism, only in the emulation of the life of Jesus.

Bertholt Brecht believed that truth is always "concrete." Islamic mysticism is centered in personal experience. Any assertion about God, within Sufism, becomes a declaration about the individual's experience of God and not of the divine nature. Moreover, mysticism retains the crucial rejection of the need for a mediator between God and creation. In Sufism, the task of mediation to attain salvation is left to individuals through meditation and spiritual insight.

For Christians, the primary benefit of dialogue with Islamic mysticism may come from the lack of a strict adherence to codified dogma and, subsequently, an openness to hear about other experiences that people have gained in "knowing" God. Sufi writers enjoin others to "leave argumentation to the anti-Christ and befriend the Jesus of the Spirit."[33] Individuals can gain further dependence on God (*tawakkul*) as they continue in their search for God through learning. Al-Ghazali observed that Jesus called people to be "yielding earth,"[34] not hard rock where insight is not free to flourish. The desire for the next world, emphasized in Sufism, has fostered an elasticity not familiar in Islamic orthodoxy. At the same time Sufism encouraged a syncretistic toleration that avoids any limitations and, thus, defies definition.

In Sufism, unlike orthodox Islam, the emphasis on the role of Jesus has grown through time. The stories of Jesus' miracles, the suffering, and the "sweet words"[35] of His teaching, have touched a respondent chord within folk expressions of mystical Islam. As Christ was increasingly accentuated within Sufism, the frail links between the description of Jesus in orthodoxy began to weaken and to become strained. An illustration of this is the Sufi emphasis on Jesus' preaching on love.

The Sufi idea that Christ was one with God probably also emerged as a response to external influences. Further, the emphasis on Christ as a teacher of wisdom and His life in poverty were much easier to employ for the transmission of their message than was the life of the Prophet Muhammad. The Jesus presented in Sufism increasingly came to be used as a source of authority for unorthodox ideas. Without exception, these portrayals of Christ are complementary, supernatural, ascetic, and compelling.

Sufism's largely positive portrait of Christ may foreshadow a willingness on the part of Islamic mystics to learn more about Christian theological ideas. At least, it might predispose Sufis from dismissing the prospect of dialogue in which Christ is the central concern.

For Sufis the name of Jesus is synonymous with love. Let this be a starting point!

> Know possessions as the anti-Christ
> And look on Jesus as Love
> Once you've joined the band of Jesus
> You can slit the other's throat
>
> — Sana'i

> Happy news, O heart!
> The Jesus-breath has come!
> From his wholesome spirit
> wafts the fragrance of the One.[36]
>
> — Hafez
> (died 792/1389)
> from the *Diwan*

NOTES

1. Kenneth Cragg, *The Mind of the Qur'an* (London: Allen and Unwin, 1973), 8.

2. Cited in R. A. Nicholson, *The Mystics of Islam* (London: Routledge and Kegan Paul, 1963), 40.

3. Lawrence Browne, *The Prospects of Islam* (London: SCM Press, 1944), 67.

4. Kenneth Cragg, *Jesus and the Muslim* (London: Allen and Unwin, 1985), 63.

5. Muhammad Ibn al-Arabi, *The Wisdom of the Prophets,* trans. Titus Burkhardt (Salisbury: Beshwara Publications, 1975), 72.

6. Ibid.

7. Ibid., 71.

8. Ibid.

9. Browne, *The Prospects of Islam,* 68.

10. His other major work was the twenty-five-thousand-verse treatise called the *Mathnawi.*

11. Cited in William Chittick, *The Sufi Path of Love: The Spiritual Teachings of Rumi* (Albany: State University of New York Press, 1953), 130. The earlier reference in this paragraph is also from p. 130.

12. Ibid., 73.

13. Ibid., 123.

14. Ibid., 145.

15. Browne, *The Prospects of Islam,* 68.

16. Chittick, *The Sufi Path of Love.*

17. Ibid., 264.

18. Ibid., 241.

19. Ibid., 62.

20. J. Windrow Sweetman, *Islam and Christian Theology,* 3 vols. (London: Lutterworth Press, 1947), vol. 2, part 1, 309.

21. W. Montgomery Watt, *Faith and Practise of Al-Ghazali* (London: Allen and Unwin, 1953), 21.

22. Mysticism in most religions may relate to the fact that God is often described as absolute, and paradoxes are used to explain that His absoluteness encompasses a wide spectrum of contrasting dimensions. A God without personality who, at the same time, contains everything within Himself invites opposites to be identified within Himself.

23. This abandonment was based on the idea that union with God signified a non-differentiation between the individual and the essence of God. The individual ceases to exist and only God remains.

24. Mahmoud M. Ayoub, "Towards an Islamic Christology II: The Death of Jesus, Reality or Delusion (A Study of the Death of Jesus in Tassir Literature)," *Muslim World* 70, no. 2 (April 1980): 120.

25. Javad Nurbakhsh, *Jesus in the Eyes of Sufis,* trans. Hamid Mashkurk (London: Khaninqanhi-Mimtallunhi, 1983), 81.

26. Ibid., 34.

27. Ibid., 92.

28. Ibid., 53.

29. Ibid., 51.

30. The Prophet Muhammad, in contrast to Jesus, has reached ultimate perfection (the seventh heaven). Jesus' lack of attaining this higher level will be resolved after He descends to the earth, marries, announces to be a Muslim, and dies. Neal Robinson, *Christ in Islam and Christianity* (Albany: State University of New York Press, 1991), 180.

31. Abdul Al-Affifi, *The Mystical Philosophy of Muhammad Ibn al-Arabi* (Cambridge: Cambridge University Press, 1939), 213.

32. Nurbakhsh, *Jesus in the Eyes of Sufis,* 51.

33. Ibid., 57.

34. Ibid., 75.

35. Ibid. p. 52.

36. Ibid., p. 39.

Bibliography

Abdul-Haqq, Abdiyah Akbar. *Sharing Your Faith with a Muslim*. Minneapolis: Bethany, 1980.

Ahmad, Kurshid, ed. *Islamic Perspectives: Studies in Honour of Mawlana Sayyif Abdul 'Ala Mawdudi*. London: Zafar Ishaq Ansari, undated.

Ahmad, Shah E. *Theology: Muslim and Christian*. Lucknow: Lucknow Publishing House, 1970.

Ainger, Geoffrey. *Jesus, Our Contemporary*. London: SCM Press, 1967.

Akhtar, Shabbir. *A Faith for All Seasons*. London: Loewellew, 1990.

Alfahim, Abdul Rahim. *The Two Hundred Hadith*. Makkah, Saudi Arabia: Makkah Printing and Information Establishment, 1990.

Al-Ghazali. *The Alchemy of Happiness*. Trans. Claude Field. London: Octagon Press, 1980.

———. "Christ in the New Testament and the Qur'an." *International Review of Missiology* 3 (July 1976).

Ali, Abdullah Yusuf. *The Holy Koran*. Lahore: Muhammad Ashraf, 1934.

Ali, Maulana Muhammad. *A Manual of Hadith*. London: Curzon Press, 1977.

Anderson, J. N. D. *Christianity and World Religions*. Downers Grove, Ill.: InterVarsity Press, 1984.

———. *The Mystery of the Incarnation*. London: Hodder and Stoughton, 1978.

Andrae, Tor. *Muhammad: The Man and His Faith*. Trans. Theophil Menzil. New York: Barnes and Noble, 1935.

Anwati, Georges C. "Kalam," in *The Encyclopedia of Religion,* ed. Mircea Eliade, 8:231–42. New York: Macmillan, 1978.

Ashgar, Ali E. *Islam and Muslims: A Critical Re-Assessment*. Jaipur, India: Printwell, 1985.

Ataur-Rahim, Muhammad. *Jesus: A Prophet of Islam*. London: MWH, 1979.

Ayoub, Mahmoud. "Towards an Islamic Christology: An Image of Jesus in Early Shi'i Muslim Literature." *Muslim World* 46, no. 3 (July 1976).

———. "Towards an Islamic Christology II: The Death of Jesus, Reality or Delusion (A Study of the Death of Jesus in Tassir Literature)," *Muslim World* 70, no. 2 (April 1980): 91–121.

Baillie, D. M. *God Was in Christ*. London: Faber and Faber, 1956.

Bell, Richard. *The Origin of Islam in Its Christian Environment*. London: Frank Cass, 1968.

Berdayev, Nicholas. *Freedom and the Spirit.* New York: Scribner's, 1935.

Bonhoeffer, Dietrich. *Christology.* London: Collins, 1966.

Borrmans, Maurice. *Guidelines for Dialogue Between Christians and Muslims.* Trans. R. Marston Speight. Mahwah, N.J.: Paulist Press, 1981.

Bouquet, A. C. *Christian Faith and Non-Christian Religions.* Westport, Conn.: Greenwood Press, 1958.

Bray, Gerald. *Contours of Christian Theology: The Doctrine of God.* Leicester: Inter-Varsity Press, 1993.

Broeman, Cecily. *In the Shade of the Moon.* Southdale, South Africa: Sigma Press, 1990.

Bromiley, Geoffrey W. *An Introduction to the Theology of Karl Barth.* Edinburgh: T. & T. Clark, 1979.

Brown, Stuart. *Meeting in Faith.* Geneva: World Council of Churches Publications, 1989.

Browne, Lawrence. *The Prospects of Islam.* London: SCM Press, 1944.

Brunner, Emil. *The Christian Doctrine of God.* Philadelphia: Westminster Press, 1961.

———. *The Mediator.* Philadelphia: Westminster Press, 1957.

Cave, Sydney. *Redemption: Hindu and Christian.* London: Oxford University Press, 1919.

Chapman, Colin. *You Go and Do the Same.* London: Church Missionary Society, 1983.

Christensen, Jens. *A Practical Approach to Muslims.* Upper Darby, Pa.: North Africa Mission Publishers, 1977.

Cohn-Sherbok, Daniel, ed. *Islam in a World of Diverse Faiths.* New York: St. Martin's Press, 1991.

Commission for Inter-Faith Dialogue, eds. *Guidelines for Dialogue between Muslims and Christians.* Cochin, India: KCM Press, 1977.

Cooper, Ann. *Ishmael, My Brother.* Kent: STL Books, 1985.

———, ed. *In the Family of Abraham: Christians and Muslims Reasoning Together.* Tunbridge Wells: Gospel Communications, 1989.

Cracknell, Keith. *Christians and Muslims Talking Together.* London: British Council of Churches, 1984.

Cragg, Kenneth. *The Arab Christian: A History in the Middle East.* London: Mowbray, 1991.

———. *The Call of the Minaret.* London: Oxford University Press, 1956.

———. *The Christ and the Faiths: Theology in Cross-Reference.* London: SPCK, 1986.

———. *The Dome and the Rock.* London: SPCK, 1964.

———. *The Event of the Qur'an: Islam and Its Scripture.* London: Allen and Unwin, 1971.

———. "Greater Is God." *Muslim World* 71, no. 1 (January 1981).

———. *Jesus and the Muslim.* London: Allen and Unwin, 1985.

———. *The Mind of the Qur'an.* London: Allen and Unwin, 1973.

———. *The Pen and the Faith.* Delhi: SPCK, 1988.

Creed, John Martin. *The Divinity of Jesus Christ.* Cambridge: Cambridge University Press, 1938.

Crim, Keith, Roger A. Bullard, and Larry Shinn, eds. *The Abingdon Dictionary of Living Religions.* Nashville: Abingdon, 1981.

Dretke, James P. *A Christian Approach to Muslims: Reflections from West Africa.* Pasadena: William Carey Library, 1979.

Dods, Marcus. *Muhammad, Buddha and Christ.* London: Hodder and Stoughton, 1937.

Dorman, Henry Gaylord. *Towards Understanding Islam.* New York: Columbia University Press, 1948.

Elder, John. *The Biblical Approach to the Muslim.* Fort Washington, Pa.: Worldwide Evangelization Crusade, 1978.

Forsythe, P. T. *The Person and Place of Jesus Christ.* London: Hodder and Stoughton, 1909.

Frieling, Rudolf. *Christianity and Islam.* New York: Floris Books, 1957.

Gibb, H. A. R. *Islam: A Historical Survey.* Hyderabad, India: Henry Martyn Institute, 1979.

———, and J. H. Kramers, eds. *The Shorter Encyclopedia of Islam.* Leiden: E. J. Brill, 1991.

Goldsmith, Martin. *Islam and Christian Witness.* London: Hodder and Stoughton, 1982.

Goldziher, Ignaz. *An Introduction to Islamic Theology and Law.* Trans. Andrae and Ruth Homari. Princeton: Princeton University Press, 1981.

———. *Muslim Studies.* London: Allen and Unwin, 1971.

Green, Michael, ed. *The Truth of God Incarnate.* London: Hodder and Stoughton, 1977.

Guillaume, Alfred. *The Traditions of Islam.* Beirut: Khayats, 1966.

Hahn, Ernest. *Jesus in Islam: A Christian View.* Hyderabad, India: Henry Martyn Institute of Islamic Studies, 1991.

Hanna, Mark. *The True Path.* Colorado Springs, Colo.: International Doorways Publishing, 1975.

Hengel, Martin. *The Atonement: The Origins of the Doctrine in the New Testament.* Trans. John Bowden. London: SCM Press, 1981.

Heschel, Abraham. *The Prophets.* New York: Harper, 1957.

Hirjir-Walji, Hass. *Escape to Freedom.* Claremont, South Africa: Life Challenge, 1982.

Hussein, Muhammad Kamel. *The City of Wrong.* Trans. Kenneth Cragg. Amsterdam: Djambatan, 1959.

———. *The Hallowed Valley.* Trans. Kenneth Cragg. Cairo: American University in Cairo Press, 1977.

Iqbal, Muhammad. *The Reconstruction of Religious Thought in Islam.* London: Oxford University Press, 1934.

Jeffery, Arthur, ed. *A Reader on Islam.* The Hague: Mouton, 1962.

Jennings, George. *All Things, All Men, All Means — to Save Some.* Le Mars, Iowa: Middle East Missions Research, 1984.

Jomier, Jacques. *How to Understand Islam.* London: SCM Press, 1988.

Jones, E. Stanley. *The Christ of the Indian Road.* New York: Abingdon Press, 1925.

Jones, L. Bevan. *The People of the Mosque.* London: SCM Press, 1932.

Jungel, Eberhard. *The Doctrine of the Trinity.* Trans. Horton Harris. Edinburgh: Scottish Academic Press, 1976.

Kaiser, Christopher B. *The Doctrine of God: A Historical Survey.* London: Marshall, Morgan and Scott, 1982.

Klein, F. A. *The Religion of Islam.* London: Curzon Press, 1985.

Koyama, Kosuke. *Waterbuffalo Theology.* Maryknoll, N.Y.: Orbis Books, 1974.

Küng, Hans. "Christianity and World Religions: The Dialogue with Islam as One Model." *Muslim World* 77, no. 1 (January 1987).

Lenning, Larry G. *Blessing in Mosque and Mission*. Pasadena: William Carey Library, 1980.

Lewis, C. S. *Beyond Personality: The Christian Idea of God*. London: Centenary Press, 1944.

MacDonald, Duncan Black. *The Development of Muslim Theology, Jurisprudence and Constitutional Theory*. New York: Russell and Russell, 1965.

Macquarrie, John. *The Humility of God*. London: SCM Press, 1978.

Mansood, Stephen. *Into the Light*. Bromley, Kent: STL Books, 1986.

Marsh, Charles R. *Share Your Faith with a Muslim*. Chicago: Moody Press, 1975.

Marshall, I. Howard. *The Origins of New Testament Christology*. Leicester: Inter-Varsity Press, 1976.

Martin, Richard C., ed. *Approaches to Islam in Religious Studies*. Tucson: University of Arizona Press, 1985.

Martinson, Paul Varo. *A Theology of World Religions*. Minneapolis: Augsburg Press, 1987.

Masih, Akbar. "The Death of the Lord Jesus on the Cross." *The Bulletin of the Christian Institute of Islamic Studies* 3, no. 3–4 (January–April 1970).

McAuliffe, Jane Dammen. *Qur'anic Christians: An Analysis of Classical and Modern Exegesis*. New York: Cambridge University Press, 1991.

McCurry, Don, ed. *The Gospel and Islam: A 1978 Compendium*. Monrovia, Calif.: Missions Advanced Research Center, 1979.

Miller, William. *Ten Muslims Meet Christ*. Grand Rapids, Mich.: Eerdmans, 1969.

Moltmann, Jürgen. *The Crucified God*. Trans. R. A. Wilson and John Bowden. London: SCM Press, 1974.

———. *The Trinity and the Kingdom of God*. Trans. Margaret Kohl. London: SCM Press, 1981.

Musk, William A. *The Unseen Face of Islam*. Modesto, Calif.: Missions Advanced Research Center, 1992.

Naaman, Ghulam Masih, and Vita Toon. *The Unexpected Enemy*. London: Marshall Pickering, 1985.

Nasr, Seyyed Hossein. *Ideals and Realities of Islam*. New York: Praeger Books, 1967,

———. *Islamic Life and Thought*. Albany: State University of New York Press, 1981.

Nazir-Ali, Michael. *Frontiers in the Muslim-Christian Encounter*. Oxford: Regnum Books, 1987.

———. *Islam: A Christian Perspective*. Exeter: Paternoster Press, 1983.

Neill, Stephen. *The Christian Faith and Other Faiths*. London: Oxford University Press, 1961.

———. *The Christian's God*. London: Lutterworth Press, 1976.

———. *The History of Christian Missions*. Baltimore: Penguin Books, 1964.

———. *Salvation Tomorrow*. London: Lutterworth Press, 1976.

Newbigin, Lesslie. *The Finality of Christ*. London: SCM Press, 1969.

Newby, G. D. *The Making of the Last Prophet*. Columbia: University of South Carolina Press, 1989.

Nolin, Kenneth. "Al Ustadh al-Haddad: A Review." *Muslim World* 60, no. 2 (April 1970).

————. "Christ in the Qur'an, The Taurat and the Injil: A Continuing Dialogue." *Muslim World* 61, no. 61 (April 1971).

Nurbakhsh, Javad. *Jesus in the Eyes of the Sufis*. Trans. Terry Graham, Leonard Lewisohn, and Hamid Mashkuri. London: Khaniqahi-Nimatullahi, 1983.

Olyott, Stuart. *The Three Are One: The Christian Doctrine of the Trinity*. Reading: Evangelical Press, 1979.

O'Shaughnessy, Thomas. *The Koranic Concept of the Word of God*. Rome: Pontificio Istituto Biblico, 1948.

Padwick, Constance. *Muslim Devotions*. London: SPCK Press, 1961.

Pannenberg, Wolfhart. *Jesus, God and Man*. Trans. Lewis L. Wilkins and Duane A. Priebe. London: SCM Press, 1968.

Parrinder, Geoffrey. *Jesus in the Qur'an*. New York: Barnes and Noble, 1965.

Parshall, Phil. *Bridges to Islam*. Grand Rapids, Mich.: Baker Books, 1983.

————. *The Cross and the Crescent: Reflections on Christian-Muslim Spirituality*. Wheaton, Ill.: Tyndale House, 1989.

————. *The Fortress and the Fire*. Bombay: GLS Press, 1975.

————. *New Paths in Muslim Evangelism: The Evangelical Approach to Contextualization*. Grand Rapids, Mich.: Baker Books, 1980.

Paul, Muhammad. *Why I Became a Christian*. Rikon, Switzerland: Good Way Publishing, n.d.

Peters, F. *Judaism, Christianity and Islam: The Classical Texts and Their Interpretation*. Princeton: Princeton University Press, 1990.

Pickthall, Muhammad Marmaduke. *The Meaning of the Glorious Koran*. New York: New American Library, n.d.

Rahman, Fazlur. *Islam: A History*. New York: Holt, Rinehart and Winston, 1966.

Raisanen, Heikki. "The Portrait of Jesus in the Qur'an: The Reflections of a Biblical Scholar." *Muslim World* 70, no. 2 (April 1980).

Raschid, M. S. *Muhammad Iqbal's Concept of God*. London: Routledge and Kegan Paul, 1981.

Rasooli, Jay M., and Cady H. Allen. *The Bitter and the Bold*. Westchester, Ill.: MD Publications, 1991.

Rippin, Andrew. *Muslims: Their Religious Beliefs and Practises*. London: Routledge Press, 1990.

————, and Jan Knappert. *Textual Sources for the Study of Islam*. Totowa, N.J. : Barnes & Noble, 1986.

Ro, Bong Rin, and Mark C. Albrecht, eds. *God in Asian Contexts*. Taichung, Taiwan: The Asian Theological Association, 1988.

Robinson, Neal. *Christ in Islam and Christianity*. Albany: State University of New York Press, 1991.

Robson, James. *Christ in Islam*. London: John Murray, 1929.

————, trans. *Mishkat Al-Masabih*. Lahore: Sheikh Muhammad Ashraf, 1981.

Saab, Hassan. "Communication Between Christianity and Islam." *Middle Eastern Journal* 18, no. 1 (1964).

Sachedina, Abdul-Aziz Abdul Hassan. *Islamic Messianism*. Albany: State University of New York Press, 1981.

Safa, Reza. *Blood of the Sword, Blood of the Cross.* Bromley, Kent: STL Books, n.d.

Sangster, Thelma. *The Torn Veil.* London: Marshall Pickering, 1984.

Schlorff, Samuel P. "The Hermeneutical Crisis in Muslim Evangelization." *Evangelical Missions Quarterly* (July 1990).

Schuon, Frithjof. *Dimensions of Islam.* Trans. P. N. Townsend. London: Allen and Unwin, 1970.

———. *Understanding Islam.* Trans. D. M. Matheson. London: Allen and Unwin, 1963.

Seale, Morris S. *Muslim Theology.* London: Luzac, 1964.

———. *The Qur'an and the Bible.* London: Croom Helm, 1978.

Shariati, Ali. *Man and Islam.* Trans. Fatallah Marjani. Houston: FILINC, 1974.

Shayegan, Daryush. *Cultural Schizophrenia: Islamic Societies Confronting the West.* Trans. John Howe. London: Saqi Books, 1989.

Sheikh, Bilquis. *I Dared to Call Him Father.* Eastbourne: Kingsway Publications, 1979.

Smith, Jane I., and Yvonne Yazbeck Haddad. *The Islamic Understanding of Death and Resurrection.* Albany: State University of New York Press, 1981.

Smith, Wilfred Cantwell. *Islam in Modern History.* Princeton: Princeton University Press, 1957.

———. *On Understanding Islam.* The Hague: Mouton, 1981.

———. *Towards a World Theology: Faith and Comparative History of Religion.* London: Macmillan Press, 1981.

Sooehdeo, Patrick, ed. *Jesus Christ, the Only Way: Christian Response in a Multi-Cultural Society.* Exeter: Paternoster Press, 1978.

Spencer, H. *Islam and the Gospel of God.* Delhi: SPCK Press, 1956.

Stott, John. *The Cross of Christ.* Leicester: Inter-Varsity Press, 1989.

———. "God in the Gallows." *Christianity Today* (January 27, 1987).

Subhan, John A. *How a Sufi Found His Lord.* Lucknow, India: Lucknow Publishing House, 1942.

Sweetman, J. Windrow. *Islam and Christian Theology: A Study of the Interpretation of Theological Ideas in the Two Religions.* 3 vols. London: Lutterworth Press, 1947.

Taylor, John V. *The Go-Between God.* London: SCM Press, 1972.

Thomas, David. *Anti-Christian Polemic in Early Islam: Abu Isa al-Warraq's "Against the Trinity."* London: Cambridge University Press, 1992.

Tillich, Paul. *Systematic Theology.* Vols. 1–2. Chicago: University of Chicago Press, 1951.

Tisdall, W. St. Clair. *The Sources of Islam.* Trans. William Muir. Edinburgh: T. & T. Clark, n.d.

Toon, Peter, and James D. Spiceland, eds. *One God in Trinity.* London: Samuel Bagster, 1980.

von Grunebaum, Gustave, ed. *Logic in Classical Islamic Culture.* Wiesbaden: Otto Harrassowitz, 1970.

———. *Medieval Islam: A Study in Cultural Orientation.* Chicago: University of Chicago Press, 1961.

Wainwright, Arthur. *The Trinity in the New Testament.* London: SPCK, 1962.

Wansbrough, John. *Qur'anic Studies: Sources and Methods of Scriptural Interpretation.* London: Oxford University Press, 1977.

Ward, Keith, and Basil Blackwell. *The Concept of God.* Oxford: Oxford University Press, 1974.

Watt, W. Montgomery. *The Faith and Practise of Al-Ghazali.* London: Allen and Unwin, 1953.

———. *Islamic Philosophy and Theology.* New York: Columbia University Press, 1988.

———. *Muslim-Christian Encounters.* London: Routledge, 1991.

———. *What Is Islam?* London: Longmans, 1968.

Welch, Alford T., and Pierre Cachia. *Islam: Past Influence and Present Challenge.* Albany: State University of New York Press, 1979.

Wensinck, A. J. *A Handbook of Early Muhammadan Tradition.* Leiden: E. J. Brill, 1960.

———. *The Muslim Creed.* Cambridge: Cambridge University Press, 1932.

Williams, John Alden, ed. *Themes of Islamic Civilization.* Berkeley: University of California Press, 1971.

Wingate, Andrew. *Encountering in the Spirit: Muslim-Christian Meetings in Birmingham.* Geneva: World Council of Churches Publications, 1988.

Wismer, Donald, ed. *The Islamic Jesus: An Annotated Bibliography of Sources in English and French.* New York: Garland, 1977.

Wolfson, Harry A. *The Philosophy of the Kalam.* Cambridge: Harvard University Press, 1976.

Woodbury, J. Dudley, ed. *Muslim and Christian Along the Emmaus Road.* Monrovia, Calif.: Missions Advanced Research Center, 1989.

Wootton, R. W. F., ed. *Jesus, More Than a Prophet.* Leicester: InterVarsity Press, 1982.

Zahniser, A. H. Mathias. "The Christian View of God's Unity." A paper presented at the Wilmore United Methodist Church, Wilmore, Kentucky, January 1993.

Zeidan, David. *The Fifth Pillar: A Spiritual Quest.* Carlisle, England: OM Publishing, 1993.

Zwemer, Samuel. "The Allah of Islam and the God Revealed in Jesus Christ." *Muslim World* 36, no. 4.

———. *The Moslem Christ.* Edinburgh: Oliphant, Anderson and Ferrier, 1912.

———. *The Moslem Doctrine of God.* London: Oliphant, Anderson and Ferrier, 1905.

Index of Qur'anic References

Index of Biblical References

Index of Subjects and Names

OTHER TITLES IN THE FAITH MEETS FAITH SERIES

Imagining the Sacred, Vernon Ruland, S.J.

Christian-Muslim Relations, Ovey N. Mohammed, S.J.

John Paul II and Interreligious Dialogue, Byron L. Sherwin and Harold Kasimow, editors

Transforming Christianity and the World, John B. Cobb Jr.

The Divine Deli, John H. Berthrong

Experiencing Scripture in World Religions, Harold Coward, editor

The Meeting of Religions and the Trinity, Gavin D'Costa

Subverting Hatred: The Challenge of Nonviolence in Religious Traditions, Daniel L. Smith-Christopher, editor

Christianity and Buddhism: A Multi-Cultural History of Their Dialogue, Whalen Lai and Michael von Brück

Islam, Christianity, and the West: A Troubled History, Rollin Armour Sr.

Many Mansions?: Multiple Religious Belonging, Catherine Cornille, editor